COMPUTERS

Promise and Challenge in Education

David Woodhouse

MA DPhil MSc DipEd

Dean, School of Mathematical
and Information Sciences,
La Trobe University, Melbourne

Anne McDougall

MSc MEd

Lecturer in Computer Education,
Monash University, Melbourne

D1445700

Blackwell Scientific Publications
Melbourne Oxford London Edinburgh Boston Palo Alto

© 1986 by
Blackwell Scientific Publications
Editorial offices:
107 Barry Street, Carlton
  Victoria 3053, Australia
Osney Mead, Oxford OX2 0EL, UK
8 John Street, London WC1N 2ES, UK
23 Ainslie Place, Edinburgh
  EH3 6AJ, UK
52 Beacon Street, Boston
  Mass. 02108, USA
677 Lytton Avenue, Palo Alto,
  Ca. 94301, USA

First published 1986

Typeset in Australia by Davey Graphics Pty Ltd
Printed in Singapore by
Singapore National Printers Pte Ltd

DISTRIBUTORS

USA and Canada
  Computer Science Press Inc
  1803 Research Boulevard
  Rockville, Maryland
  20850, USA

Australia
  Blackwell Scientific
  Publications Pty Ltd
  107 Barry Street, Carlton
  Victoria 3053

South-East Asia
  P G Publishing Pte Ltd
  Alexandra PO Box 318
  Singapore 9115

Others
  Blackwell Scientific
  Publications
  Osney Mead, Oxford
  OX2 0EL, UK

Cataloguing in publication data
Woodhouse, David, 1940–
  Computers: promise and challenge in
  education.

  Bibliography.
  Includes index.
  ISBN 0 86793 160 4.

  1. Computer-assisted instruction.
  2. Computers — Study and teaching.
  3. Microcomputers. I. McDougall, Anne,
  1945–   . II. Title.

371.3'9445

CONTENTS

INTRODUCTION

Changes occur rapidly in computing. This book has been a year in the writing, and has had to be thoroughly revised to keep pace with the new developments of that year. Therefore, to avoid its early obsolescence, we have looked as far ahead as possible. We dismiss as out of date some topics and methods that are still current; and we describe as standard some that are only just emerging. Not being clairvoyant, we shall doubtless be wrong on some counts (perhaps, for example, Prolog will not be the language of the future, after all, but will be overtaken by a new-look Lisp). However, sufficient will be correct for this book to be of use for some time as a teacher's guide to the growing area of computer use in schools.

The book is for all teachers who intend to use computers in schools. It is not about teacher training *per se*, nor is it a general introduction to the structure and use of computers. Rather, it covers the intersection of these two fields of study. The two major topics in this intersection may be categorized crudely as 'learning with computers' and 'learning about computers'. The former topic is the subject of Part I of this book. The nature of the computer as an information processor means that it can be used to enhance teaching and learning processes. The decreasing cost of computing facilities means that it is increasingly feasible to consider them as possible aids to teaching and learning. As such an aid, the computer has its own particular strengths and weaknesses. However, it is potentially a valuable teaching aid right across the curriculum, and all teachers should know sufficient about it to be able to decide whether, and if so when and how, to use it in their teaching. Part I describes the theory and practice of using computers to assist the processes of teaching and learning. This use of computers has been given a multitude of names, including CAL, CAI (Computer Assisted Learning or Instruction), CBL, CBI, CBE (B for Based, E for Education), CSL and CSI (S for Supported). We prefer 'Learning' to 'Instruction', and use the term CAL throughout. We assume that the reader is, or is training to be, a teacher, but we make no more specific assumptions about the reader's area of expertise. Instead we illustrate the range of applicability of the computer by reference to its use in various subject areas. These examples may indicate to the reader ways of applying in his or her own discipline the general principles given.

Not only is the computer applicable, from time to time, in all disciplines across the curriculum, it is also of use to teachers in primary schools (chapter 7) or special education (chapter 8). Therefore, most of the material covered outside these two chapters is also relevant to these areas. Part I does not demand computer knowledge on the part of the reader.

Part II describes aspects of 'learning about computers', and hence is essentially 'methods of teaching computer studies'. For this part, it is assumed that the reader has computer knowledge appropriate for the level s/he proposes to teach. However, as we argue strongly throughout the book, teaching with computers is the best way to initiate teaching about them, and so Part II is in fact relevant to all teachers. It covers courses in computer awareness or computer literacy, as well as senior secondary computer science, together with discussions on computer languages and on what computer science entails. All teachers are therefore encouraged to at least skim through this section, ignoring what they find unhelpful or unintelligible. This part is quite short because, contrary to popular belief, most general educational principles still apply: another reason why everyone can profit from this section. We concentrate on material that is specifically relevant to teaching computing.

Part III deals with some practical considerations that arise whenever the use of computers in schools is contemplated. Selection, purchase, management and the provision of resources are the main topics. In addition other computer uses, which are relevant to teachers, are described (including school administration, library work and computer managed learning). In conjunction with this, the roles of the principal, the librarian and the computer resource person are described.

The Bibliography lists the books and articles referred to in the text. We particularly draw to the reader's attention *Mindstorms* (Papert 1980) for inspiration; *Computer Science* (Woodhouse *et al*

1984) for general background; and the Oxford *Dictionary of Computing* (1983) for reference. For the reader who wishes to learn a programming language, books on Logo by McDougall *et al* (1982, 1984) are available for two models of microcomputer. The Appendix lists useful resources, including people, organizations, journals and the various CAL programs mentioned in the book.

The book is not addressed to the computer consultant, nor to the specialist software writer, nor does it provide a detailed description and comparison of specific machines. The former would have over-extended the scope of the book, while the latter would have become obsolete very quickly.

Developing a new educational environment inevitably entails some difficulties and frustrations. The experienced teacher is unsettled by being once more in the situation of having no bank of personal experience to draw on; and both new and experienced teachers suffer from the absence of an accepted body of tradition or extensive practical results. However, even if only a fraction of the rich and exciting possibilities that the computer promises in the educational sphere are realized, such initial disturbances will prove to have been worthwhile. This book should ease the transition from the first thought of computer use to a smoothly-running, computer-conscious educational environment.

Our thanks are due to Tony Adams for discussions on Logo, Russel Baader for his camera work, Gillian Barclay for the cartoons, Marjorie Clamp for her typing, Owen Hughes, Chris Durham and Jeff Richardson for ideas on primary school use, Peter Edwards for comments on special education, Tony Jones for general discussions, and Margaret Whitstock for information on libraries; to Harvey Cohen, Geoff Cumming, Iain Macleod, John Traeger and the Apple Computer Co. for providing photographs; and to our students who have, both wittingly and unwittingly, provided a lot of help.

David Woodhouse   Melbourne
Anne McDougall

PART I

LEARNING
WITH
COMPUTERS

Chapter One

Computers in the classroom

The things taught in schools are not an education, but the means of an education
R. W. Emerson (1803–1882)

1.1 INTRODUCTION

In the title of this book, we refer to the promise and the challenge of computers in education. The computer's capabilities promise to improve both the quality and the extent of the learning experience. The challenge lies in using these capabilities to achieve this desirable result. Many teachers are taking up this challenge, or have already done so. Many others feel they should, but are afraid to try. And others again feel that it is not relevant to them.

It is still commonly believed that the computer is a sort of calculator, or that great technical expertise is required to use it. These dual misconceptions have pre-conditioned mathematics and science teachers to consider the possibility and utility of using computers in some way, and conversely, have resulted in many teachers of non-science subjects believing that the computer is not relevant to their work, and that its use would in any case be beyond their capabilities. The aim of this chapter is to show that computers are relevant to all (or almost all) teachers. The rest of this book is intended to assist all teachers to meet its challenge successfully.

1.2 THE COMPUTER AS DATA PROCESSOR

It is certainly true that the first electronic computer was designed for arithmetic calculation. However, within a very short time, it was realized that the computer is a general information or data processor. Data refers to the symbols we use to record facts, ideas, etc. Information is the meaning attached to the data. The computer takes data and processes it to produce new data. Certainly, the computer can process numerical data. For example, the data could be two numbers and the rules for addition, and the computer could produce the sum. The data could be an English–French dictionary and an English word, and the computer could produce the French equivalent. Again, the data could be some words and the rules for writing haiku (a type of Japanese poetry), and the computer could produce a poem using the given words. Or if it was given a specification of some of Schubert's works, it could write a short passage of music in the style of Schubert.

A machine with such a generally applicable capability should presumably be useful in education, also. However, one should not start with the fact of the computer and ask: How can we apply it? Our proper starting point is: What are we trying to do in education? Then: What facilities does the computer offer? Then: Can the latter help with the former? We propose that the computer be used, not just 'because it's there', but, firstly, because it enables some things to be done differently and variety is of great value in teaching; secondly, because it can be used to do some things better than is possible at present; and thirdly, because it allows us to do some things that are totally impossible otherwise.

IF I'D HAD A COMPUTER — I WOULDN'T HAVE HAD
To LEAVE THIS DARNED SYMPHONY UNFINISHED.

1.3.   WHAT ARE WE TRYING TO DO?

Firstly, we must answer the question: 'What is it that we are trying to do in education.' This is not an easy question to answer. In the first place, the answer depends on your philosophy of life, and in the second place, it depends on your starting point. The former may be illustrated by reference to a commercial organization, where the aim of those in charge is likely to be to maximize profit; and the use of computers, or any other tool, is directed towards achieving this goal. This singleness of purpose is possible because the organization was founded for this purpose, is under unified control, and has no external forces pushing it in some other direction. Employees have accepted the profit motive, as this has also been to their advantage. However, they are increasingly seeking 'quality of life', 'job satisfaction', etc., and to this end want some control of the running of the firm. Thus there are different groups, with conflicting ideas, each feeling they have the right to a share of the decisions.

Education exhibits similar characteristics to this new, confused, commercial environment. Politicians, administrators, councils, teachers, parents, students, and academics may all have different views, and also feel that they have the authority and right to influence all decisions that are made. Often, the different views are contradictory, leading to arbitrary decisions, conflicting actions, or long delays while differences are resolved. In particular, any one of these outcomes can apply in the matter of introducing computers into a school. Thus, as in all aspects of teaching, each individual chooses (or accepts) a particular ideology, and then bases his or her teaching activities on it.

Even assuming a particular point of view or educational philosophy, the question 'What are we trying to do?' can be answered at various levels, depending on how far back one wishes to go, what one is willing to assume as a starting point, and how much one is willing to change.

Some possible answers, in increasing order of generality, are as follows.

1 We are trying to implement a particular lesson plan. Can we slot the computer into an existing lesson plan to do a particular task?
2 We are trying to achieve a particular goal. Can the computer be used to permit a different presentation aimed at achieving this existing goal?
3 We are trying to achieve a particular aim. Can the computer facilitate the presentation of a different course to achieve existing aims?
4 We have other aims in mind, that have so far been unrealizable. Can the computer be used to extend existing courses to achieve these new aims?

5   We have a new style of education in mind. Can the computer be used to promote a new approach within existing structures?
6   We espouse a new educational philosophy, different from that which has evolved to date. Can we take advantage of the advent of a radically new machine to implement radically new policies?

Whichever level of change is sought, there are problems. Many people are very busy now: any change involves extra time, and this is often a sufficient deterrent. This, together with the cost of computer use, leads to an unwillingness to change again once the effort has been made, and tends to ossify computer supported activities. Therefore if one has not gone far enough down the above list for a start, one may be committed to an increasingly irksome philosophy, or even a specific syllabus. But starting a long way down the list will be more time-consuming, and might delay computer use unacceptably.

However, just as the ability to drive a car is worth the effort involved in learning, so the ability to use computers apropriately and with confidence in one's teaching is well worth the effort involved in coming to grips with the task.

1.4   THE SCHOOL AS MICROCOSM

While it is clear that the purpose of teaching a subject in school is not to make all students experts therein, nor to train them for a career in that discipline; nonetheless the school curriculum should be influenced, in both content and method, by the current activities of practitioners in the field, and by the likely imminent developments in professional practice. This is not an entirely new insight. Document work is central to the activities of the practising historian, and so it has been accepted that history students at upper secondary levels should be involved in some document work. However, in many disciplines, this connection has not been made. Science students have done well-defined, rather artificial, stereotyped experiments. Mathematics students have been set tractable problems with straightforward solutions. French students have been taught grammar and vocabulary, with no literary or cultural context. In the last 20 years, this has changed, with the new mathematics, discovery learning, project work, a wider interpretation of foreign language studies, and so on. However, no professional or academic area stands still. All disciplines are developing, and so the school curriculum must change too, if it is to maintain its close relation with practical content and method. In particular, the computer is now being used in many disciplines, and so the teachers of the corresponding school subjects should take cognizance of this and act appropriately.

One example of this is in the production of architectural and technical drawings and blueprints. The whole design process is being increasingly automated, with the designer using a computer terminal with keyboard and screen, in place of a drawing board, with a file stored in the computer being the result of the design process. The computer can then produce plots directly from the file. In this situation, what should be taught in technical drawing classes at school? While there is still need for an appreciation of accuracy and perspective, it is totally unrealistic to act as if the outside world of draftsmanship had not changed. Clearly the syllabus needs to take account of computer applications, and the method needs to involve computer use.

The subject of the social scientist's study is people, and people are so varied in their nature, motives and actions, that the sociologist can easily amass enormous quantities of data — and needs to do so in order to obtain representative results. However, the more data s/he has, the more need there is for computer storage (because of its capacity) and computer analysis (because of its speed). Such large quantities bring their own problems of scale, and it is quite unrealistic, and unconnected with contemporary social science, to set the student only the restricted sort of problems that can be handled without the help of the computer.

The historian is in a similar position. Increasing amounts of historical data are being discovered and generated. Whether it is documents relating to the role of organized labour in the Spanish Civil War, or an on-going record of known aboriginal middens, the quantity is likely to be such as can only really be used if it is computer based, and gathered into a data base designed to facilitate the addition of information and the posing of various questions. This is part of the world of the historian in the 1980s, so some concept of it must be part of the world of the history student in the 1980s.

1.5   EDUCATIONAL TECHNIQUES

Some topics which are already in the curriculum can be much better taught, and hence more readily learned, if computers are used appropriately as part of the educational environment.

1 *Biology.* If a biology teacher wishes to give concrete experience of genetics and hereditary characteristics, the normal approach involves the rearing of generations of fruit flies. However, the techniques of feeding, handling and inspecting fruit flies and keeping them alive are not essential to the understanding of transmitted characteristics. The alternative approach is to program a computer to simulate the production of generations of fruit flies, given the relevant genetically determined characteristics, and the probabilities of their occurrence in successive generations. One well-known PLATO (see Chapter 2) simulation does this, and also draws pictures of the various fruit fly variants on the terminal screen. This approach not only omits the irrelevant part of fruit fly rearing, but permits many more families and generations to be studied. Simulation is covered in detail in Chapter 6, where it is also observed that practice in handling experimental equipment is also necessary, but that it can profitably be distinguished as a distinct skill for the beginner to learn separately.

2 *Nutrition* (in physical education or home economics). Appropriate nutrition depends on many factors. These include the amount of various essential nutrients in the diet and their contribution to energy, body maintenance and resistance to infection; the activities carried out and their corresponding energy requirements; personal details such as height, age, sex; and medical conditions, such as diabetes. Adequate teaching of nutrition and dietetics requires the calculation of many example diets for particular individuals, and the assessment of many proposed recipes. This can be extremely tedious, detract from the essential learning, and limit the number of examples which can be covered. To overcome this, a number of computer programs are available, which can quickly perform the desired analyses and the corresponding calculations. One such program is the *Dietary Planning, Health and Fitness Program* (Ima Computer Co. Ltd, Melbourne), while another is *Diet* (Cambridge University Press).

3 *History. The First Fleet Data Base*, prepared at the Elizabeth Computer Centre, Hobart, contains information on the 777 convicts who sailed in 1787 on the first fleet to Australia (Fig. 1.1). An associated query language allows students to carry out historical research by interrogating the data base. How many convicts were female; what age were the convicts; what were their crimes; what trades were represented? Such questions may be of intrinsic interest, but also lead to wider considerations, such as the criminal population, attitudes to crime and punishment, relative severity of different assizes, and trades which are now extinct. Students are able to form hypotheses and test them against the data.

Fig. 1.1

4 *Social studies.* The investigation of the *First Fleet Data Base* readily leads to questions of society, such as the problems of satisfying basic needs in the Port Jackson settlement, the probable life span of the colony, problems of the very old and the very young, and comparison of twentieth and eighteenth century societies. Note that many associated activities, such as role plays, further research, and mapping, are not computer centred. This program has been used successfully from Year 2 upwards.

5 *Grammar.* The biggest problem in teaching English grammar is motivation: "Why should we learn words like 'participle', and phrases like 'adverbial phrase': we can talk without knowing such words and phrases. And anyway yous can still catch us drift, even if we don't talk real good." McDougall & Adams (1982) show how an oblique approach has the desired effect. As in much of the Logo environment (see Chapter 5), the student is put in the driving seat by being asked to 'teach the computer' to do something — in this case, to teach it to write sentences. To do this, the student must provide lists of words, and simple output statements. The output produced will probably be so far from satisfactory English, that the student will be moved to group the words into classes to achieve, first, grammatical and next, meaningful, output. The rules which the student gradually builds into the growing program, are exactly the rules of English grammar!

6 *Foreign languages.* Similar concepts were used in a number of programs designed by S. Zammit of St Catherine's College, Melbourne, to assist in the teaching of French. A program for beginners codes French words using a variety of substitution ciphers. A more advanced program generates a large number of sentences, using the students' basic vocabulary. As the students' vocabulary increases, the computer-based dictionary is augmented, and the number of possible sentences grows. Another program involves the children in understanding complicated street directions to navigate from point to point on a town plan. These programs were written by the teacher — a language specialist, but not a programmer — not for the children to operate, but to enable the teacher to provide extra variety in the lessons.

7 *Commercial studies.* In this area it would be natural to use a computer to assist the learning of typing. In all other activities, the computer terminal is only representing something. If a program simulates the breeding of fruit flies, for example, pressing a key may represent creating the next generation. If the user is learning to type, however, each key is used simply for its own sake, and not as representing some totally different action. A passage of text which the student is to type, could first be input to the computer, by the teacher, and the student could then type the passage, using the computer terminal as a normal typewriter (indeed some ordinary typewriters double as on-line terminals). The computer could indicate the errors, time the typist and print out the typing rate. Over a period of time, it could produce a graph of (increasing) rates and (decreasing) error counts. There is current debate over the amount of keyboard skill required by all children with the increased use of computers in schools. It is clear that insisting on a preliminary touch-typing course is unrealistic. (It would be like returning to old style writing practice, and anyway children's hands are too small.) The predominant current view is that children should just pick up keyboard skills 'on the job'. The question is highly relevant to the next application.

8 *Creative writing* (Ninedek 1984). The problem with encouraging creative writing is the conflict between the initial rapid flow of ideas and the production of a final polished composition. This conflict is resolved by the professional writer by the production of several drafts. The school child, however, does not have the same motivation, and can scarcely be persuaded to produce two versions (the first and the last). A word processor is a computer program which facilitates the amendment, editing and correction of any piece of text which has been typed in at a terminal. There are a host of such programs, including *Bank Street Writer, Gutenberg, Vic Writer, Visiword, Wordstar* and *Zardax*. Some, like *Bank Street Writer*, have been designed for children, with simplicity of operation as the main aim; others, like *Zardax*, have been designed to offer greater power for the word processing task. All however, allow the distinct essay writing skills, such as idea conception; topic ordering; syntax correction; and calligraphic production; to be applied in sequence with little extra effort.

1.6   ATTAINING THE UNATTAINABLE

Some topics cannot be directly taught in schools, but can be included in the curriculum through the medium of computers. Many dangerous, unrepeatable, or inaccessible processes fall into this category, as they can be modelled by simulation programs (see Chapter 6). In this way, the science curriculum can be extended to include radioactive elements and biogenetic engineering; the economics curriculum can include the management of a large company or of the nation; and the geography curriculum can include a close involvement with places too distant for field trips. In all such areas, if the school child is given any practical experience at all, it is normally with a much reduced and totally sanitized version. The computer simulation, while not involving the handling of actual materials, is nonetheless more realistic, as it embodies the scope of the real-life situation. Some of the examples which follow are extensions of those in the preceding section.

1 *Genetics*. Once genetic inheritance is modelled by computer, the application may be extended to species which cannot be bred in school laboratories for enough generations to provide adequate experience for the students. *Catlab* and *Birdbreed*, produced by J. Kinnear at Melbourne State College, are programs which allow students to mate cats or birds, selected on the basis of colour and pattern. The aim of the programs is not only to teach genetic principles, but also to give practice in defining research problems, controlling variables, analyzing and interpreting data, studying causal relationships, and generating, testing and refining scientific hypotheses.

2 *History*. Use of a prepared data base (such as the First Fleet) presents only one aspect of historical research. Users of the program *Archaeological Search* (Anderson 1984) have the task of organizing the excavation of an historical site, including problems of time, money, staff available, competition and assessment of findings. A similar program (*Saqqara*, developed in Cambridgeshire, UK) focuses on an actual site in Egypt, and users must first seek permission for the expedition, then seek grants to fund it, and then report on the expenditure.

3 *Information handling*. It is because historians and social scientists now use data bases that the *First Fleet Data Base* is an appropriate aid to the study of history. However, because data bases are used in so many contexts, it is appropriate for children to learn more generally how a data base is established, augmented and accessed. *Factfile* (Chapter 7) is a program, designed for 7–13 year olds, which enables them to create and use data bases on topics of their own choosing. The user must decide on the subject (e.g. postage stamps) and the headings (e.g. country, design, colour, size, value, age). The learning experience lies principally in the gathering of information (selection and rejection), ordering the information (coding and categorizing) and using the information (formulating questions). The computer's task is simply to store the information, in the desired categories, and provide rapid answers to questions about it. As with the dietary program of the preceding section, the computer takes over the drudgery, and allows concentration on the essentials.

Factfile was developed under the UK Microelectronics Education Programme (MEP). *Quest* is another data base management program for slightly older children. Like *Factfile*, it is content free, allowing the establishment of data bases on any topic.

Prolog is a computer programming language which can be used to build data bases (see Chapter 12). While it does not provide the specific data base assistance of *Quest* or *Factfile*, it can be used for other purposes as well.

4 *Process writing* (Henderson-Lancett 1984). The word processor not only reduces the necessary drudgery of re-drafting, as described above, but actually permits an approach to learning which had been advocated in the pre-computer era, but was too time consuming

without the assistance of the computer. The process approach to children's written language includes conferencing, providing a sense of audience, and repeated revision. The screen display of text is an excellent basis for discussion with the teacher or other children (conferencing); the printed version is easier to proof read than a manuscript, and immediately gives the air of having been read (sense of audience); and, of course, revision is much simpler.

1.7   APPREHENSIONS AND PITFALLS

Some people are worried about computers because they are new. It is a common experience, when computers are on public view, that children rush in and use them, while the adults hang back. The adults take an active part only after establishing an incipient understanding of the machine and how to use it, by observing the children's performance. This difference is presumably because children are only just learning about the world, and hence are constantly facing the unknown, and making mistakes, and integrating new experiences into the pattern they are constructing of the world around them. The adult, by contrast, has an established world view, and finds it hard to accommodate something like the computer whose effect is so significant that it is changing the world, and so must affect our view of the world (if that view is to continue to be realistic). The adult also has an adequate working knowledge of the things s/he is supposed to do, and is not accustomed to making the embarrassing mistakes of the learner.

Another fear is of things technical, in which category the computer clearly fits. The prospective user should realize that a car is also a technical artefact but few people feel themselves incapable of learning to drive. While the first computers needed a lot of expert knowledge to operate, using today's microcomputers is very much easier than driving a car.

Related to the widespread fear of things technical is the conservative attitude that rejects any new development, just because it is new: 'The old ways are best', 'What was good enough for ...', 'Better the devil you know ...'. This is a general tendency, not specific to teachers or to computing, and it is not part of the explicit purpose of this book to attempt to rebut it. We may just observe that such an attitude is particularly unfortunate in teachers, who are acting now for the future. They have the difficult task of communicating what is good from the past, and yet preparing their students to recognize good in the future when they encounter it.

A converse pitfall is the technological imperative. There are those whose attitude — explicit or implicit — is: 'if it's possible we shall do it'. There are many who take this attitude to the use of nuclear power, to biogenetic engineering, and to the exploitation of natural resources. Unfortunately, this also occurs with computers: sometimes the computer has been introduced with no very clear idea of its expected use, and with no one competent to manage it. Resources are then wasted as the machine gathers dust on the shelf.

1.8   POTENTIAL

The main aim of this chapter has been to show that the computer is being used to good effect in a wide variety of subjects. Therefore, all teachers should consider the possibility of using computers in their teaching. It is particularly important that non-science teachers understand the potential of the computer as a tool for their use, lest a mistrust and awe of computers be perpetuated in their students. Teachers need not be proficient programmers, nor skilled technicians. Indeed, the major skills required are those teaching skills which they already possess. The examples given in Sections 1.5 and 1.6 should show that the computer need not play a dominant role when it is used. It may not even be the focus of activity, but simply a resource or tool which is used as and when necessary. Properly applied, computer use is beneficial for the learning process itself, and also accustoms the children to the role and capabilities of the computer far more effectively than any superficial 'computer awareness' course can do.

Chapter Two

Approaches to computer use in education

You can do anything with children if you only play with them

Otto von Bismarck (1815–1898)

2.1 INTRODUCTION

In this chapter, we survey the history of and philosophical approaches to the use of computers in education. In so doing, we touch on topics that are described in more detail in later chapters. Here, however, the emphasis is less on 'what?' and more on 'why?' The answer to this second question is a composite one, based on both the educational principles deemed to be appropriate, and also the style of computer power currently available. So we can trace in the evolution of educational computing, the influence of the mainframe computer (1960s), the minicomputer (1970s) and the microcomputer (1980s). In all cases, however, it has been accepted that computers for use in education must normally be accessible to both student and teacher via on-line terminals (although there are some exceptions). In the case of a microcomputer, the terminal and computer usually form the same unit; while a mainframe may be some distance from the terminals which are attached to it.

In the 1950s, horizons for computer applications were widening rapidly, but often unrealistically so. In 1957, Sputnik I was launched, and the whole educational system of the USA convulsed in an attempt to 'catch up' with the Russians. The 'new math' was born; and during the 1960s computers were pressed into the service of the cause. Millions of dollars were spent, but ultimately there was little impact on mass education. Some of these early applications failed to meet their own objectives, while others met objectives that were later felt to be educationally undesirable. These early failures have coloured attitudes to computer use in education, alienating teachers, kindling suspicion of computers, and establishing a body of rigid material for computer aided instruction which is still used as the pattern by many authors in the field.

2.2   AUTOMATED TEACHING: THE TEACHER IS DEAD

2.2.1   Computer managed learning (CML)

When the question 'How can the computer help in education?' was posed in the late 1950s, a number of possibilities sprang to mind, starting with those activities that seemed closest to existing computer applications. Since computers had been used in commercial applications, the management of the learning process seemed a possible candidate. An early attempt at computer managed learning (see Chapter 13) was the Individually Prescribed Instruction (IPI) project, in which a computer was programmed to provide daily tests and lesson assignments for students. Teachers, freed from record keeping, and from deciding what and how students should learn, were to function as tutors, helping the children maximise the learning from their computer-prescribed lessons. A more ambitious project was set up to teach reading and writing to 2 and 3 year olds. This was O.K. Moore's 'Talking Typewriter' project at Yale University (e.g. Moore 1966). This project had some success, but was enormously expensive.

Although these initial applications of computers to education were motivated principally by the existence of the computer, naturally they had specific objectives, and could be counted successful if these objectives were achieved. The next question to arise, however, is of the wider utility of any particular computer application. This raises the question of whether the application is effective. However, the concept of 'effectiveness' in this context has been defined in vastly different ways (cf. Chambers & Sprecher 1980). Criteria that have been used include the amount of learning; the rate of learning; the cost of learning; the thoroughness of learning as measured by tests at the end of the course; the thoroughness of learning as measured by tests at a later stage; the change in attitude towards computers; the drop-out rate; or simply the fact of the construction of educationally oriented computer based materials. This plethora of opinions makes it difficult to assess individual reports of computer use, or to compare different ones.

2.2.2   Computer aided instruction (CAI)

After CML, the next rather repetitive task which seemed ripe for computer intervention was the presentation of simple exercises on work studied — the sort that typically cover several pages at the end of a chapter of a text book. Such textbook exercises have a number of defects, including the common availability of answers (in the back of the book) and the needs of some students for more practice than others on any particular topic. Thus, the computer was programmed to present such exercises giving answers only when necessary, and allowing students who were performing well to skip some of the questions. It also kept a count of the questions attempted, and those answered correctly. In this last activity, it overlaps the IPI project. This application has come to be called 'drill and practice'.

Limited as is such an application, it opened the door to much more extensive possibilities. Firstly, it was observed that such lists of exercises only follow a chapter for convenience, and that ideally exercises should be spread more evenly throughout the book. This suggested using the computer, not merely to present the exercises (or test items), but also to present the material to be taught. This material would be presented in short sections, with each section followed by one or two exercises. Secondly, it was realized that such an arrangement was a computer form of the programmed instruction that was just coming into vogue, based on the work of Professor B.F. Skinner of Harvard University (Skinner 1968). Skinner described teaching as a situation in which we want students to learn things faster than they could usually do in the natural environment — and far faster than mankind has discovered or learned them over the years. To accelerate such learning processes, Skinner invented the method of 'programmed instruction', for use either by teachers, or by the student directly from books. This method was a natural candidate for computer implementation, giving rise to CAI.

In the first flush of enthusiasm for CAI, the 1960s can be seen as the 'the teacher is dead' era. The picture was painted of a gradually falling need for teachers, as more and more topics were computerized. Professor Patrick Suppes of Stanford University foresaw the time when every child could have what Alexander the Great enjoyed as a royal prerogative, namely the personal services of a tutor as well-informed and responsive as Aristotle. As a start in the creation of such a tutor, he began to break down the learning of arithmetic into minute steps, with associated learning objectives and reinforcements.

Meanwhile, at the University of Illinois, Professor Donald Bitzer, in collaboration with Control Data Corporation embarked on the PLATO (Programmed Logic for Automatic Teaching Operations) system (See, e.g. Smith & Sherwood 1976). PLATO was based on a very large computer, controlling very many (up to 4000) terminals. The specially designed terminals incorporate a touch sensitive screen (since, as Bitzer observed, "children and medics won't use a keyboard"), high resolution graphics, provision for a graphics template (to project figures onto the screen from behind), and voice output (See Chapter 14). Not surprisingly, such a terminal is expensive.

Another product of the PLATO project is the author language Tutor (see Chapter 10). Over the years, about 16 000 hours of CAL material have been produced for the PLATO system, principally by teachers. This has involved of the order of 800 000 hours writing time, and about a quarter of the available material is used fairly regularly. The terminal network can also be used for user to user communication.

2.2.3   A cloud on the horizon

However, despite the early promise, by the end of the 1960s computers had made little impact on practical education. In 1972, the Educational Testing Service in the USA surveyed the field and observed that these approaches and programmes had not been widely adopted because

1   hardware cost too much;
2   software development cost too much;
3   systems were unreliable;
4   systems' capabilities had been overrated;
5   teachers were afraid of technology;
6   teachers were afraid of losing their jobs;
7   there was little provision for relevant teacher training;
8   schools are conservative

(Anastasio & Morgan 1972; Murphy & Appel 1977). It was found that the benefits of CAI reported in the small were not realized in the large. It is one thing to take a limited, circumscribed topic; analyze its components; devise appropriate pathways through it; take into account all possible student responses at each step; and deal with all these responses appropriately. It is another matter entirely to do this for a larger, more complicated, more diverse topic, which is perhaps less susceptible to the complete postulation of incremental behavioural objectives and in which it is more difficult to predict all possible plausible student errors.

One valid application of this technique is in revising previously learned work. Once skills are learned, they need to be practised or refreshed if they are not to be lost, and drill and practice CAI can continue to play a useful role in this respect, no matter how the skills have been learned.

However, the majority of projects which persisted into the 1970s did so by changing direction. PLATO simply incorporated other aspects of computer assisted learning (Chapter 3), particularly simulations (Chapter 6). Patrick Suppes has probably stayed closest to the spirit of CAI and has achieved success through discarding the general Aristotle in favour of more specific projects, confining himself mainly to those areas identified in Chapter 3 as being appropriate for CAI. In each case, the subject matter is thoroughly analysed, and various learning strategies developed and considered before program development begins.

2.3   INDIVIDUAL INSTRUCTION: THE TEACHER'S ROLE CHANGES

The next class of applications arises through identifying particular categories of student. Suppes' earliest work, dating from 1963, was on basic mathematical, reading and language skills for disadvantaged students. This involved no change in the existing curriculum, but rather its presentation in a manner appropriate to each individual student. The next project focussed on handicapped children, with the development of mathematical and linguistic material for deaf children. Another group of children who are often ill-served by their own schools are those with a very high IQ. For this group, Suppes followed through his interest in logic, and developed a course in formal logic, which the students could pursue on home terminals (Taylor 1980, chapters 19 and 20).

At the university level, Suppes has concentrated on elementary courses (such as formal logic) which are susceptible to his CAI approach, and courses (such as Chinese and Russian) with low enrolments and/or few staff. Pursuing the goal of efficient use of staff time, Suppes himself no longer gives lectures, but supports his computer-based courses and gives advanced seminars. Experience at La Trobe University with the formal logic course (VALID) shows that while it frees the staff member from lecturing, and setting and marking exercises, his time is fully occupied in one-to-one tutorials as students require individual assistance. "Most students demand quite a bit of individual tuition, not I think just because they are stuck, but because they are excited about new ideas and want to talk about avenues the computer will not let them explore, and sometimes too because the medium can be lonely" (Richards 1983). As this sort of pattern has been recognized, the view of the computer as replacing the teacher has disappeared. In its place is the view that 'the teacher is still needed, but his/her role has changed'. We could see this as the designation of the 1970s.

The other major worker in the CAI field in the 1970s was Professor Alfred Bork of the University of California at Irvine, where he directs the Physics Computer Development Project. He has produced CAI dialogues for teaching physics to first year students at UCI, and more recently for teaching science in high schools and in further education courses. Bork insists that the computer should contribute something unique to the learning activity, and his work has been relatively successful, due in particular to the heavy emphasis on the use of the graphical capabilities of the computer. As Bork says, "a dialogue which recreates a book or some other teaching method is not likely to have long survival value" (Taylor 1980, chapter 2). He further admits that "much of the existing computer material is less than impressive" (Taylor 1980, chapter 3), and says that "it is too early to prepare a 'complete' computerized course".

Bork emphasizes the merits of stand-alone systems, rather than large timesharing systems of the PLATO type, although he notes the benefits to be obtained from a network of computers, especially for development. Conversely, PLATO materials developed on a large system can now be run on a microcomputer (Sugarman 1978).

Thus far, the computer had been seen as a teaching agent, firstly through CAI, and then through simulation programs, also. However,

> "If the computer is so powerful a resource that it can be programmed to simulate the instructional process, shouldn't we be teaching our students mastery of this powerful intellectual tool? Is it enough that a student be the subject of computer administered instruction — the end-user of a new technology? Or should his education also include learning to use the computer (1) to get information in the social sciences from a large data-base enquiry system, or (2) to simulate an ecological system, or (3) to solve problems by using algorithms, or (4) to acquire laboratory data and analyze it, or (5) to represent textual information for editing and analysis, or (6) to represent musical information for analysis, or (7) to create and process graphical information? These uses of computers in education cause students to become masters of computing, not merely its subjects."

So wrote Professor Arthur Luehrman in 1972 (Taylor 1980, chapter 9) in a paper whose title is reminiscent of Papert's work with Logo, namely "Should the computer teach the student, or vice-versa?" Luehrman was at Dartmouth College and associated with the development of the Basic programming language. Throughout the 1970s, first on minicomputers, then on micros, Basic has been the means of introducing many students to the possibilities inherent in being able to write their own programs. Luehrman stressed that no-one today should be accounted educated unless they are computer literate (Section 11.6), and that computer literacy includes the ability to write programs.

Some educators wanted to go further than simply automating existing teaching (CAI) or adding a new subject to the existing curriculum (computer programming), and to use the computer to revolutionize education. So we come to the 1980s, the microcomputer, the work of Dwyer and Papert, and the era of 'The teacher is more necessary than ever, and must be very good'.

2.4   FACILITATING LEARNING: THE TEACHER IS ESSENTIAL

Professor Thomas Dwyer of the University of Pittsburgh has worked on the teaching of secondary school mathematics, and emphasizes the need for 'student-controlled' computing. By this, Dwyer means the use of simulations, computer programming, and model-building [what Rushby calls "revelatory and conjectural computer aided learning" (chapter 3)]. The teacher's role is to help the students to do things for themselves (Taylor 1980, chapter 5), for the best learning takes place when the learner takes charge (Papert 1980). "The history of education has been the emancipation of the child from mastering 'learning' imposed from outside, freeing him to discover for himself the world of reality and his own place in it" (Boyle 1969).

Dwyer defines education as "that which liberates human potential, and thus the person" (Taylor 1980, chapter 5). A curriculum to achieve this must nurture growth in the knowledge of, understanding of and practice of existing ideas; and in creativity through problem solving. Teacher–student controlled computing provides exactly such a setting (Taylor 1980, chapter 7). Piaget maintains that learning is not spontaneous, but provoked by situations, and his analysis of intellectual growth as the accumulation of operational thought proceeding through a number of well-defined stages suggests situations for learning. The task of pedagogy is therefore to set up learning situations, wherein the experience of reality can be assimilated into an intellectual structure (Boyle 1969). One aspect of this task is so to influence technological development as to increase the range of appropriate learning environments. The computer should not be an end in itself, but should act as a catalyst to the establishment of relationships between people. Unfortunately, "the best methods are the most difficult ones" (Piaget 1970), and such a varied and flexible approach to learning demands more expertise of the teacher. However, many people are finding that the thoughtful use of computers enables them to carry out their jobs more creatively, effectively and enjoyably. Taking up the challenge of structuring appropriate 'curriculum-free' learning environments could enable teachers to experience a similar increase in job satisfaction.

2.5   HOMO LUDENS

There is a paradox here, similar to that exemplified by Falstaff's phrase: let us "have a play extempore", when Hal suggested they enact Falstaff's encounter with highwaymen, which he had just rehearsed. Learning environments should be rehearsed and yet extempore: they are to be planned, and yet give rise to spontaneous and joyful action, since learning and play go hand in hand. The notion of a formal learning situation is relatively new in human history. John Dewey expressed a nostalgia for earlier societies where the child becomes a hunter by real participation and playful imitation. Very young children are still ignorant of formal learning situations, even in our society, and for them education is a natural outgrowth of play. "Concepts and rules can be derived more readily from active play, exploration and investigation than from listening to or reading about them" (Piaget 1972). "Play is a way of gathering, under highly motivating circumstances, a variety of experiences. An experiential basis is a vital ingredient in the learning process" (Bork *in* Taylor 1980, chapter 3). "The active play of young children appears closely related to their cognitive development, and children often use play to help them assimilate new information from the environment into their existing modes of understanding" (Piaget 1951). These factors also operate in primitive societies, as is described at length in *Homo Ludens* (Huizinga 1955). This historical view is relevant to modern practice, as the growth of the intellect in the individual is of essentially the same nature as the progress of understanding over the centuries (Boyle 1969).

The theme of learning through playing has been taken up most strongly by one of Piaget's disciples, namely Seymour Papert. "Since children learn by doing and by thinking about what they do ... the fundamental ingredients of educational innovation must be better things to do and better ways to think about oneself doing these things" (Papert 1970, *in* Taylor 1980, chapter 13). Papert set himself the task of developing computer based learning situations which would be conducive to the assimilation of mathematical ideas. In order to do this, he had to invent a language that would allow children really to communicate with computers. The language he invented was Logo, and the mathematically oriented learning environment is based on a small robot, known as a turtle. (The importance of Logo to the use of computers in education is so great that a separate chapter (5) is devoted to the topic.) The turtle can be either an actual device with wheels and a pen that can be driven around the floor under computer control, leaving a trace of its route drawn by the pen (Fig. 2.1); or a small triangle on the screen of a computer terminal that can be moved around the screen under computer control, leaving a line to mark its passage. This brings the child firmly into contact with geometry. The traditional way of introducing geometry is very abstract, and has no connexion with the child's previous experience. Such learning usually demands an effort of will power and much repetition. However, most children could obey if told to walk in a circle or square, etc., so it is obvious that geometric concepts are part of their experience. The turtle forms the bridge between their existing experience and the abstract mathematical concept. They 'intuitively' know how to walk in a circle; when they try to teach the turtle how to do this, they are forced to make this knowledge explicit, and hence they come to understand it. Papert calls this learning syntonic, to imply that it goes together with the child's existing world view. This syntonicity has a number of aspects, and Papert distinguishes (i) its personal resonance: Logo mathematics brings out the knowledge of body geometry which the

Fig. 2.1

student already has (but could not verbalize); (ii) its social resonance: because children spend a lot of time watching television, making a picture on a television screen gives them a definite, relevant authority; and (iii) its utility: it can be used at once to do interesting and exciting things. "The right way to learn mathematics is first learning it as a concrete thing that actually works in the world, and then gradually move into pure mathematics". In the Logo context, mathematical principles become sources of relevant (syntonic) power (Papert *in* Taylor 1980, chapter 15).

The Logo programming language has great power, and is applicable to many topics other than mathematics. Logo programs can be run on most of the common microprocessor systems.

When one speaks of computers and games in the same breath, one of the first images that springs to mind is the video game. Some current studies (including one at Murdoch University, Western Australia) are using video games to investigate how people develop new skills, and to chart the development of people's understanding. Video games (like most games) involve using strategies and anticipating patterns. They entail acquiring and building up knowledge about the rules of the games, and applying and modifying that knowledge as the game progresses.

Despite the value of games, a warning is in order. No football coach would let his players kick a ball around unsupervised, and then claim they had been training: he plans the training sessions very carefully. However, one sometimes encounters teachers who do nothing with the computer but let the children play games at will, then refer to 'learning through play', and claim that the time has been profitably spent. This is the lazy way out: it is as great a dereliction of duty as the failure to plan any other lesson, and is only possible because the students find computer games more entertaining than the average unplanned lesson.

2.6   NEW APPROACHES TO EDUCATION

The rapid spread of microcomputers in the home and the school since the introduction of the Apple, PET and Tandy in 1977 has raised the possibility of a totally new approach to education.

When one considers what a person needs to know to live everyday life, the amount of mathematics is minimal: a little arithmetic will do it. Much of the mathematics curriculum exists only because the concepts were once necessary. However, the curriculum has not kept up with technology: calculators are a fact of life, and rarely fail. Similarly, the average person needs little formal knowledge of grammar; foreign languages are irrelevant for most people; concepts of mountain formation or knowledge of mediaeval wars are not going to assist in earning a living; etc. In most cultures, education has been for what you need to know. We, however, have built complicated educational structures, driven by the increasing amount of knowledge, not by the students' need to know. Hence the emphasis at each stage is on those who will continue to the next stage, rather than the (often larger) group who will cease formal education at this point. However, the recent sudden exponential increase in knowledge has brought people up short with the realization that one cannot teach everything, and must therefore teach how to learn.

Learning is validated when one can (and wants to) put it into practice; hence the liberalizing of curricula, emphasizing politics, social issues, etc. Unfortunately, one quickly exhausts these topics until the student has had a lot more experience of life. This is where the computer permits an improvement in learning, by affording some experience of otherwise inaccessible situations. For example, simulations permit experiments in economics, Prolog in historical research, and Logo in geometry. The computer offers the opportunity to carry out projects of greater complexity than is usually possible even in the real world, let alone the school context. Even if they are not directly relevant to one's later life, the 'totality' of the experience makes it enjoyable and worthwhile. Furthermore, it can be adopted by the student and made part of his or her own experience if it exhibits syntonicity, in terms of personal resonance, social resonance and utility.

Illich (1970) proposed the abolition of educational structures as we know them, because education has become a self-serving organization. He suggested the creation of flexible learning webs, including those people wishing to learn and those willing to teach, with appropriate rewards, educational credits, etc. A Papertian revolution in education offers a real possibility of achieving the benefits Illich seeks from 'de-schooling'.

In contrast, Professor Tom Stonier of the University of Bradford proposes far *more* education, in order to meet both the current unemployment problem (by taking hordes of students off the streets and creating a demand for more teachers), and the future unemployment problem (by educating more appropriately for the information revolution) (Stonier 1982). The problem with this is two-fold. Firstly, the provision of the necessary teachers; secondly, students who leave before the end of secondary schooling are often bored and disruptive in class for 12 months before they leave. Keeping them in school for even more years could be disastrous. Jones (1982) refers to Illich's work, but agrees with Stonier in viewing education as a significant area of employment: "we should recognize and pay for the concept of 'education for education's sake', rather than 'work for work's sake' ... We must recognize that psychological needs are at least as important as physical ones, and that education has always been (and will continue to be) our greatest industry in terms of the employment (meaning 'occupation', both paid and unpaid) of vast numbers of people." Ironically, the new developments in education could probably be used to implement the Stonier pattern, just as well as the Illich pattern.

2.7   THE 1990s AND ARTIFICIAL INTELLIGENCE: CAI RE-BORN

We said above that CAI failed to be widely applicable, because it did not reproduce person-to-person teaching, and because behaviourism is not sufficiently comprehensive to deal with the varieties of learning that take place in the classroom — certainly at tertiary level. The death-knell of behaviourism was sounded by the rise of cognitive psychology as the dominant paradigm for learning theory in the 1970s (Wilkinson 1983).

Researchers continued to ask, 'what is it that a teacher does that the machine is not doing?' The answer is that the teacher responds intelligently and creatively to the student's intermediate steps or false starts. The most advanced CAI systems represented course materials and teaching procedures separately, so that different problems and remedial comments could be generated for each student. However, this attempt to tailor courses to the individual student had limited success, because the good teacher must understand and respond appropriately to what the student is actually doing, and not just what s/he is supposed to do. This requires insight into the subject matter, the student's existing knowledge (and lack of it), the student's character, and good teaching principles. While this is clearly likely always to be beyond the scope of total automation, some of it does relate to an area of computing research, namely artificial intelligence.

It is not easy to define artificial intelligence, and many texts discursively slide around a definition. However, a reasonable definition is as follows: Artificial intelligence (AI) is the study of (i) how humans carry out tasks we class as intelligent; and (ii) how to produce machines which carry out such tasks. That the two parts may be different may be seen by analogy with flight: we study how birds fly, and how to build machines that fly, but our flying machines do not use the principles of avian flight. Research into the two areas of artificial intelligence has resulted in a number of very valuable and flexible learning tools, such as Logo (Chapters 5 and 12), Prolog, Smalltalk and Boxer (Chapter 12).

It will be evident that part of the difficulty in defining AI is the need to refer to intelligence, a term which is itself not well defined. In practice, AI is often defined simply by listing topics considered to fall under its umbrella. Such topics include understanding and translation of natural languages, understanding speech, vision systems, theorem proving, and playing chess. Clearly most of these relate to communication between people, and it was this fact that suggested the use of AI methods to improve the practice of computer assisted learning. The new, AI-based CAI systems have three components, namely an expert module; a teaching module; and a student module (Barr & Feigenbaum 1982)

1 *Expert module.* This contains the knowledge that the system is to impart. Originally conceived as a static data base, it is now more often a multi- dimensional network. A lot of work is proceeding on the representation of knowledge (knowledge engineering) and on expert systems. An expert system is one which exhibits the behaviour of a (human) expert in a particular area of specialization, based on a large domain of knowledge in that area. Expert systems have been devised to assist in the diagnosis of blood diseases (MYCIN) and to produce legal arguments in damage cases (LDS). In the CAI area, the expert module has the task of generating problems and checking the student's solutions. Some expert systems can describe the decision steps that led to a problem solution. This is only useful if the steps correspond to those of a human problem-solver.

2 *Teaching module.* This module communicates with the student, selecting problems, monitoring, criticizing, assisting on request, and selecting remedial material. It communicates in natural language rather than in highly coded form; it embodies a variety of teaching methods; and it has access to the student module. The aim is to say 'the right thing' to the student, so that s/he will realize his or her own errors.

3 *Student module.* This represents the student's understanding of the material to be taught, and is crucial if the teaching module is to 'say the right thing'. This understanding can be represented as a subset of the expert system's knowledge, or as a deviation from it. The latter makes it easier to recognize where the student's reasoning differs from that of the system. The contents of this module are built up over time by asking the student questions, and by making deductions based on his or her problem-solving activities.

Other aspects of expert systems are described in Section 4.5.

One advantage of the flexibility of the computer is that it can be programmed to reflect any view of the student which is considered appropriate. In early CAI work, the view embodied was a mechanistic, behaviourist one. The conscious application of AI techniques, and the explicit identification of a separate program module to represent the student and his or her current stage of understanding, makes much greater use of the computer's capabilities.

This new wave of tripartite CAI systems dates from the mid-1970s, and has already shown some significant success. However, we have associated it with the 1990s, as there is still a long way to go in the development of systems which exhibit the level of intelligent conversational communication that humans take for granted, and which do all the things a teacher would do in developing a student's knowledge and understanding. This is also the target date for the Japanese fifth generation project, which is AI-based, and includes ambitious proposals for expert systems based on cheap machines.

Chapter Three

Overview of computer assisted learning

When I use a word, it means just what I choose it to mean Lewis Carroll (1832–1898)

3.1 INTRODUCTION

In Chapter 2, we sketched a chronological view of computer use in education, both historical and predictive. In this chapter, we focus on the present, and on computer assisted learning (CAL). By CAL we mean what occurs when a computer (or computers) forms part of a learning environment. This does not include the presence of a computer, used only for administration, in the school office: this is considered in Part III. We also consider separately (in Part II) the teaching of computer topics.

It is most appropriate to use computers in the educational process, since learning involves the flow of information, and the computer is an information processor. However, there are distinguishably different styles of computer use for educational purposes. Taylor (1980) suggested that the computer may function as "tutor, tool or tutee", while Kemmis *et al* (1977) identified four approaches to education which they called (i) emancipatory; (ii) instructional; (iii) conjectural; and (iv) revelatory; and which are further described in Rushby (1979). It is convenient to use these headings to categorize CAL. However, the categories should not be interpreted rigidly, as emphases are constantly changing as new applications are developed.

3.2 EMANCIPATION: THE COMPUTER AS TOOL

This is the age of the labour-saving device. Mechanical and electronic gadgetry has been developed to reduce the human effort involved in many tasks, from tooth-cleaning to house-building. The analogous use of the computer to carry out boring tasks in education may be called emancipatory CAL. However, computer use in this sense should not be overdone, as there are circumstances, especially in learning or training situations, when expenditure of effort cannot be avoided, or the whole purpose of the activity is defeated: if you want to run a marathon, you should not avoid long training runs by always travelling by car. Thus, although the computer can quite easily take over a lot of the effort in educational tasks, the educator must first consider carefully whether the effort itself is an integral part of the desired learning (authentic effort) or whether it is simply a necessary evil to enable learning to take place (inauthentic effort). The authenticity of a particular activity may, of course, depend on the context. For example, simple arithmetic calculations are authentic in grade 3; but extensive ones are inauthentic at university. It is differences of opinion over authenticity of arithmetical calculations that have given rise to the extensive and continuing debate on the use of calculators in schools. In general, emancipatory programs should not be used too early before an understanding of the embodied concepts has been developed.

Availability in this role is making the computer an accepted part of the educational scene. It is no longer an arcane device, invoked only on special occasions, but a tool whose use comes as naturally as a pencil or blackboard. The computer has been called both 'electronic pencil' and 'electronic blackboard' to emphasize that its use by both students and teachers should be a normal event. So, for example, word processing was developed to save time and effort in office work in re-drafting documents, but is becoming a tool for thinking and creating. Computer-based information handling procedures were developed to assist businesses to process large amount of data, but are becoming a tool to remove the drudgery from learning to select, classify and use information.

It is no accident that many of the examples of CAL given in Chapter 1 can be placed in this category. It is discussed further in Chapter 4.

3.3   INSTRUCTION: THE COMPUTER AS TUTOR (CAI)

3.3.1   Much of the early use of computers in education could be classed as instructional, in its explicit attempts to instigate and control learning (see the previous chapter). This use was referred to indiscriminately as CAL or CAI (Computer Assisted Learning or

Instruction), despite the difference between (pupil-centred) learning and (teacher-centred) instruction. This style of CAL has now been largely superseded, except for special applications, such as remedial and revision work. Some people still use the terms CAL and CAI synonymously; however, CAI is increasingly being reserved to denote this instructional subset of CAL. Many CAI programs are still written, as they are generally easier to write than programs in the other three categories. For example, over 60% of the 1600 programs listed in a 1982 microcomputer educational software catalogue were of this type (Dresden 1982). We give CAI a larger section in this chapter, because it does not merit a chapter of its own. CAI may be divided into four subtypes.

Drill and practice CAI

This is the automation of those endless repetitive exercises that occur at the ends of chapters or on work sheets. The list of simple problems is stored in the computer, rather than on paper, and the student communicates with the computer via a terminal. The computer presents a problem and compares the student's answer with the correct one. What happens thereafter depends on the particular drill and practice program. If the student answers wrongly, the question is presented again. On a second incorrect response, the computer announces the right answer and moves on to the next question. Or the student is told (by the computer) to seek the teacher's help. Or

the question is re-presented until the right answer is given. Or an earlier similar question is re-presented. A correct answer, of course, causes the presentation of another question, which may be the next in sequence. Or the computer chooses questions at random from its list. Or the computer skips through the list if the student answers correctly the first time. In any case, a tally is kept (by the computer) of the number of questions presented and the number answered correctly. It may stop only at the end of the list; or only when the student has given a specified number of correct answers; or on request. It is claimed that such variability of behaviour permits the computer to respond appropriately to each user, and hence leads to 'individualization of learning'.

Tutorial CAI : programmed learning

Attempts have often been made to automate programmed learning texts, as follows. The topic to be studied is divided into a sequence of short numbered sections (called frames), each followed by questions on that section. Instead of simply proceeding to the next section in sequence (as in reading a normal book), or searching the index to locate desired revision material (again, as in a normal book), the reader is told which section to read next on the basis of answer(s) to the questions set. This format is clearly amenable to implementation by computer, with each frame being less than a screenful of text. This gives us tutorial CAI.

Generative CAI

In further pursuit of individualized instruction, the computer is programmed to generate questions within a basic framework about a particular topic. Questions can be generated randomly. This avoids knowledge of the correct answers becoming common currency in the class, but it makes it more difficult to compare the progress of different students. Alternatively, question generation can be made to depend on a student's previous responses. Such an approach to CAI is called generative. Clearly, drill and practice and tutorial CAI can be generative.

Dialogue/enquiry CAI

The computer's ability to generate questions relating to a given subject can be extended to enable the computer not simply to ask but also to answer questions in a limited subject area. This permits the student and computer to conduct a limited dialogue. The aim is to remove all restrictions on the student's input, and provide the computer with the ability to respond sensibly. In the first three forms of CAI, control of the situation rests with the computer, in that it initiates the student's activity. In dialogue/enquiry CAI, however, the pupil has some control.

The concept of conducting a dialogue with the computer has been greatly extended in recent years. This is the basis of Weizenbaum's *Eliza* and *Doctor* programs (Weizenbaum 1966), and of expert systems generally (Chapter 2). Thus, dialogue/enquiry CAL shades over from CAI into other styles of CAL. The following is a sample of dialogue with *Eliza* (human input in lower case; computer response in upper case):

Men are all alike.
IN WHAT WAY
They're always bugging us about something or other.
CAN YOU THINK OF A SPECIFIC EXAMPLE
Well, my boyfriend made me come here.
YOUR BOYFRIEND MADE YOU COME HERE
He says I'm depressed much of the time.
I AM SORRY TO HEAR YOU ARE DEPRESSED

It's true. I am unhappy.

DO YOU THINK COMING HERE WILL HELP YOU
NOT TO BE UNHAPPY

I need some help, that much seems certain.

WHAT WOULD IT MEAN TO YOU IF YOU GOT
SOME HELP

Perhaps I could learn to get along with my mother.

TELL ME MORE ABOUT YOUR FAMILY

We shall not consider the CAI or instructional style of CAL
further in any specific manner.

3.3.2   Disadvantages of CAI

CAI is now generally regarded as being based on an inappropriate
educational philosophy (cf. Howe & du Boulay 1979), and being too
rigid, and hence is subject to wide-ranging criticism, some of which
is outlined below. A cosmetic change of terminology from 'drill and
practice' to 'structured reinforcement' has not reduced the criticism.

1   Individualization may not be achieved. It is often claimed that
CAI offers personalization of tuition, and puts the student (rather
than the teacher) in the driving seat. However, this 'individual
instruction' often means only individual access, not specific teaching
for the student's strengths and weaknesses (Howe & du Boulay
1979).

2   A program may not be precisely right for a particular class, and
may not be easily modifiable, either. For example, there are many
methods for doing subtraction, and the program may not use the one
the teacher wishes to use. When a teacher uses a text or other printed
material, s/he often adapts it, to overcome such inconsistencies. CAI
material rarely offers teachers this opportunity.

3   Drill and practice programs often fail to respond appropriately to
wrong answers. Clearly, they should not just say 'wrong'.
Unfortunately, there are so many possible responses which a
thoughtful teacher might use, that it is infeasible to build them all
into the program. Some drill and practice implementations present
reinforcement feedback. This is a description of what the answer

should have been. Unfortunately, this generally fails to improve student performance. Better still is information feedback, which leads the student through the steps involved in producing the right answer, preferably by a sequence of questions and responses. Clearly it is difficult to plan such subsequences in advance.

4 CAI is inconsistent with many modern syllabi: it is inappropriate to drill ideas which make sense only when taught through discovery learning. (This problem is not confined to CAI, of course.) Howe and du Boulay contend that the widespread use of drill and practice would turn back the educational clock, and would be an abuse of the potential of advanced technology.

5 Drill and practice often makes use of multi-choice or short answer questions, and so it shares the possible repressive effects that such questions may have when used in other contexts. For example, 'What was the main reason for Governor Macquarie's downfall?' suggests that there is just one right answer, and leaves no room for opinion, discussion or challenging 'facts'.

3.4   CONJECTURE: THE COMPUTER AS 'TUTEE'

The major criticism of tutor mode CAL is that the computer is in control. This is not only psychologically inappropriate, but also educationally unsatisfactory, since as has often been observed, the best way to learn something is to try to teach it. This suggests that the roles be reversed and the student control the computer. Now, the way to control a computer is to write a program, and this can be a complicated process, requiring a lot of learning. We therefore have a dilemma: to learn best, the student should teach, but first needs to learn how to teach. It was to cut across this dilemma that Papert developed Logo. His aim was that it should be a language "with no threshold", so the beginner can use it almost immediately. However, it also has very powerful facilities, so it continues to be useful as the student's ability increases and horizons expand. (Logo learning environments and microworlds are discussed in Chapter 5.) Other languages now exist that offer a gentle entry to programming, and hence open up the learning that can take place *through* programming. Prolog and Smalltalk are two examples. A natural extension to the Logo concept of 'teaching a turtle to draw a circle' is to write a CAL program designed to teach another person. A computer program may be a model of some aspect of reality, so the ability to program empowers a student to build various models and test various hypotheses (conjectures). Another benefit of this mode of computer use is the opportunity to solve problems of manageable dimensions. Unfortunately, the general problem-solving skills developed in programming do not appear to transfer automatically to other domains. This may be because people think more specifically in terms of the structure of the problem under consideration at any time, rather than more broadly in terms of the language being used to solve it. Transfer effects have been more evident in highly structured situations where the student's attention is drawn explicitly to the principles s/he is unconsciously applying, rather than in the open, exploratory Papertian mode. Lewis (1980) presents carefully graded exercises and procedures designed to teach problem solving processes. Further aspects of problem solving and programming are discussed in Chapter 11.

It is important to remember that the learning of programming should never be an end in itself, but a means to other concurrent and subsequent ends.

3.5   REVELATION: SIMULATION

Here, the computer acts as a mediator between the student and a model of some real-life situation. The model simulates a nuclear power plant, a sick patient, genetic inheritance, or the economy, for example, and the student is led through a process of learning by discovery as s/he inputs data and observes the results. Sometimes s/he is free to use any data; sometimes the leading process is more structured being designed to guide the student's investigation of the model along a pre-determined route.

Computer-based simulations are very useful in the science laboratory, where they permit students to gain experience with substances that are too expensive (like gold) or too dangerous (like uranium) to be actually used in school experiments. However, simulation is no substitute for experimental skills. Simulation is also useful in social sciences, but it is no substitute for actual experience in interviewing. If the aim is to teach the handling of equipment, making measurements, or interviewing people, then this must be done through the medium of genuine experiments and experience.

Some of the better simulations involve both computer-oriented work and non-computer-oriented work (see the examples in Chapter 1).

This form of CAL is related to each of the others. Firstly, in an obvious sense, the computer as simulator is a tool, permitting experiments to be carried out. Secondly, the dialogue/enquiry form of CAI shades into simulation. Thirdly, in conjectural mode, the user is actually building models, rather than just changing the inputs to them.

Simulation is considered in detail in Chapter 6.

3.6   ADVANTAGES OF CAL

The effectiveness of CAL is difficult to define. Amount of learning; retention of learning; reduction in drop-outs; attitude to the topic of study; attitude to study in general; and attitude to computers; these are all possible criteria for measuring its effectiveness. In general, well-designed, tightly controlled evaluative studies of the use of CAL are rare, because it is difficult to control the number of variables.

In practice, therefore, studies tend to be statistical concentrating on CAI, and behavioural objectives, and comparing 'the use of a computer' for teaching a particular course segment, with 'the non-use of a computer' for the same segment. Unfortunately, this entirely misses the point, which should be evident from the examples in Chapter 1, that the computer is used best if it is integrated into the learning environment, as a tool, laboratory apparatus or catalyst. To measure learning rather than performance, attitudinal studies are required.

However, the following advantages have been reported or surmised from time to time (cf. Chambers & Sprecher 1980). Most relate specifically to CAI, but some are more generally applicable.

1   Frees teachers for other necessary work, and hence increases educational productivity.
2   By enabling students to manipulate concepts directly, and explore the results of such manipulation (especially in emancipatory mode), it reduces the time taken to understand difficult concepts. Note that superficial learning time need not necessarily be reduced. Just as with any other labour-saving device, one may do more in the same time, rather than the same in less time.

3 It individualizes instruction by responding appropriately to current student input, possibly taking into account also the student's performance to date. This could extend to the presentation of alternative materials or methods. It also allows the individual student to have some control over the content, sequence, and pace of his or her course.

4 It forces active participation, in a way that a text book cannot, and a lesson often does not.

5 Partly as a result of interactive student participation, it offers fast feedback. This, of course, is essential for feedback to be truly effective. Periodic tests can adopt an instructional as well as a monitorial role.

6 It permits students to make their mistakes in private. Many students are embarrassed to ask a question lest they seem stupid, or inattentive. They then waste a lot of time seeking the answer. If the computer can get them started, they can bring the deeper questions to the teacher with more confidence.

7 Offers a wider range of experiences than are otherwise available to the student (especially through simulations).

8 Captures the interest of some reluctant learners (and, as a result, has been observed to reduce truancy, where this is a problem).

9 Good for low-aptitude students and for revision.

3.7   CAL CONSIDERATIONS

3.7.1   Educational

1 The computer is educationally neutral, and, by appropriate choice of software and techniques, can be used to support any educational philosophy. On the one hand, it has been used to implement behaviourist theories (Section 3.3) that had already been implemented without the use of computers. On the other hand, it is facilitating long-standing educational aims which had not previously been fully achievable. It has long been recognized that the student learns better if s/he is in control of learning, and is forced to take meaningful initiatives in the process. The computer, especially in conjectural and emancipatory modes, permits the learner to be in control. The computer acts like a magnifying glass, amplifying whatever approach is taken to curriculum.

2   In all education one should first set the educational goals, then consider ways of achieving them. This approach should also be applied to the use of computers. If, when the educational goals have been set, the computer is deemed to be useful, it can be introduced as an integral part of the learning experience.

3   Care may need to be taken to avoid the computer's being regarded as a special novelty, but rather as an integral part of the educational process.

4   Simulation programs permit the execution of chemical and biological experiments, and so teach about reactions etc. They do not give practice in laboratory procedures, such as handling equipment, rearing fruit flies, etc.

5   The time required for computer use must be considered. Good simulations generate personal interactions, and use a lot of class time. Tool programs theoretically save time, but in practice are often used to do more.

6   Only a few instances of CAL can be presented to the student with no prior explanation. Usually, just as with other educational activities, some background must be provided, including some explanation of how to interact with the program(s).

3.7.2   Personnel

There have been significant problems in this area. These include the following.

1   Lack of teachers with the ability to make use of computers in education.

2   Lack of money in teacher training to change this.

3   Teachers' fear of a new device.

4   Teachers' rejection of a system which was originally touted as being their ultimate replacement.

5   Domination of school computer use by the mathematics department.

6   Lack of communication between teachers using CAL material.

7   Lack of expert support for teachers using the material.

8   Tension between educational and administrative use of the computer: this may make choice of a configuration difficult.

9   Extra time may be needed for lesson preparation using the new facility.
10   Software selection skills must be developed.

These problems are being, and in some places have been, overcome. We mention them to assist in the diagnosis of adverse undercurrents which may sometimes be felt.

3.7.3   Hardware

1   Some available hardware offered for educational use was not designed for that purpose.
2   The diversity of hardware makes it difficult to select a system, and difficult to build a base of expertise and software for a given machine.
3   The rapid development of hardware makes it difficult to select a system before it becomes obsolete.
4   Costs include purchase, maintenance, repair, enhancements, and the administration of the augmented instructional system.
5   The system must be managed, and the class and hardware be in the same room at the right time.

3.7.4   Courseware

1   The time taken to develop programs. Factors of 50 or 100 hours to develop 1 hour of CAL material are often quoted (although these are principally for extensive CAI programs).

2 Probably as a result of this, the dearth of good quality courseware. Chambers and Sprecher (1980) quote a review of 4000 CAL programs written in Basic, of which only 3–4% were found acceptable by teachers in the relevant discipline.

3 Various skills are needed to write good courseware, which suggests the need for a team approach.

4 As a result of **1** and **3**, the high cost of CAL courseware.

5 Lack of portability. This is due to the variety of languages (cf. Chapter 12) which in turn is due largely to the variety of systems in use. Even the programs mentioned in **2**, all nominally written in the same language (Basic), were sufficiently different that it would have taken about 100 hours work per program to make them sharable. Increasingly, however, the specifications of what the CAL programs should do are being written first, and programs to do this being produced for several different computers. An example of this is the Jacaranda Wiley series of programs on mapping skills.

6 Extra costs. Despite early claims, CAL is usually in addition to, not instead of, a lot of existing activities, and schools lack the money to meet these extra costs.

Chapter Four

The computer
as a tool

Man is a tool-using animal. Without tools he is nothing, with tools he is all
Thomas Carlyle (1795–1881)

4.1 INTRODUCTION

Humankind has been characterized as *Homo habilis*, 'man the tool-maker', and the computer is one of his latest and most versatile tools. Never content with any particular tool, man constantly improves old ones and develops new ones. Thus, the digging stick is superseded by the rotary hoe (or rotavator); the automatic washing machine is an improvement on using heavy stones in a stream; etc. In each case, the more advanced tool permits a given amount of work to be done in less time, or more work to be done in a given amount of time. Similarly, the computer is an improvement on the manual processing of information and permits information to be processed in greater quantities or at a greater rate. Considered in this light, every use of the computer is as a tool, emancipating people from otherwise tedious and time-consuming activities. However, it is helpful to identify different emphases of educational computer use, and this we did in the previous chapter.

In the educational context, the 'computer as tool' contrasts with the 'computer as focus' of the learning activity. In CAI mode (Section 3.3), for example, the computer leads the user through the activities to be carried out. In simulation mode (Chapter 6), a model is built in to the computer, so it is the machine that maintains the thread of the activity (even though extensive non-computer activities may take place). Even in conjectural mode (Chapter 5), the distinction is still present, as although the user is more in control, the computer is the milieu within which the models are being built. By contrast, in tool (or emancipatory) mode, the thread of activity is independent of the computer, even though the computer may be used extensively from time to time. The use of the computer as a quiescent tool or resource, to be called into play as and when required, is very valuable and effective. As computers are integrated into the educational process and activities, more and more computer use is seen as being in this category.

In any field, the potential contribution of computers is initially viewed in terms of the processes already present, and not in terms of activities which are currently impossible precisely because they require the computer. This is inevitable, because until one is aware of the capabilities offered by computers, one is unaware of the novel activities they make possible. However, computerization of an existing system can have the unfortunate consequence of irrevocably entrenching it. This is because people spend a lot of time, effort and money in implementing and learning to use the computer-based system. Then, when use of this system suggests totally new ideas, people are strongly resistant to changing yet again to implement these new ideas. It is ironic that innovative people who introduce computers at an early stage, without waiting for 'everyone else' to do it first, can be the ones who are thus locked in to an obsolete system. Of course, this phenomenon is not restricted to computers.

In any such situation, the existing system is reaffirmed, with its bad points as well as its good ones. Garson (1979) points out that some current educational systems have unhealthy aspects. For example, they place pupils in a passive recipient role, they postulate mandatory examinations, and they over-educate for jobs. The

introduction of computers could reinforce these unhealthy aspects of the system and, furthermore, add a dimension of training people in mechanistic skills. The only way to avoid this completely is to be able to predict the future. In the absence of this ability, it may be possible to minimize the ill effects by designing the computer, not around the concept of surrogate teacher, but around the concept of student resource, or tool. This approach assists in the maintenance of flexibility, because new computer uses can be implemented and incorporated as they are recognized or developed. Students can be relieved of tasks (such as extensive memorizing) which are better done by the computer. At the least, this frees them to develop essential skills and knowledge (such as social interaction and information handling). It is possible to go further, however, and design the computer applications so that its use actually assists in the development of such skills and knowledge. Some of the many uses of the computer as an educational tool are described in this chapter. (See also the examples in Chapter 1.)

4.2   THE COMPUTER AS CALCULATOR

4.2.1   Statistical calculations

The topic of statistics received little attention in schools until recent years. This was partly due to the extensive calculations necessary for worthwhile applications: even a simple mean and standard deviation calculation of data obtained about the members of one school class took a long time. However, statistics has (rightly) been given increasing prominence in school curricula, and careful use of a computer can add immeasurably to the subject. Note that this is an excellent example of the distinction between authentic and inauthentic labour. By the time a student is studying statistics, simple arithmetical processes should be well understood, and computer calculation of running totals, square roots, etc. quite reasonable. The authentic labour at this point is the work necessary to understand the significance of the statistical parameters computed.

There are a number of computer packages for statistical analysis. A package, in this sense, is a group of programs. Use of the package is via commands designed to be relevant to the topic of the package. Some statistical packages are *SAS* (*Statistical Analysis System*), *Minitab*, and, the best known, *SPSS* (*Statistical Package for the Social Sciences*). *Minitab* is available on some microcomputers, and *SPSS* is available for many computers. It puts statistical manipulations conveniently into the hands of many people and hence can be abused: it is as easy to request 100 correlations as 10 — but can take hours of computer time and reams of printer paper; it is easy to request a statistic which will not be significant — again wasting time. It is vital in these applications to think first about what calculations one wants. Many novice users of such packages are like someone who, given his first electric saw, cuts every piece of wood in sight 'because it's so easy' rather than first calculating and measuring to determine which cuts are required.

4.2.2   Numerical methods

In school calculus, one learns Simpson's rule for integration, and possibly the Newton–Raphson method for the solution of equations. Before computers were available, these numerical methods were fringe topics, because applying them is laborious. Now, however, it is possible to carry out many more steps of an iterative method; possible to compute numerically some of the many integrals that cannot be handled analytically; possible to calculate non-integral roots of equations; etc. In fact the educational role of the computer becomes slightly fuzzy here. On the one hand, it is a tool, making feasible long calculations to exemplify the methods being learned. On the other hand, however, it is also an object of study, since most such calculations in the 'real world' are also carried out by computer.

Some fascinating possibilities exist. For example, the mathematics teacher says that if you add 1 and ½ and ⅓ and ¼ and ..., then the sum gets bigger and bigger (albeit slowly). If you program a computer to do the addition, however, the sum stops increasing after a while. Such an observation, made by the student at first-hand, provides an excellent starting point for the discussion of topics such as infinity, precision and errors.

4.2.3   Spreadsheets

The statistics learned may be applied in social and biological sciences; the numerical methods in mathematics and engineering;

and another tool, the spreadsheet, is used in economics and accounting. A spreadsheet is a page, usually large, divided into many columns and rows, whose significance and use depends on the individual entries. A spreadsheet used for company budgeting might have one column allocated to each department, and each row to a category of income. Another spreadsheet could represent expenditure in similar fashion. There are usually some entries that depend on others, such as totals, subtotals, percentages and so on. Thus, the changing of one or two entries may entail much eraser work and re-calculation of dependent entries. It is here that an 'electronic spreadsheet' shows its value (Fig. 4.1). Displaying on a terminal screen a table of rows and columns (usually 254 rows by 63 columns), a program allows the user to enter mathematical formulae to specify how the values of particular entries are to be calculated from others. The user then inputs the independent entries, and all the totals, balances or whatever are calculated and displayed automatically by the computer program. Now, when an entry is changed, the computer re-calculates all the entries which depend on it, and displays all the updated values.

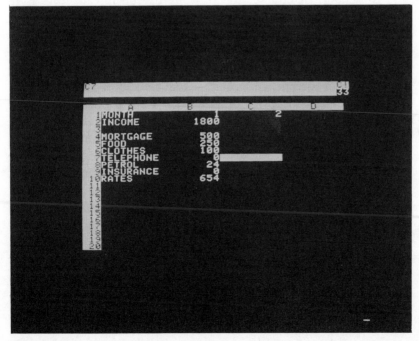

Fig. 4.1

The first, and best-known, electronic spreadsheet program was *VisiCalc*, developed in 1978 at Harvard. This is available for many computer systems (including microcomputers). Other spreadsheet programs are available, and include *Lotus 1-2-3*, *Multiplan*, *SuperCalc*, *CalcStar*, *Logicalc*, *Magicalc*, *ParaCalc*, *PlannerCalc*, *CalcResult*, *InfoCalc*, *MicroModeller* and *IFPS*. It is clear from the above brief description of spreadsheet usage, that the computer-based spreadsheet lends itself to the answering of questions of the 'what if...?' kind. The manager of a company can enter possible instead of actual figures and formulae, and observe the result. Used thus, *Visicalc* and the others verge on model-building or simulation programs. In fact, *MicroModeller* and *IFPS* are designed more for use by long-term economic model-builders than for managers interested in day to day effects. In addition to financial modelling, spreadsheets can be used in other business areas, such as stock control, and estimation. *Multiplan* is thought by some people to be easier to use than *Visicalc*. Apart from *IFPS*, the systems mentioned above would be within the financial range of many schools. Some, such as *Lotus*, combine the spreadsheet facility with graphics and data base capabilities.

In school, of course, the obvious use of spreadsheets is in business and accounting courses, as well as mathematics. Fractions, decimals, ratio, simple and compound interest, income, income tax, inflation, money management and investment are all possible applications areas. However, Hayes (1983) has some interesting applications of spreadsheet programs that could be used to introduce the spreadsheet concept to other students not actually studying a commercial subject. It can also be used to present and afford practice with matrices (in mathematics, perhaps). Another point, valuable in the subject computer studies, is that the spreadsheet is a simple introduction to non-algorithmic problem solution. The spreadsheet does not exhibit the sequence of steps of the typical flowchart or pseudocode algorithm. Rather, it is a static structure designed to encompass the entire procedure all at once. The computer itself, of course, must carry out the necessary steps in some well-defined sequence. However, the user need not be concerned with this. This characteristic makes the spreadsheet a useful introduction to fourth and fifth generation, non-procedural, computer languages, such as Prolog.

4.2.4   Symbolic mathematics

Sometimes the mathematician does not immediately require a numeric solution to a problem, but wishes to manipulate algebraic and numeric symbols, to integrate, for example, or to differentiate, or to factorize a polynomial. Computer programs can be written to do this, and symbolic manipulation packages such as muMath are available to enable this to be done on a microcomputer.

4.3   THE COMPUTER AS WORD PROCESSOR

The computer is a general data processor, not merely a processor of numerical data. Alphabetic characters may be input to, coded in and stored by the computer just as readily as numeric ones. This means that the computer can store words, sentences and whole books. Furthermore, it can be programmed to perform the sort of operations we should like to perform on the text of any letter or document we have written.

One such operation is editing, and most computers have an editor program. This program enables one to review any text which has been typed in to the computer, and amend it. Typical amendments are the correction of spelling errors, deletion of unwanted sentences, interchanging paragraphs, etc. When the content of the text is satisfactory, it must be set out for printing or typing. To this end, many computers have a text formatting program, allowing the user to specify such things as number of lines per page, size of margins, page numbering, section and subsection numbering, paragraph indentation, and tabular output. The text of this book was input to and edited on a VAX computer. It was then output on magnetic tape which was used as input to the typesetter.

Some computer systems (both the hardware and the associated software) are designed to be particularly convenient for editing and text formatting. Such systems are called word processing systems. These were quickly adopted in situations where similar documents had frequently to be produced: in a solicitor's office, for example, where the same deed, contract, etc. is frequently produced, but with different names, addresses, numeric entries, etc.; in a college, to prepare handbooks or course notes, which need to be revised from

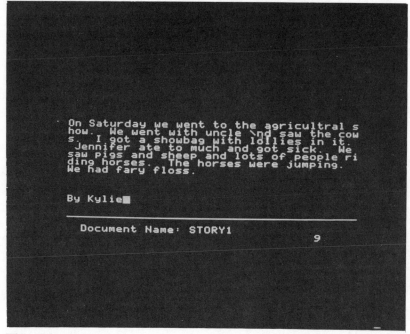

On Saturday we went to the agricultral s
how. We went with uncle \nd saw the cow
s. I got a showbag with lollies in it.
Jennifer ate to much and got sick. We
saw pigs and sheep and lots of people ri
ding horses. The horses were jumping.
We had fary floss.

By Kylie

Document Name: STORY1

9

Fig. 4.2

year to year. Increasingly, however, word processors are replacing typewriters in many offices because of the ease with which letters and reports can be amended or produced in different formats. Word processing packages are now available for most general purpose computers, and some are only a little less convenient than the specialized word processing systems. Some, such as *Zardax*, *Wordstar* and *Spellbinder* run on a variety of computers; while others, such as *Applewriter* and *Wordbee*, are specific to one machine.

Use of word processing in the classroom can both prepare students for its use in the workplace, and be used to assist with school work. We have already described (Section 1.6) how word processing can enable the implementation of the process writing approach to creative written work. First drafts can be produced without too much concern for spelling, etc. (Fig. 4.2). Corrections and amendments can then be made progressively, without having to re-write the whole essay manually. Theses or long projects can be gradually assembled, typing in a chapter or section at a time, not necessarily in the final order, and then re-organized as desired. Many word processors will keep an automatic index of specified words. Reports can be drafted, and then printed in different layouts for different purposes, such as checking by the student, checking by the teacher or submission to an external examiner. Most word processors can automatically number paragraphs and subparagraphs. Clearly, using a word processor does not teach the skill of handwriting. Therefore handwriting must be taught separately. This division can be useful, as it permits the student's attention to be concentrated on one thing at a time. This does seem, prima facie, to be better than seeking creativity in a story, and simultaneously insisting on concentration on spelling and on careful attention to handwriting.

Quill (Bolt et al 1983) is a set of microcomputer-based writing activities for Years 4–6. Quill addresses six characteristics of writing instruction via six specially designed facilities. A Planner encourages organized note taking; a Library stores and provides access to text; a Mailbag permits the sending of messages; an editor (Writer's Assistant) facilitates revision; a formatter (Publisher) produces finished text; and Story Maker is a story construction tool.

Many word processors have an associated thesaurus of words, which can be used for spelling correction. Each word in a text is checked against the thesaurus; if it does not appear therein, it is displayed on the screen, possibly with suggested corrections, namely the word(s) in the thesaurus most like it. Used thus, the system actually teaches spelling (to some extent), as it points out mistakes, and (often) the correct word alongside. Sometimes, of course, the word is correct, albeit absent from the thesaurus. The user signals this fact, and the computer adds the word to the thesaurus. Sometimes, however, a listed word is correctly spelled, but is not the one intended. For example, if 'bare' is in the thesaurus, it will always be accepted as correct, even if the user meant 'bear'. Such errors can only be detected if the system is designed to take the context of a word into account as well, and then we are into the area of understanding natural language, not simple word processing. In practice, an automatic spelling corrector works best if the desired allowable words are few in number and quite different in form.

One approach to spelling correction is to include common misspellings in the thesaurus, associated with correct spelling. This is not done in practice (Peterson 1980), because of the difficulty of deciding just which errors are common. A more widely used approach is to check each word in the text which is not in thesaurus to see if it differs from a thesaurus word by: (i) transposition of two letters; (ii) one letter extra; (iii) one letter missing; or (iv) one letter wrong.

These four rules cover 80% of spelling errors. Such checking is not cheap, but neither is it prohibitive. A thesaurus of 10 000 words would be quite reasonable for a small community of users. This requires about 100 K bytes of storage — less than one single-sided single density floppy disc.

The computer's word processing facility makes the use of the cloze procedure for both teaching and testing a very simple matter (Sullivan 1984). It is easy to specify the words to be omitted (every fifth one has been found to be best) and to give the student immediate feedback as s/he chooses words to fill the gaps in the given text.

One natural area of computer use closely associated with word-processing is the teaching of typing (Section 1.5). A useful, integrated course in commercial studies can be based on the computer and include both the learning of typing and of general word processing skills.

The above description of the computer's capabilities in the word processing field has not included pedagogical considerations. These must be taken into account before sensible decisions on actual computer use can be made. The first decision is whether the use of the computer is in fact easier than manual re-drafting involving crossing out and inserting or cutting and pasting. Relevant considerations are the availability of the computer system for input and editing; and the production of printouts for inspection and correction. Secondly, what skills are currently to be learned? If one is manual dexterity in writing, then keyboard use is inappropriate; if one is spelling, then automatic correction is inappropriate. Clearly, this sort of computer application will work best with children who are already reasonably familiar with the computer, and can therefore use it as a tool without the use obtruding on their consciousness. Used properly, the word processor, like Logo (Chapter 5), is a tool for thinking.

4.4   THE COMPUTER AS LABORATORY ASSISTANT

4.4.1   The computer as controller

Much modern machinery is controlled by computer. Indeed the

control of microwave ovens and automatic washing machines was among the most common uses of microprocessors when they were developed in the early 1970s. In laboratories, many devices need controlling, including stepping motors, cameras and feeding mechanisms for animals. Most school experiments are so reduced in scope that no automatic control is necessary. However, if a computer is available, together with a means for converting computer output into signals to control the devices, then more extensive and more precise experiments can be conducted (Fig. 4.3).

Fig. 4.3

Automatic control usually involves a feed-back loop: that is, the current state of on apparatus is sensed and used to determine the next control signal. Some automatic controllers are simple devices, as for example in temperature directed control of a heater, and time directed control of lights. A computer is needed when significant calculations must be performed between the observation being made and the consequent control signal being sent, and the computer's capability for recognizing and acting on a great variety of conditions is essential. In chemical kinetics, for example, which is the study of the rates of chemical reactions, traditional methods can be used only on slow reactions (of half-life 10 minutes or more), and involve lengthy calculation of results. Fast reactions can be studied using a computer-controlled spectrophotometer, provided the resulting data analysis is also carried out by computer.

Another exciting application is in a music laboratory. It is possible to obtain keyboard and synthesizer attachments for an Apple computer (among others). With such a system, the student can be required to play the notes on the keyboard which correspond to sounds emitted by the synthesizer. Used thus, the computer is functioning as a sophisticated teaching tool, perhaps only in CAI mode. However, the system can also be used as a composing tool: the student can play at the keyboard, while the synthesizer produces the corresponding sounds and the computer records the corresponding notes. This could be a significant aid to creativity.

4.4.2   The computer as data recorder

Many experiments will continue once initiated, and the experimenter simply needs to make successive observations: of temperature, perhaps, or voltage, or pressure or radioactive decay or the number of items that have passed a certain point. Work with a solar heater could be based on the regular and frequent recording of collector input and output temperatures, the ambient temperature, and the solar radiation striking the collector. Often, now, an appropriate data-logging program can be written to record all the data that is input to the computer by the apparatus via an appropriate interface device. This use emphasizes the input part of the feedback loop mentioned in the last section, but simply recording the input, rather than taking any input-dependent action.

Sometimes, it is more helpful to have the computer represent the data by displaying it graphically on a screen, rather than (or as well as) printing numerical observations for later inspection. The screen of an oscilloscope is a common example of a similar effect, where voltages etc. are observed by the machine, and a graph of the values is shown on a screen.

In general, a lot of money can be saved by writing simple programs to enable the computer to function as an instrument simulator, instead of buying a lot of specialized equipment that will be used only occasionally. Often, a program can be modified quite easily to record other observations, or counts. This is not only economical, but also demonstrates the similar nature of apparently dissimilar processes.

4.5   THE COMPUTER AS EXPERT

4.5.1   Information handling

In Section 1.5 we mentioned the *First Fleet Data Base*, which provides a milieu for historical and sociological study. Another data base established by the Elizabeth Computer Centre in Hobart is *Birds of Antarctica*. This lists the sightings of birds on an Antarctic expedition in November and December 1982, together with time, date, place, weather conditions, and the bird's activity. Interrogation of the data base permits the student to practice scientific investigation, building up a picture of the habitat and behaviour of sea birds. This leads to non-computer activities in studying climate, ecosystems, history, etc.

Work with an established data base focuses on the subject matter, and on techniques for information retrieval. The next step is for students to construct their own data bases. These will probably be less extensive and less detailed, but possibly more motivating. Furthermore, students are then practising techniques of information collection, categorizing and storage. Two systems designed to help students to do this are *Factfile* and *Quest* (Section 1.6). Another system is *Query*, an application of which to geography studies is described in Eisenstadt (1982). Students collected data from a rural area about the shopping and travelling habits of the residents. As the data grew, the scope of project work increased, but data analysis became more time-consuming. Using computer-based storage and handling permitted hypotheses to be tested easily.

4.5.2   Expert systems (cf. Section 2.7)

Systems for handling data bases provide specified ways of accessing the data. In recent years, systems have been developed which permit the user to ask any question at all. To accomplish this, a system needs the following characteristics.

1   In-depth knowledge. Humans use a lot of implicit information in all their communication. The system must contain a lot of knowledge to even begin to match this.
2   Responsiveness. Through dialogue with the user, the system should be able to explore the intention of a query it does not at once

understand, and eventually either produce the answer or indicate that it is unable to answer the question.

3 Convenience. The system should accept queries in any form, the closer to the user's natural language the better, so the user does not have to learn a computer language. This requirement is also a partial consequence of 2 above.

Point **1** can clearly be satisfied most readily if the scope of the knowledge is restricted. The resulting system 'knows' a lot about a rather specific topic, and hence behaves rather like a human expert on the domain of knowledge it encompasses. Such systems have come to be called expert systems. More precisely, however, an expert system should: (i) perform at a level close enough to that of the human expert for the system to be useful; and (ii) perform the expert's task in basically the same way that the expert performs it [unlike the aeroplane and the bird (Section 2.7)].

There are several reasons for this second requirement, which diverges from common AI (artificial intelligence) practice. The power of an expert system lies in its knowledge base. This body of knowledge and its interrelationships is coded and set down by an expert in the area and an expert on expert systems! This is done iteratively in a codify, test, revise, ... cycle, with the domain expert commenting on shortcomings and suggesting modifications. Clearly, if the system uses its knowledge in a totally different manner from that of the expert, s/he will not be able to relate deficiencies in system performance to inadequacies in the knowledge base. Furthermore, we put a lot of trust in experts, and expect them to be able to justify their recommendations or answers. If a human expert is to be replaced by an expert system, to control a nuclear power station or air traffic movements, for example, then it must be able to explain itself on request, and we want to be able to understand the explanation.

A number of expert systems exist and are in common use. They will become increasingly common in all areas of information retrieval. If a library is automated using an expert system, electronic browsing is simplified, and serendipity learning — that is, chancing upon new ideas and information — enhanced. Clearly, many data bases would be appropriate for embedding in an expert system. Since the Prolog language (Chapter 12) has brought the construction of data bases, and the rules associated with them, within the capabilities of school children, expert systems will become increasingly relevant in schools. In fact, one could sum up the Japanese fifth generation project as the use of Prolog and data bases to build expert systems.

4.6   THE COMPUTER AS ARTIST

Much effort has been devoted to endowing computers with sophisticated graphical capabilities, for in all applications the value of graphical output is being recognized. Pictures and diagrams can enliven and enlighten an otherwise rather obscure list of figures or block of text. It is said that a picture is worth a thousand words, and there is probably some corresponding conversion factor for pictures vis-à-vis numbers. Even microcomputers permit the drawing of complicated coloured pictures, while there are large special purpose computers that can produce pictures with the facility of the cartoon and the reality of a motion picture. Art educators at all levels should therefore consider the impact of computer graphics on their subject (Deken 1983). Art students need to extend their design knowledge, perceptual skills, visual awareness, technical knowledge and skills, and critical skills to include the use of computers for graphical work. Conversely, art students should consider the openings for graphic designers to work in the computer field. These aims are achievable in schools, since many colour graphics and computer-aided design packages are available for microcomputers. With these, students can

Fig. 4.4

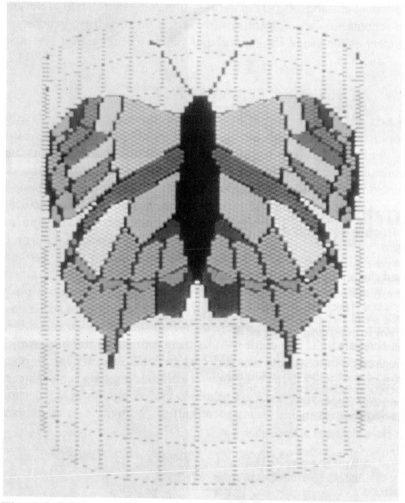

Fig. 4.5

draw various charts and graphs; three-dimensional diagrams, including perspective views; and pictures of all sorts. Computer-based graphics enable a student to draw quickly and accurately, and hence they form the pictorial analogue of the word processor.

The ability to draw accurately permits the investigation of patterns and shapes. Symmetry is a topic which has appeared in the mathematics curriculum in recent years. Understanding of this concept is enhanced by the ability to move patterns around the screen, and see where and how they fit together. *Tesselator* is a program from Addison-Wesley which runs on the BBC microcomputer. The user is able to produce tessellations (that is, coverings of a flat surface with shapes or tiles leaving no gaps). Escher tessellations use different shapes; while Penrose tesselations use just two shapes (Fig. 4.4). Another program (also from Addison-Wesley for the BBC) is *Graphito*, a colour graphics package for geometry, permitting two-dimensional transformations, three-dimensional linear transformations, spirograph drawings and rubber band drawings (Fig. 4.5).

A graphics package can also be a useful tool in the study of vectors, drafting, technical drawing, dynamics (moving springs, balls, etc.), calculus (curve drawing, equation solving), linear programming (dynamic convergence on solutions), and geography (mapping, scale drawing, compass work). Logo (turtle geometry) is very useful in geometrical areas. Also, wherever data bases are relevant, graphics can be used in conjunction therewith to display information from the data base.

Hardware to support the computers' graphical capability is discussed in Chapter 14.

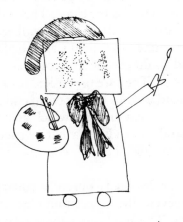

ME IN MY NEO-IMPRESSIONIST PERIOD!

4.7   LEARNING ABOUT THE TOOL

In using the computer, we learn about the computer. Using it as calculator, we learn about its accuracy, its precision, its finite storage capacity that leads to rounding errors. Using it as a spreadsheet, we can learn about non-algorithmic processes. Using it to control a model railway we can learn about process scheduling, resource management and deadlock. The Reality In Mathematics Education (RIME) project of the Victorian Department of Education has used this effect. In some of the mathematics lessons designed in this project, a computer is used, and the teacher is encouraged to take the opportunity to draw to the students' attention some aspects of computers, and their advantages and limitations. With learning environments structured in this way, the use of the computer as a tool provides a significant measure of computer awareness (especially if it is used in a variety of ways), and forms a good basis and context for further explicit instruction under this heading. This approach can often be used when only one computer is available per class, and when the teacher lacks the experience or confidence to teach about computers directly.

One example from the RIME project will serve to illustrate the idea (cf. C. Lovitt, 'Ready made lessons in mathematics/computer classes: a teacher education project', *in* Salvas 1983). Eleven to thirteen year old pupils are to be introduced to the concept of summing an arithmetic series, by pairing the numbers in the series so that the sum of each pair is the same. This is done for series starting 1, 2, 3, ... and ending with an even number. In the classroom is a computer, programmed to sum any specified arithmetic series. The pupils are asked to do several examples, and use the computer to check their answers. They are then asked to devise ways of extending the method to handle series ending on an odd number, then to series not starting with 1, then to series which go up in steps greater than unity. When a student produces a tentative technique, s/he uses it to find a few answers, and then, by checking these on the computer, tests the theory.

Thus far, the lesson is purely mathematics, with computer assistance. However, the opportunity exists to teach something about computers. The computer should be programmed to add the series 'the long way'. Despite this, it is still 'fast' in human terms on series of length less than about 100. No series tested up to this stage should be longer than this. The teacher may now invite the class to try to 'beat the machine'. The initial response is likely to be that it is impossible to beat a machine, which can solve any problem almost instantly. However, before reaching series of length 3000, most students are 'beating the machine'. This begins to put machine ability in context. If now, the machine is asked to check $1+2+3+\ldots+1\,000\,000$, the students may be asked how long they think it will take. Almost all are still likely to be well off the mark, which may be more than two hours!

The teacher should explain, of course, that the computer is programmed to do the addition the long way. This leads to the suggestion that the computer be programmed to use the short cut. This in turn provides a basis for pointing out that there are good and bad programs, and comparing the efficiency of these two.

Oldknow and Smith (1984) and Kelman *et al* (1983) suggest how to use microcomputers, computing concepts and computing techniques to explore ideas in mathematics.

Chapter Five   Logo and learning

Tortoises formulate only Educated Guesses. Ah, yes — the power of the Educated Guess D. Hofstadter (*b*. 1945)

5.1   INTRODUCTION

Logo is perhaps the only computing environment available at present which has been deliberately developed from a model of education based on a theory of learning. The philosophy and educational background of Logo is best explained in *Mindstorms: Children, Computers and Powerful Ideas* (Papert 1980).

Papert acknowledges strong influence from Piaget's model of children as builders of their own intellectual structures, and he emphasises the importance of learning that takes place 'without being taught'. Logo is designed to enable children to use computers in a masterful way, as tools for actively exploring, planning and programming projects that interest them. This should lead to encounters with many powerful ideas, some of which are present in the existing curriculum, in areas such as mathematics; while others, such as debugging, recursion and problem solving techniques are new to the school context. Papert believes that children will be helped to think about their own learning processes in new ways as they use computers as tools for thinking.

Many books on Logo programming are available (see the bibliography). Our purpose here is not to teach the language, but to discuss the role and use of Logo in various educational contexts.

5.2   MICROWORLDS AND LEARNING

The word microworld has been used to describe several of the Logo applications outlined in the next section. Although an exact definition of the term is still emerging, and different researchers seem to have different interpretations, some features of computer-based microworlds as learning environments are distinctive and we shall attempt to summarize these below.

Papert describes a microworld as a subset of reality, or a constructed reality, whose structure matches that of a given cognitive mechanism so as to provide an environment where the latter can operate effectively (Papert 1980). The definitive computer-based microworld is his turtle geometry, in which the state of the turtle can be defined completely in terms of its position (where it is) and its heading (which way it is facing). A learner explores the effects of changing the turtle's state, using state change operators which alter either the position (e.g. Forward) or the heading (e.g. Right) of the turtle. The turtle acts as a transitional object, a concrete object whose movements are closely related to the learner's own familiar body movements, but with which abstract and powerful ideas from mathematics can be explored. Papert illustrates this with the example of a child realizing that he or she can make the turtle draw a circle by first walking in a circle, describing the act of doing so (e.g. as "going forward a little and turning a little, going forward a little and turning a little") and finally transforming this description into commands for the turtle, REPEAT [FD 1 RT 1]. He notes that the program is really a differential equation expressing the characterization of a circle as a curve of constant curvature, so the child has made contact with a fundamental mathematical notion by using old schemata as an assimilative basis for building new structures. He contends that the turtle geometry microworld is rich in occasions for this kind of encounter. An important task for educators is the invention of more microworlds, so structured as to allow learners to exercise particular powerful ideas or intellectual skills.

MICROWORLD ?

There are several important features of the microworld approach to computer-based learning environments. In a microworld the learner must be able to initiate the activities, to explore, to hypothesise and test these hypotheses, and to work on problems and projects of his or her own making (Fig. 5.1). While the modelling of reality might well be part of a microworld, many powerful abstract ideas can be explored only if the computer-based environment is not restricted to the modelling of real world processes.

It is impossible to predict or measure, and possibly difficult even to observe, the learning outcomes which might result from experience with a microworld, and herein lie challenges for researchers and for those concerned with educational accountability. Nevertheless the approach, like Logo itself, is solidly based on educational theory, and as more work is done on developing microworld software and the microworld concept itself, this approach will have increasing impact on the ways computers are used in education.

5.3   LOGO ACROSS THE CURRICULUM

In this section we shall look at some ways in which Logo has been used in various curriculum areas. While its use in some areas, such as mathematics, physics and language development, are relatively well established, other areas of application are still quite new at present, so the examples below are presented in the hope that they will give teachers ideas from which to build newer and better applications that are appropriate to the curriculum areas and levels with which they are involved.

It should be noted that in some applications the curricular aims are served by students actually programming in Logo itself, while in others a set of pre-written procedures should be provided for the student to use simply by typing English commands (which are in fact the names of Logo procedures), but without necessarily understanding the internal structure of the procedures being used.

5.3.1   Logo for learning mathematics

Several distinctly different ways in which Logo can be used in the teaching of mathematics have emerged.

Papert's approach, clearly stated in the title of his paper 'Teaching children to be mathematicians versus teaching mathematics' (Papert 1972) is presented more fully in his book (Papert 1980): "The computer-based Mathland I propose extends the kind of natural Piagetian learning that accounts for children's learning a first language to learning mathematics ... No particular computer activities are set aside as 'learning mathematics'."

Logo can provide an environment in which this natural learning takes place as a child is exploring and making hypotheses, creatively engaged in the pursuit of a personally meaningful project. Most of the work based at MIT has taken this approach, and has produced reports of individual children participating in a wide variety of interesting and valuable mathematical experiences (e.g. Lawler 1980; Watt 1979a).

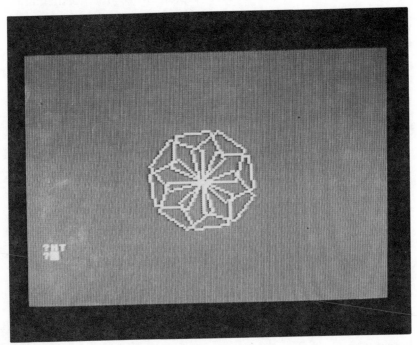

Fig. 5.1

Work on Logo and mathematics learning at Edinburgh University has taken a rather different approach. Here Logo procedures are used as a 'kit of parts' to enable students to model mathematical processes (Howe *et al* 1981). The learning environment is far more structured than is suggested by Papert. Students work individually, but from prepared worksheets. These worksheets are on topics prescribed in the Scottish school mathematics curriculum (Howe & O'Shea 1978). Results of this work show improvements in performance over students in control groups (Howe *et al* 1980) and "the pupils taking part in the study gained in self confidence, became more positive in their attitude to school mathematics and were much more willing to talk and argue about maths problems with their teacher" (Howe 1980).

The role of Logo in mathematics learning is examined in detail in a review paper by Hall (1980). He discusses bothof the approaches mentioned above, and reviews a variety of smaller projects, with students ranging from primary to undergraduate level.

Some excellent books that exploit Logo for mathematics learning are appearing. Thornburg (1983) presents some beautiful work combining turtle graphics and mathematics in topics such as tessellations, squirals and spirals, and recursive fractals and trees. Abelson and DiSessa (1980) have written a substantial textbook treating undergraduate mathematics topics such as vector methods, topology, non-Euclidean geometry and general relativity using turtle geometry, confirming clearly the wide range of levels at which Logo has much to offer to mathematics learning.

5.3.2   Logo and language

The list processing capabilities of Logo, coupled with powerful screen editing, allow children to use it in the development and modification of written materials. A study by Lawler (1980a) investigated at some length the introduction of a 6 year old girl to creative writing using a computer-based environment. To alert the child to the importance of structure in composition, and to distinguish between this and their content, Logo procedures establishing standard beginnings and endings for short stories and letters were used. Lawler reports that developments in her writing some years later suggested that she had gained a sense of structure from the computer experience, and he notes the recurrence in later work of thematic material from the earlier computer compositions.

Watt (1979a) reports three different ways in which sixth-grade children in the MIT-based Brookline project used Logo for writing activities. One student, having mastered the use of control keys for editing, wrote a Logo procedure to print a long story, line by line. Another, a child who had "great difficulty with academic work" and had not completed any assignments during the year, was offered a ready-written Logo procedure which allowed her to type letters and stories directly into the computer. The facility to correct and completely obliterate errors as soon as they were made was most important to this child, and she completed nine short letters and stories, showing a steady development of style and proficiency in grammar and punctuation.

The third student prepared a 'madlib' story procedure, in which the computer substituted randomly chosen nouns, verbs and adjectives in grammatically correct positions in the story, producing a different story each time the program was run.

Working in Edinburgh, Sharples developed computer based language workshops (Sharples 1980, 1981). Children used his programs to explore language as an object, to improve their understanding of its use and to broaden the style of their written English.

Following this work, a computer-based environment in which children might try teaching a computer to write poetry has been developed (McDougall & Adams 1984). Here children engage in activities such as sentence generation and the building of small poems on the computer, from dictionaries or word lists assembled (as Logo lists) by the children themselves. The teaching is done by the children, with the computer as the learner. The aim here is not necessarily the production of superb poetry as such — a very difficult task for a computer — but the creation of an environment in which the skills and techniques of human writers and poets can be detected, distinguished and discussed.

First of all, to have the computer generate sentences, will it be enough to teach it some words, and tell it to put them together in threes and fours, followed by full stops? Several tries, using the computer procedures provided, soon raise the need for classifying words according to their functions in a sentence. Once lists of nouns, verbs and so on have been set up and problems of tense and gender agreement are solved, templates for sentences or for small poems can be set up for the computer to fill in, selecting words randomly from the appropriate lists. The word lists might be something like

```
MAKE "NOUN [DOG PLANE HOUSE CAR CHILD]
MAKE "VERB [RUNS SMELLS FLIES SINGS SLEEPS]
MAKE "ADJECTIVE [TINY FRIENDLY MISERABLE
BLUE QUICK]
MAKE "ARTICLE [THE A]
```

and a sentence template could be set up by

MAKE "TEMPLATE1 [ARTICLE ADJECTIVE NOUN VERB]

On the command

WRITE :TEMPLATE1

the computer might produce

THE TINY CHILD SLEEPS

or

A MISERABLE HOUSE FLIES

The children control the computer-generated material by altering the word lists from which the computer makes its selections. Some children will design lists of words so that the computer's sentences will not only be correct, but also sensible; others will delight in computer-generated nonsense sentences, and design word lists to make them even more improbable.

A great variety of templates can be set up, including templates for groups of sentences formatted into structures for poems. Whether the computer-produced poems are interesting, evocative or nonsensical again depends on the contents of the word lists from which the computer selects as it 'writes'. Meaning or rhyming could be introduced into the poetry by preparation of appropriate word lists, and similarly poems which are beautiful, scary, sad, and so on could be made. Exploring the relationships between different types of word lists and the computer-generated poems that result from them could provide a context for discussions of many facets of language use and poetry writing, at a depth which is suited to particular classes or teacher aims.

The *Beach* microworld (Lawler 1982) has been devised to assist very young children to learn to read. Using Logo sprites (Section 12.3.3), scenarios containing many moving objects of different shapes and colours can be created (Fig. 5.2). Because Logo gives the user freedom to define and name procedures, appropriate descriptive English words can be used. For example, SUN can be the name of a procedure that creates a yellow ball on the screen. The word UP can name the command that causes a sprite to move upwards, and words such as SLOW or FAST can name procedures that set the sun, or any other shape in the picture, in motion. By typing in these words, the child can then generate and animate a picture on the screen. New procedures are easily defined, and the child or a teacher can add actors or actions to the scene so the microworld can be tailor-made to suit any child, and can be to a large extent designed by the child.

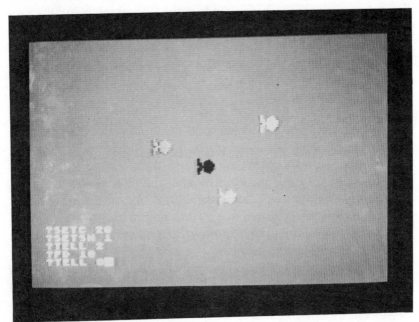

Fig. 5.2

5.3.3   Logo and physics

As the graphics turtle allows exploration of geometric concepts, so the dynamic turtle, or dynaturtle, developed by DiSessa (DiSessa & White 1982), enables exploration and experience of a world of Newtonian motion. The dynaturtle remains at rest or travels with uniform velocity in a straight line except when acted on by forces. These forces are specified by a student at the computer keyboard, and, depending on their direction, they can cause the dynaturtle to speed up, slow down or change direction. Details of the dynaturtle procedures can be found in the book by Abelson (1982).

5.3.4   Logo music

Using a computer controlled synthesizer for sound generation, quite powerful systems are being developed in which Logo can be used for interactive, composition-like projects (Bamberger 1982). More limited systems are available already in the Logo implementations on several microcomputers. These permit some musical explorations using the procedural techniques of Logo, to examine musical structures, patterns and components (McDougall *et al* 1984).

5.3.5   Logo and art

Logo turtle graphics have been used in visual art teaching (Sharp 1984). Sharp uses turtle graphics as an independent form of expression, with a special set of skills and techniques to be learned, a unique set of aesthetic possibilities and limitations, and outcomes that clearly distinguish it from other forms of expression. She uses the turtle to study line lengths, shapes and textures, and ways of generating lines. Then procedures written by students which place colours in multiple juxtapositions of simple shapes are used to study interrelationships of colours. This provides a context for discussing the use of colour by human artists, just as the computer-generated poetry provides a basis for understanding the work of human poets.

Chapter Six

Simulation

Oft on the dappled turf at ease
I sit, and play with similes

W. Wordsworth (1770–1850)

6.1   INTRODUCTION

For many years, pilots in training have used flight simulators. A flight simulator is a machine with seats, controls and instruments in the same positions as in the flight deck of a particular kind of aeroplane: a Boeing 767, for example. In a real aeroplane, pushing the control column forward changes the position of the elevators, which in turn causes the aeroplane to start descending. The effects of this descent register on the aeroplane's instruments: for example, the altimeter reading decreases, the rate of climb indicator shows a negative reading, and a marker moves down on the artificial horizon. The simulator, on the other hand is controlled by an appropriately-programmed computer, and the movement of the simulator's control column does not move an elevator, but results in new input to the computer. The computer calculates the effect the movement would have on a real 767, and what the corresponding changes in the 767's instrument readings would be. The program then outputs signals that change the simulator's instrument readings to these new values.

The trainee pilot attempts to fly at a specified height, speed and direction, and then to descend, turn, slow down, etc., and can monitor success by reference to the instruments — without being penalized for failure by hitting very hard earth with a very big bang!

Comparing the flight simulator with a real aeroplane, one sees that they are similar in that the same movements of the controls cause the same changes to instrument readings; they differ in that, in the simulator, there is no corresponding change in motion, no windscreen through which the pilot can monitor progress — and no fatal consequences of errors. The simulator is therefore a model of a Boeing 767.

A model is a concrete or theoretical representation of a system, designed to provide a framework for predictions about the system and for the manipulation of variables for certain purposes, including the better understanding and appreciation of the system. A model is analogous to that which it models: that is, the model and the original are alike in some respects, and unlike in others. The intent of the model maker is that they be alike in the relevant respects. Which respects are relevant depends on the purpose for which the model is being made. The flight simulator possesses characteristics of a Boeing 767 which are relevant to the trainee pilot. A small toy plane is another model, which possesses features relevant to the child who wants it as a toy — but which would be useless for pilot training. Conversely, the young child may not recognize the flight simulator as an aeroplane.

The process of building and using a model is called simulation. In the two examples given, the models are concrete, physical entities. Such models are used in many contexts. A civil engineer, for example, might build a scale model of an estuary, and experiment with it to investigate methods of flood control or patterns of dissipation of effluent; an architect makes models of the buildings in a new shopping complex and then tries different arrangements of them; a physics teacher uses an orrery to demonstrate planetary movement.

Such concrete, physical models are sometimes called iconic (from the Greek word for image) to emphasise that there is another sort of model, namely the theoretical or mathematical model. A mathematical model is a description of a system in terms of interrelated processes, and the equations and inequalities which govern their interaction. Initially, such a model seems less satisfying, because it is less tangible. However, it is also far more flexible: building several physical models of a flood-control system will take longer and cost more than amending some equations and carrying out a new set of calculations. It is this last phrase that indicates the role of the computer in simulation. Until the advent of the computer, it would have taken longer to carry out the calculations for a complicated mathematical model than to build a physical one. Now, however, the theoretical model is more common, and special languages have been devised (simulation languages) to assist in representing and manipulating theoretical models on a computer.

The mathematical model is not only more flexible than the physical one: it is also more widely applicable, and usually cheaper. It cannot only be used to represent tangible physical systems, such as a Boeing 767 or a river estuary, but also intangible systems such as the national economy or a commercial organization. In general, models are used whenever it would be difficult to experiment with the real life situation. Such experimentation may be dangerous: testing a nuclear power station, or letting a student pilot fly a 767. It might be infeasible: firing a missile at an actual target or trying different ways of running a company. It might be uneconomic: building boat after boat to obtain the best hydrodynamic shape or using up large quantities of an expensive raw material in various versions of a manufactured article. It might be impossible : trying different patterns of industrial development in an area, or changing the weather.

As we have said, a model embodies some aspects of the system it represents, and not others. Of course, when the real life system includes dangerous aspects, we deliberately omit these from the model: the flight simulator is fixed to terra firma, the nuclear power station model includes no actual radioactive substances. Otherwise, however, we usually want the model to be as close to reality as possible. However, if it is an iconic model, it usually costs more to make it more like the original. If it is an abstract model, it involves a more complicated mathematical formulation, and this in turn is more difficult to analyse. In fact, abstract simulation (that is, the construction and use of abstract models) did not become widespread until after the advent of the computer which permitted the analysis of more complicated problems, and the performance of many more calculations in a reasonable time.

To appreciate the implications of closeness to the real system, let us return to the flight simulation. As described, the simulator would be useful for practising instrument flying, that is flying with reference to the instruments only, as is done when the aeroplane is in cloud. However, normal flying involves much more visual reference to the outside world for feedback about whether the controls are being handled properly. Incorporating this into the simulator is very difficult. In order to do it, where windows would be in the aeroplane, the simulator has television screens, and what is projected onto them is changed in accordance with the pilot's movement of the controls. This can be arranged in one of two ways. One way is to film all possible views that the pilot might see through the windscreen, store these in the computer somehow, and have the computer select the right sequence of frames. Even if one confines the simulation to flying around one particular airport, it would clearly be impossible to film every view the pilot might see, and very difficult to select the correct one moment by moment. The other way is to store in the computer a description of a particular airport, and have the computer calculate moment by moment what view it should generate and project on the screen. This takes a lot of computing power, and so it takes a big computer to do it fast enough for a realistic simulation. The difficulty of this process means that flight simulators with visual simulation are used mainly to simulate night landings at specified airports. (At night, the pilot's view is a pattern of lights rather than the whole detail of the scene, and this is easier to represent.)

The other dimension omitted from the original simulator was that of motion. Some simulators are now totally mounted on a movable framework and are rotated in response to movements of the controls. Again, an increase in similarity leads to an increase in complexity, and hence an increase in cost of construction and an increase in the calculation required at each stage.

6.2   SIMULATION AND EDUCATION

In the last section, we observed that simulation permits the investigation of systems which would otherwise be inaccessible; and that a theoretical model furnishes a reasonably cheap way of doing this (provided that adequate computing power is available). These two factors immediately make computer-based simulation very attractive in education. Many investigations cannot be carried out in schools because they are dangerous, infeasible, too expensive, or totally impossible, and yet students will leave school and be involved in these (or similar) problems. Computer simulation offers a way of enormously extending the student's range of educational experience. Because of the many benefits to be gained from them, the stated policy of the Chelsea Computers in the Curriculum Project throughout the 1970s was to concentrate on the development of simulations, including such units as *Pond Ecology, Radioactive Decay* and *Mass Spectrometer* (Watson 1982).

The general modelling consideration (that the model must not be so simplified as to become misleading, yet not so complex as to be intractable) gains the extra dimension here that it must not be so complex that students of the intended level are unable to manipulate it. Furthermore, the assumptions used in constructing the model must be made explicit so that students can recognize which aspects of the given system are being simulated, and in which aspects the model differs from reality. They should also study the model critically, assessing its validity by reference to other sources.

Computer-based simulations can be used to promote a range of educational goals (cf. Coburn *et al* 1982):

1 motivation for study;
2 discovery learning;
3 learning of content;
4 mastery of skills;
5 development of concepts;
6 social interaction.

These goals, of course, are not mutually exclusive. Furthermore, (almost) all the comments also apply to simulations which do not involve the computer (of which there are many). However, as observed in the last section, the power of the computer permits the manipulation of models which are far more realistic, and hence much more interesting.

6.2.1   Motivation for study

The introduction of a new topic to a class can be a problem, as there is often a lot of introductory material to be covered before the students have enough information to do anything interesting. Such an extended introduction can be so boring for the students that not only do they not enjoy the introduction, but they are so turned off by it, that they take no interest in the topic when it eventually arrives. Teachers use a lot of devices to overcome this initial hurdle. One common one is to bring some (familiar or unfamiliar) item into the classroom and initiate a discussion about it. A simulation can do an excellent job of introducing the topic and raising questions, so that the subsequent work has a firm basis to build on, and might even be presented totally in response to students' questions.

When a simulation is used like this, it can be presented as a game (Section 6.3), with certain rules, and then the students, singly or in groups, play the game.

6.2.2   Discovery learning

Simulations, especially computer-based ones, encourage the user to ask 'What would happen if ... ?' The nuclear power plant simulation may be able to answer the question 'what would happen if I withdrew the carbon rods?' The flight simulator: 'what would happen if I applied full left aileron?' A medical simulation: 'what would happen if I doubled the dose prescribed?' The simulation of the national economy : 'what would happen if I increased income tax by 10%?' Often much more complicated hypotheses can be tested than would be the case in a real-life situation. The introduction of discovery learning has been strongly advocated for a number of years, because the student has greater interaction with the subject matter and is thus

more likely to assimilate the knowledge, skills and concepts involved. The introduction of computer simulations makes discovery learning much more feasible.

6.2.3   Learning of content

It is clear that, by trying different inputs to a model and examining the outputs, facts about the model may be learned. The fruit fly and cat breeding simulations mentioned earlier permit genetic effects in successive generations to be examined in a single lesson. Similarly, long, expensive and/or dangerous chemical reactions can be studied and learned at first hand, while in geology, the stages in the formation of the earth's crust can be studied in academic time, rather than geological time. Such simulated experiments also eliminate the frustrations resulting from faulty apparatus or technique.

6.2.4   Mastery of skills

Skill derives from the application of learned facts or content, and simulations give plenty of scope for such application. The skills in question can be very diverse: motor skills; basic arithmetic; map-reading; analysing, recording and interpreting data; formulating and refining hypotheses; planning strategies; and general problem-solving are all goals of various simulations.

6.2.5   Development of concepts

Concepts include those inherent in the subject matter, and those involved in its study. Examples of the latter are the processes of logical reasoning, induction/deduction and hypothesis testing. Concept development involves extrapolation from the knowledge and skill that has been acquired, to an understanding of, for example, general genetic or economic principles. The usual approach to the development of concepts is to study a number of related topics and then induce from these the general principles. Concept learning rarely occurs without a great deal of groundwork of content learning. Some students bypass the latter stage, and, as a result, develop half understood pseudo-concepts (and a good line in waffle to hide their lack of knowledge). Other students, despite every assistance, fail to make this transition. Computer simulations assist the induction process by permitting the study of a greater variety of topics, and by telescoping some normally lengthy processes into a much shorter time span. The effect of this is frequent re-emphasis of the salient features, hence making them more apparent, and assisting in an appreciation of the underlying concepts.

6.2.6   Social interaction

Students should normally work on a computer-based simulation in groups of two or three rather than singly. Not only are 'two heads better than one', but also in working together they are more likely to verbalize what they are doing, and this is a great aid to learning. Many simulations *require* several users. *Gold Dust Island* (Gare 1983), for example, involves several people marooned on a desert island. What happens to them depends in large measure on whether they co-operate or compete. Such activity gives practice in working together, in learning to allow for other people as individuals, and in accepting that others will act in ways one cannot anticipate.

Several economic simulations represent a number of companies in competition. While one person can run each company, with some of the more complicated models it is sensible to have a team running the company, with separate people as chairman, production manager, sales manager and advertising manager. The result of such simulations is not only learning about the subject matter, but also about how to work, co-operatively and/or competitively, with others. *Lemonade* is a well-known, simple instance of an economic simulation, set in the context of making and selling lemonade from a roadside stall.

6.3   GAMES

Games and simulations are sometimes regarded as the same thing and sometimes distinguished from each other. Just as we discussed simulation in general, with computer simulation as a special case, so let us do with games. A game is a competitive amusement, played according to a set of rules. A simulation involves a model which produces certain outputs for certain inputs. If we define the set of rules to be the model together with some of the possible outputs, then the task of finding the inputs which give rise to those particular outputs is a game, according to the above definition. The competition is against the other users, or against oneself. Thus, most simulations can be viewed as games. The converse, however, is not true. Snakes and ladders, for example, is a game, but does not simulate anything. *Monopoly*, on the other hand, considered simply a game for many years, is now seen to be also a crude economic simulation. Yet another board game, namely *Diplomacy*, however, is essentially a simulation of some events of World War 1. In fact, there is a whole class of simulations, known as war games, that provide much more precise simulations, incorporating troop numbers, actual battles, and so on. There are also economic simulations, known as business games. War games and business games are used in military and commercial training, respectively.

Although there are games which simulate nothing, they should not be rejected, but simply subjected to the same criteria: does their use tend towards the achievement of the stated educational goals (Clayson 1982)? The game of *Wff 'n' Proof*, for example, is not a simulation. It aims to teach logical inference, problem-solving and reasoning, by having the students apply logical principles to make deductions from given facts and relationships.

6.4   THE TIME FACTOR

All the simulations referred to in this chapter involve a time factor. Going back to the flight simulator, the answer to the question 'what happens if I apply full left aileron?' could be 'you write off the plane (and yourself)'. However, a more informative response would be a sequence of positions and attitudes of the aeroplane, say after 5 s, 10 s, 15 s. The answer to the nuclear reactor question 'what happens if I withdraw the carbon rods?' could be 'you initiate the China syndrome'. However, a more informative response would be a sequence of indications of the ongoing state of the reactor. In the case of the question 'what happens if income tax is increased by 10%?', there is no final answer, and the only possible response is a sequence of values of GNP, employment statistics, etc.

It is typical of simulations that they produce a sequence of outputs, representing the state of the model (and hence the system being modelled) at successive moments in time. As a simple example of this, suppose we wish to simulate a dog chasing a rabbit (Woodhouse *et al* 1984). The rabbit is at R(0,0) when seen by the dog at D(0,100) (Fig. 6.1). At that moment, the dog starts to run towards the rabbit, and the rabbit to run towards its burrow, B(100,0). Assuming that these distances are in metres, and that the rabbit runs in a straight line at 18 kph, while the dog always runs towards the rabbit at 29 kph, will the dog catch the rabbit? (If the dog reaches the horizontal axis before catching the rabbit, it turns left and heads along the axis towards the burrow.) It is an adequate answer to the problem to have a program print 'dog catches rabbit', or 'rabbit reaches burrow'. However it is much more informative to have a table like Fig. 6.2, as it gives a better feel for whether it was a near thing etc.

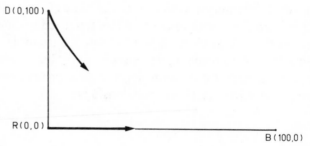

Fig. 6.1

Time (s)	Dog's position	Rabbit's position	Rabbit's distance to burrow (m)	Dog's distance to rabbit (m)
0	(0,100)	(0,0)	100	100
1	(0,92)	(5,0)	95	92.1
2	(0.4,84)	(10,0)	90	84.5
3	(1.3,76)	(15,0)	85	77.2

Fig. 6.2   Pursuit simulation: tabular form

It would also be useful to offer the user the choice of whether the whole program should be run and all the output produced, or only one line produced at a time in response to the user pressing a key on the keyboard. If the output device has a screen, a graph (based on Fig. 6.1) would be a better form for the output than a table (Fig. 6.2). Such a program could be run repeatedly with different values for dog and burrow position and dog and rabbit speed.

If a computer is used for a payroll calculation, it does not matter whose salary is calculated first, nor whether union dues are deducted before health service payments. Simulations are different. In a game, players move alternately; in business, time passes and certain events occur, actions have to be carried out, etc; in a shop, it makes a difference when people come in; on the road, the time when traffic passes is relevant. Simulations therefore move through time, and we can adjust the rate at which this simulated time passes: slowing down the dog/rabbit race so we can appreciate the relative positions; speeding up the formation of the earth's crust so that it fits into the time we have available. Other simulations which slow down real time are of chemical, biochemical and nuclear reactions. Others which accelerate real time relate to population changes, decision making processes, and the succession of generations (of cats or fruit flies).

Most simulation systems (and, in particular, simulation languages such as Simula and GPSS) have a time flow mechanism. Time passes in jumps, which may be all of the same size (as in the dog/rabbit or the flight control simulations), or can be of unequal sizes. The latter would be useful for simulating a traffic flow at an intersection: cars do not arrive at regular intervals, and we are interested only in those moments when they do arrive. Such a simulation is a discrete event simulation, since cars are separate entities. The dog/rabbit or the nuclear reactor on the other hand are continuous simulations, since the quantities involved in the real system are changing constantly. In the model, therefore, the passage of time is split into small equal intervals, and the continuous system is simulated by a discrete model.

6.5   DETERMINISM AND NON-DETERMINISM

The dog/rabbit situation is a deterministic simulation. This means that, given the initial data, the behaviour of the model is known completely (completely determined). Such models may be called demonstrations (Coburn *et al* 1982). Possible demonstrations are of families of sine curves, the area under a curve, planetary motion, the circulatory system, geological processes, balancing chemical equations, and so on. Such demonstrations can be used without teacher intervention if desired. Some offer significant user control, while some are preprogrammed to run through a sequence without much user intervention. Demonstrations are probably most appropriate as an aid to the teacher in the primary instruction of students, and as an aid to students when they review material.

Most simulations, however, are non-deterministic. Initial data for simulation of traffic flow through a junction, for example, might be statements like: 'The average numbers of vehicles in each hour are as follows':

hour	major road	minor road
6–7 am	2000	800
7–8 am	3000	1000
.	.	.
.	.	.
.	.	.
5–6 am	700	300

For the program to run, however, actual vehicle transit times must be specified. The program therefore contains a mechanism for randomly generating times, such that the set of times generated satisfy the above data. (For example, over a large number of program runs, an average of 2000 vehicle transits are generated for the hour 6–7am.) The mechanism for this is called a random number generator. It is a small subprogram, and is the computer's equivalent of tossing a coin. A non-deterministic simulation is one which is based on the use of random numbers. Many programming languages provide a random number generator as a built-in function. RND or RND(X) in Basic is one such function; RAN or RAND or RANF(X) in Fortran is another. A full discussion of random numbers and their use in simulation may be found in Woodhouse *et al* (1984).

6.6   CLASSROOM SIMULATIONS

There are many simulations available for classroom use. We mention here only a few to get you started. Others will be available by the time

you read this, and you should also investigate what is available
locally.

6.6.1   Economics

1 *Tai-pan*. A trading game, set in nineteenth century China,
requiring memory and calculation.
2 *Hammurabi*. A similar game based on an eighteenth century BC
ruler of Babylon. (Such games provide a starting point for history,
economics, etc, and students' skill at the game should improve as
they learn the theory.)
3 *Lemonade*. This simulation has immediate appeal, as it refers to a
child gathering lemons and making lemonade, and selling it from a
roadside stall outside the house.
4 *Farm* (Eisenstadt *et al* 1982). This program is designed to show
that the farmer must make decisions about which crops to grow in
uncertain weather conditions.

6.6.2   Geography

1 A series of simulations support Jacaranda Wiley's text *Moving
into Maps* for primary children. These include *Scavenger Hunt, Sheep
Dog Trial, Cunning Running* (based on orienteering), and *Quick
Cartage Company* (R. Gare *et al* 1983, 1984).
2 *Sailing Ships Game* (I. Killbery *et al* 1983). Navigation of a large
sailing ship, including sailing ship facts, latitude and longitude,
compass directions, and Beaufort wind scale.

6.6.3   Environmental studies

1 *Route* (Squires 1983; Eisenstadt *et al* 1982). This involves the
planning and building of a motorway (freeway), taking into account
route, disruptions to local inhabitants, and costs. Students act as
geographers, environmentalists and planners, and realize that value
judgements are involved in such a project. The tedious calculation of
costs and environmental scores is carried out by the computer.

6.6.4   History

1 *Saqqara*. As mentioned before, this covers most aspects of an archaeological investigation in Egypt.
2 *Archaeological Search* (Anderson 1984) is a similar program.

6.6.5   Science

1 *Genetics.* We have already mentioned *Catlab* (Fig. 6.3), *Birdbreed* (J. Kinnear), and the PLATO fruit-fly breeding simulations.

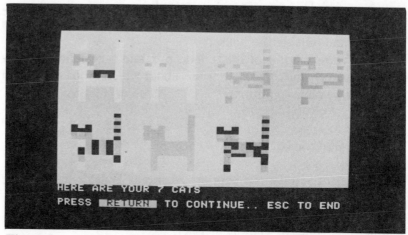

Fig. 6.3

2 *Mass Spectrometer* (Masterton *et al* 1982). Covers the physics of the spectrometer, the theory of the separation of ion beams, and the understanding of ion sources.
3 *Haber* (Shaw 1982; Eisenstadt *et al* 1982). This deals with the manufacture of ammonia, and permits students to determine the values of temperature and pressure to produce a high yield of ammonia by the Haber process.
4 *Acoustics* (Rablah *et al* 1983). An introduction to elementary acoustics, including reverberation time and the effects of room size and construction.

5   *Gas Behaviour* (Phipps & Simpkin 1983). This program for a Vic-20 simulates, graphically, the movement of gases under changes of temperature, volume and number of particles.

6.6.6   Mathematics

1   *Battleship*. An excellent way to teach co-ordinates to primary school children. The computer obviates the intricate record-keeping with pencil and paper.
2   *Pan* (Eisenstadt *et al* 1982). A demonstration of parametric equations, which permits the user to vary parameters and expressions, and displays the curves on the computer screen.
3   *Eureka* (ITMA Collaboration 1983). Aims to develop skill in interpreting and sketching graphs of realistic situations. Based on the change of water level in a bath over a period of time, under various constraints of input and output.

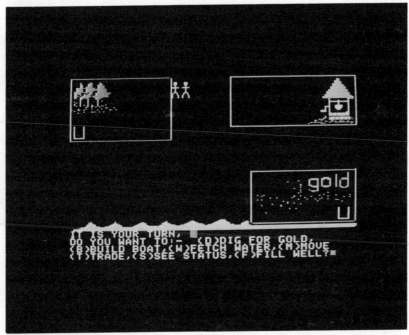

Fig. 6.4

6.6.7   General

1 *Adventure*. This is more a generic term than the name of a single game. There are now many adventure games, including *Dungeon*, *Zork* (a text only game), *Sherwood Forest* (three-dimensional graphics and text for the Apple computer, very useful at primary school), *Transylvania* (also primary), *Odessy* and the *Wizardry* series. The general form is of a quest, opposed by dragons, dwarves etc., with Tolkienian appeal. Exchanges are verbal, in contrast to the more numerical communication of some other programs. Adventure programs are being adapted for use in many areas, including reading skills, communication skills, mappings, problem solving, foreign languages and science.

2 *Litter* (MEP 1982). This uses an anti-litter campaign, to present practice in decision-making, verbal reasoning and arithmetic skills.

3 *Gold Dust Island* (Gare 1983). Set in the context of castaways on a desert island, the objectives are affective. Co-operation among players is encouraged, as individual survival depends on group co-operation and harmony (Fig. 6.4).

Chapter Seven

Computers in the primary school

Start a child on the right road, and even in old age he will not leave it
Book of Proverbs

7.1 INTRODUCTION

This chapter is rather short, but not because there are few uses for the computer in the primary school. On the contrary, it is short precisely because much of what is said elsewhere relates to primary schools as well as secondary schools: simulations are motivating, CAI can individualize instruction, the computer can be used as a tool, etc. In fact, many computer applications, which are at present mainly used in secondary schools belong pedagogically in primary schools. We refer particularly to word processing and information handling skills (via, for example, *Quill* and *Quest*, see Chapter 4), and to graphical and language skills (via, for example, Logo, see Chapter 5). There is tremendous potential for some very exciting developments in primary school computing. The purpose of this chapter is to say this explicitly, and to present some of the considerations relevant to the use of computers with primary school children.

One might, initially, think that computers have no place in the primary school, both because they are too difficult for young children to use, and because young children have more need of social intercourse with their peers than of commitment to a machine.

However, experience has shown that many primary age children confidently use computers in a variety of ways, and that this use typically generates social interaction rather than stifling it. The correct answer to the question of whether computers should be used in primary schools is not obtained by adopting some predetermined stance, but by asking educational questions. Firstly, decide, on educational grounds, what topics are to be taught. Secondly, on the same grounds, consider feasible teaching methods and equipment. These may include computer-based methods. Thirdly, again on the same grounds, choose among these methods and devices. This approach puts the horse before the cart, and neither adopts the computer willy nilly nor rejects it out of hand. Our advice is that there are many areas of the primary school curriculum in which computer use can enrich the learning environment, and assist in the development of both technical and social skills. For most effective use of the computer, varied and flexible ways of interacting with it are required. Input and output devices are described in Chapter 14.

7.2   THE EDUCATIONAL MILIEU

Computers directly affect the lives of everyone in the western world, and education should not be disjoint from the rest of the student's environment. Already, many students spend more time watching television than attending school. Now we must add the hours spent playing video games, whether at a local arcade, or at home. As the number of home computers increases, younger children will find such games more accessible, and, before long, there will be many students entering primary school with many hours of computer experience behind them. Teachers will have to cope with children for whom computer use is a normal part of life. The time is already past when one could command immediate attention, merely by bringing a computer into the class room. Now, half the class are interested (but not overawed) while the other half are asking abstruse technical questions. It might be contended that such hardened computer users in grades 1 and 2 have 'only played computer games'. This will be decreasingly true as parents buy more CAL materials; and, in any case, many so-called games have significant instructional value (see, for example, Chapter 6).

A child's world is full of intricate devices, such as cars, telephones and stereos, which are absorbed into his or her experience by a mixture of observation, direct instruction, and experiment. The child sees the computer as just another facet of the environment, and integrates it just as easily into a world view. (It is principally adults who have problems, and project these onto children.) It must be admitted that the computer is in a slightly different category from the other things mentioned: while they are each designed to do a specific task, the computer is a general purpose machine. This is why some knowledge of how a computer works is helpful. A telephone only does one thing, and a few minutes instruction on how to operate it is all most of us need: we do not need to know how it does its thing.

When we approach a computer, however, the first question is often 'what can it do?' and some knowledge of its method of operation is needed to answer this. Initially, this need can be bypassed, by the provision of specific programs. Given a disc on which is stored a program for the game *Adventure*, a few simple operations prepares the computer to play. It is now no longer a general purpose machine, but a machine for playing *Adventure*. Thus, games and other prepared programs and packages reduce the computer to an intelligible level, and enable people to gain experience in what a computer can do.

The reference to other modern gadgets indicates an appropriate manner in which to structure the use of and learning about computers at primary school, namely to integrate it into the curriculum. Many examples have been given in Chapters 1,4,5 and 6.

7.3   CURRICULUM CONSIDERATIONS

7.3.1   Curriculum content

The advent of the computer is changing the methods and contents of the curriculum. Teaching methods must now take account of the wide applicability of CAL; while the syllabus must accommodate the study both of computers themselves, and also of other topics which have become possible and necessary as a result of the use of computers in society and their availability in schools. To this extent, it is appropriate to re-design the curriculum around what the computer can do.

The aims of primary schooling must change to take account of the change in society, keeping what is still valuable, and introducing what is now necessary. We can identify the following areas which must be covered (even if only at an introductory level) in the primary school syllabus.

1   *Communication*

This involves the ability to read with understanding, to write intelligibly and to speak fluently; to assemble ideas, and express them in a story or a report. These in turn require grammatical and spelling skills.

2   *Numeracy*

The ability to perform simple calculations related to daily activities, such as budgeting, comparing quotations for a job, or estimating quantities of materials required. The necessary appreciation of abstract structures and spatial concepts to plan house extensions, garden landscaping or dressmaking, or understand weather charts and forecasts. Sufficient understanding of statistics not to be overwhelmed by the myriad figures now made public, from the unemployment trends, through the current superpower arms deployments, to the latest cricket averages; and the ability to interpret the graphs often used to present these statistics (see Chapter 4).

3   *Information handling*

Practice in selecting, collecting, collating, classifying and organizing data. How to find information. Use of reference sources: catalogues, encyclopaedias; print, video, tape and disc libraries; electronic data bases. Storing and retrieving data. Use of computers.

4 *Problem-solving*

Planning, questioning, decision making; researching, hypothesizing, experimenting, modelling, simulating; analysing, comparing, evaluating. (Also skills from 1, 2 and 3.)

5 *Social interaction*

Co-operative learning, mutual acceptance, task allocation, cross-disciplinary learning.

Now, how are these aims (to be) achieved, and does the computer have any role to play? 1, most of 2, a little of 3, and 5 have been the primary school goal for many years, and thus do not need the computer. However, the availability of the computer will affect the way these topics are tackled. We have referred (Chapter 4 and elsewhere) to the role of word processing in writing and spelling. Significant advances are also being made in using computers to assist beginning readers. Cumming (1984) points out that a skilled reader brings a range of strategies to bear, while the beginner typically relies too heavily on only a few of these. The reading problems resulting

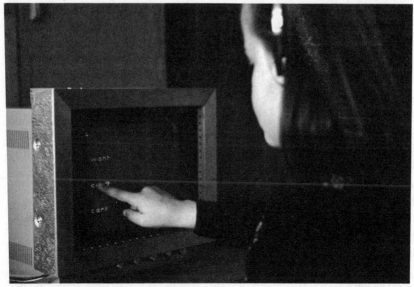

Fig. 7.1

from this imbalance can best be addressed by first identifying which strategies are being used. Cumming uses a computer with a touch-sensitive screen for input (Fig. 7.1) and voice output (see Chapter 14), at which a child works on word and sentence exercises and games. The program presenting the exercises analyses the child's errors, and is thus able to detect which strategies are being used. Further software will adapt the choice of exercises offered so as to strengthen the deficient strategies.

Effects on 2 have been mentioned in Chapters 4 and 5. Logo is particularly good for unstructured, exploratory use. Impetus has been given to 3 and 4 by today's increasing computer use, although much computer-oriented work can be done in these areas without actually using a computer. Conversely, simulations which require a group of people, whether working co-operatively or competitively, tend to the achievement of 5, and most of the interesting simulations available are computer-based.

7.3.2   Variety

Should the computer be used to do anything which is possible without its aid? In education, variety is very important. The same topic is approached in several different ways, in the hope that the child will integrate the common features. Thus, if the use of a computer provides yet another method, it is valuable. The one thing to avoid is regarding the computer as the ultimate panacea. So often, when computers are discussed, educational considerations are forgotten. One teacher says: If it can be done by computer, we should do it that way, because everyone will have to get used to computers. Another teacher says: Only do it by computer if that's cheaper. And another says: We can do it without computers, so we shouldn't use them. The right approach is the usual educational one: How much will it cost (not merely financially, but also in time, effort, disruption etc.) to do it by computer? Do we anticipate that the educational and other benefits of using this alternative method are worth the costs? The answer to this question should determine the teacher's plan of action. Aspects of cost, teacher education and classroom organization are discussed in Chapters 15 and 16.

One example of computer-based variety is provided by a word-picture matching program that requires an increasing level of participation by the student, and integrates writing, reading and word sounds (Section 7.3.1; see also Chapter 4). A similar process could be carried out without a computer, but the computer offers definite advantages. It is impossible for the user to cheat; a large repertoire can be made available without an unwieldy pack of cards; the pictures do not wear out or get defaced; the automated aspect may be more attractive to a child. When used by groups of children, a large amount of mutual assistance occurs, resulting in more social interaction (Section 7.3.1) than would occur in the more traditional teacher-directed context. However, this approach cannot replace the teacher: it should be used discriminatingly, perhaps for initial work, or practice. It can be valuable as a teacher's aide, giving extra work to the fast worker, patience to the slow worker, privacy to the diffident and positive control of the learning environment to all of them.

7.4   COMPUTER WORK WITHOUT COMPUTERS

Whatever the availability of computers outside the school, most school use must be designed to involve a minimum of 'hands-on' work. This is no bad thing, in fact. Many people make very inefficient use of computers because they are incapable of doing anything other than press a few buttons to 'see what happens'. This can be useful on occasions, such as for exploring the computer's capabilities ('browsing', as it were); or when one is completely baffled as to what to do. However, it is like tinkering with a car engine at random in the hope of doing the right thing by chance. While one is sometimes forced into this as a last resort, one's first resort should be careful thought about the problem and how to solve it, before touching the car or the computer.

Moursund (1981) points out that many normally computer-based games can be played between class members, or between the teacher and the class. This games playing activity per se can have extensive educational value, with students

1   performing mental arithmetic and/or verbal manipulation (depending on the nature of the game);
2   explaining and understanding rules;
3   improving their ability to play this game, and hence realizing that they can learn. However, since it is a computer game, and computers operate by processing data, this activity is likely to involve a lot of data handling, so the student may also realize the value of and gain practice in
4   writing;

5   organizing data, record keeping, setting up and using a data base, and information retrieval (Section 7.3.1). Furthermore, computers operate by executing a large number of conceptually simple steps. By imitating the computer in the manner of playing the game, the students may

6   not only exercise intellectual skills, but also recognize when they are exercising such skills, and recognize which intellectual skills they are using; thus, they can compare the individual steps in the game with the results of each step. Then, when they use a computer, and only the latter is apparent, they will understand what is going on inside. Thus, they will understand.

7   why a computer does what it does, and that it has no innate intelligence.

Many simple games can be treated in this way, and can prove to be very enjoyable. If/when the students eventually play the game on a computer, the above activities are legitimized and further learning experiences provided. With the above preparation, students are better able to appreciate the computer's invisible actions, its speed and its limitations.

7.5   INFORMATION HANDLING

Specific activities in this area can be designed to supplement the incidental learning referred to in the previous section. We have already mentioned (Chapter 1) the learning package called *Factfile*, which includes computer programs to manipulate a data base, and present a user interface which is intelligible to primary school children. Use of such a program again involves a lot of non-computer work first. With an appropriately designed project, the children have to consult several reference books to collect the basic data for the data base; convert the data as necessary to make them consistent (in units, form of expression, etc.); organize the data and inspect them for completeness; and selectively use one or two perhaps unusual reference sources to fill any gaps. Then the program is used to input the data base to the computer. Items can then be inspected individually, inspected in any specified grouping, and changed as necessary. The experiences of (i) collecting information from the environment; and (ii) using the computer to control its complexity; have an educational value in today's society which it would be hard to exaggerate.

In other contexts, the computer work can come first. Computer games, such as simulations, can provoke the need to refer to books, maps, graphs, etc., and then organize the resulting data, before returning to the computer for the next input to the program. A realistic simulation, such as those listed at the end of Chapter 6, can provoke incidental questions, whose answers may only found by further research in the library.

7.6   PROBLEM-SOLVING

Like information handling, this topic can be studied in some depth in a computer-oriented yet computer-less context. However, it is closely connected with computers, and indeed its full exploration at primary school has only become feasible with the advent of computers. In fact, it is less an identifiable topic than an approach, which should guide and permeate all our educational work. The computer has given us the opportunity to realize the ideas of Piagetian learning, and a decision to make this our goal could be the initial educational decision we take (cf. the end of Section 7.1). The National Council of Teachers of Mathematics (USA) has made problem-solving a major emphasis for the 1980s (cf. Billstein 1984).

Some of the basic principles of problem-solving are:

1   Understand the problem. What is the starting point, the target, the constraints?

2   Develop a tentative solution. Start at the bottom: What related problems do we know how to solve (call these primitives)? Start at the top: what subproblems can we identify whose solution would imply the solution of the original problem (call these procedures)? Divide the problem into procedures, and these into smaller procedures, until primitives are reached.

3   Debug the tentative solution. Work through the solution with data for which the solution is known, and compare the results. Do this for a variety of data until the solution procedure seems to be correct.

4   Prove the solution correct. Mathematicians realize that a theorem is not proved by the exhibition of a large number of conforming cases, and try to produce formal proofs of tentative results. Computer scientists do the same with programs, but often have to confess failure, and accept extensive tests as 'semi-proof' of correctness.

If children are learning to program, they should be guided by these steps in producing a program to solve any given problem. However, the sort of activities described in the previous section throw up many problems of how to organize data, how to play a game and how to act in a simulation, and all such situations provide the opportunity for children to practise thinking, problem solving and decision-making skills. Furthermore, they learn that data is not collected for its own sake but for some purpose, such as to provide the basis for decision making. The computer can search through the large quantities of data which the children have input, in order to gather and display those items which are relevant to the current decision which is to be made.

7.7 SOCIAL INTERACTION

We have already mentioned the repellent image of antisocial children tuned in only to machines. It should by now be clear that this is a far from accurate picture of the use of the computer in the primary school (or, indeed, at any level). The great majority of the activities in this chapter can be carried out, from time to time, singly, in pairs, or in groups. In the context of the many simulation programs, for example, far more activities take place away from the computer than directly with it. The computer can be seen not only as an organizing machine, but as a springboard.

Two advantages of CAI which are often mentioned are the personalizing of instruction, and immediate feedback. These advantages may be seen to refer not only to the answering of a list of drill questions, but also to general decisions taken in a simulation, for example. Wide-ranging decisions can be taken, with complex results, but the computer is fast enough to demonstrate the result (in the simulation) of these decisions within an acceptably short time ('immediate feedback'). This in turn allows the child(ren) to try out idiosyncratic strategies, without wasting too much time ('personalized instruction'). Through such a convenient facility for experimenting and correcting errors, children learn selfconfidence, feel more in control of their own education, are less frustrated, and are not locked into a sense of failure. Activities that establish a realistic context are much more conducive to learning. Furthermore, all this activity can involve social interaction with mutual critical evaluation of decisions, strategies and solutions, and hence co-operative learning. When such a learning milieu is provided, a further benefit is the breaking down of arbitrary discipline barriers, as questions are generated which cut across these. If this does not occur spontaneously, worksheets can be set which raise the cross-disciplinary aspects as follow-up activities or applications. This will assist in another matter, namely the ongoing use of the computer. The educational experience will be enhanced if the computer is not seen by the children as relevant to only one short segment of their school course.

7.8   PERCEIVED PROBLEMS WITH COMPUTER USE IN PRIMARY SCHOOL

7.8.1   What about non-readers using the computer?

Many non-readers can use computers, selecting discs by colour coding, recognizing pictures and shapes on the screen, responding by means of a touch-sensitive screen, a mouse, or a paddle (cf. Chapter 14). Indeed, it is perfectly possible (although not necessarily desirable) to teach pre-school children to program. In general, the teacher must inspect proposed CAL software very carefully to ensure that any directions are readable by and intelligible to children at the target level.

7.8.2   What about the 'hunt and peck' typist?

The best programs at this level require very little typing. Responses are short and consistent: press space bar to continue or press an integer to select a choice. If more typing is potentially required, as in programming, for example, the teacher could write some in advance, and then have the children find and correct bugs; or add extra capabilities to the program.

In fact, one may argue that these two points are actually advantages, because non-readers learn to read through using print to engage in discourse, and using a computer keyboard is a very active way of doing this.

7.8.3   Authentic and inauthentic work

This has already been mentioned. If every calculator has a square root key and every computer language a square root function, why teach how to calculate a square root? Indeed, why teach any arithmetic operations at all? This is just a facet of a broader question: what should students be taught? The enormous change in the answers to this question over the years suggests that there is no one correct answer. We used to require the classics 'to develop the mind'; then mathematics 'to develop the mind', and now computing 'to develop the mind'. Clearly the accepted teaching base will change with time to reflect the changes in society, and for us that means gradually accepting and assimilating the nature and implications of the computer age.

7.8.4   What computers do 'bestest'

When you write, your mind conceives an idea and formulates it into words. Automatically, with little thought, you spell out the words using the English alphabet. You leave spaces between words, insert punctuation and form sentences into paragraphs. Writing is a form of symbol manipulation. Certain aspects of writing such as spelling of individual words, indenting the start of a paragraph, capitalizing the first word of a sentence, leaving a blank space between words and ending a sentence with a punctuation mark may be quite automatic. But conceiving and formulating ideas and organizing these ideas as sentences and paragraphs require careful thought.

Similarly, certain parts of mathematical problem solving are merely symbol manipulation that can be automatically and rapidly performed by a machine. Other parts require careful thinking; indeed, that is the essence of mathematical problem solving. This cannot be done by a machine.

Much of the accumulated knowledge of the human race is represented as symbols written in books and journals. Eventually most of this will be stored in computerized data banks and will be readily available to people who use computers as an aid to problem solving. Certain aspects of problem solving are 'merely' automated symbol manipulation. The idea is that people who use both their brains and machines are much more likely to solve difficult problems than people who are restricted to just one of these tools (Moursund 1981).

The primary school of the future will not see the computer replace the teacher. It will contain a rich teacher–pupil learning environment, with the computer as the main educational tool.

Chapter Eight

Computers in special education

Our greatest glory is, not in never falling, but in rising every time we fall

Confucius (*c*551–479 BC)

8.1 EDUCATIONAL REQUIREMENTS

8.1.1 What is normality?

The 'normal' education system is based on assumptions about 'normal' human capabilities. Of course, no two people are identical in all their capabilities, so a whole range of levels of capability is recognized as being normal. We can envisage a multi-dimensional space, with each co-ordinate representing a particular capability and each point representing an individual, as defined in terms of his or her capabilities. We draw a boundary in this space, and define all those whose points lie within the boundary to be 'normal', and design our education system to cater for them. All those whose points lie outside the boundary require special educational provisions. The

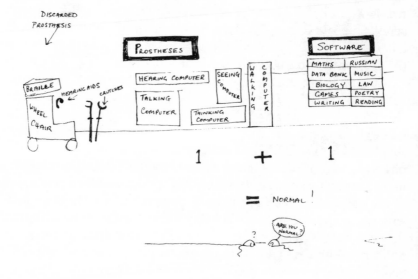

first thing to note is that wherever the boundary is drawn there will be individuals who are very close to it. There will always be children in normal education and children in special education who seem out of place, but who would seem equally out of place in the other system. This is inevitable, and our systems must be flexible enough to cope with it. This is why all primary and secondary teachers need some facility in handling both the slow and fast learners, even though they will not encounter severely disabled children. Currently (1984) there are proposals for the introduction of a segment on special education into several primary teacher training courses.

The assumptions that are made about the capabilities of the children in the normal educational system can be used as a basis for planning computer use in that system. We recognized, however, that there are significant differences between different children, so our planning includes using the computer to tailor instruction and learning situations to the individual.

8.1.2 Mental and physical requirements

If even those in the 'normal' group need special, individual consideration, how much more is this true of those whose points in capability space are far apart, outside the normal zone. There is a great variety of disablements: deafness, blindness, autism, spasticity, all in different degrees of severity. There is no obvious reason why what is useful for the blind would be useful for one with cerebral palsy. Thus, relevant computer aids must be heavily tailored, first as appropriate to the type of handicap and then towards the capabilities and needs of the individual user.

Despite this, it is useful to identify the two major subgroups within the 'special' category, namely those that differ from normality along the spectrum of mental ability (the mentally retarded and the gifted), and those that differ along the spectrum of physical ability (blind, deaf, palsied). While classroom learning involves social and physical goals, its predominant goals are intellectual, and so children in the first group are directly affected by the demands and provisions of the classroom. We have already observed that computers help with special needs, and they are very useful for this group. Neither the fast nor the slow child has specific difficulties in using an ordinary computer, and so all that is required is special software, tailored to their various needs.

Children in the second group, however, are affected only in a secondary manner: through blindness, they may not receive vital information; through palsy they may not be able to respond. As a result, they may appear retarded, and may indeed be behind some sort of 'normal' standard. This, however, is a secondary effect, resulting from the primary handicap. (Some writers prefer to see the intellectual shortfall as the primary problem, with its cause being of secondary importance. The difference is only in terminology, not in appreciation of the situation.) What these children need is an appropriate prosthesis, which involves special computer hardware (probably controlled by dedicated software), to bring them into a situation of rough parity with the 'normal' children. Then they can access all the normal software which is appropriate to their mental capabilities. We discuss the first group in Sections 8.2–8.4 and the second group in Sections 8.5–8.7.

8.2   MENTAL ABILITY

Within the range of ability we call 'normal', basic classroom teaching is often directed at the middle third of the class in terms of intellectual ability. This could leave the top and bottom thirds bored because they are idle or lost, respectively. The teacher prevents this by taking special action with these groups. Years ago, the top group were given more, harder, exercises of the same type (or asked to tutor students in the bottom group). Now they are more likely to be given research projects. Years ago, the bottom group were given more, easy, exercises of the same type. Now, they are more likely to be presented with a variety of approaches to the same material. The computer can help both these groups. For the bottom group, it provides yet another approach; for the top group, it represents a new experience to assimilate and a new tool to use in their research. Note that computer use must not be presented in a superficial fashion. Computer use by the top group must not be (and must be seen not to be) of the style of "if you finish early, Johnny, you can go and play with the computer". Conversely, for the bottom group it must not be just a time-consuming palliative that keeps them out of the teacher's hair. Contrary to current folklore, very little computer use frees the teacher from the responsibility to teach. For both upper and lower groups, the computer's place in their learning must be planned, and its use monitored.

Carl Jung observed that, while it is easy to design boxes, it is not easy to fit people into them. So, sometimes there will be children in the 'normal' class whose academic ability is far from that of the middle third. The teacher may feel that they should be in special schools, and, indeed, they may be taken out of the classroom for specific activities. However, they do not present a different type of problem (or challenge). They are simply more extreme examples of the usual classroom diversity, and so the computer's ability to personalize instruction may be used to even greater advantage.

8.3   THE SLOW LEARNER

8.3.1   Attention and motivation

Assistance to the slow learner is one area where drill and practice CAI has proved to be useful: the child does need to do more exercises before the concept 'sinks in', and remedial work must often be undertaken. It has been observed that computer-based work increases the attention span of this normally distractible category of student (Lally & Macleod 1982; see also Kleiman *et al* (1981) who have shown that computer work doubles the attention span of hyperactive children as compared with pencil and paper work on the same topic). Reasons for this seem to include: minimal extraneous distractions while the child is concentrating on the computer; the ability to require student response within a specified time; the computer's undivided attention to the student, unlimited patience and rapid reactions to answers or requests; the great variety of exercise formats; and the absolute privacy for making mistakes.

Another observed effect of computer use is an increase in motivation. We have used the phrase 'the bottom group' as a convenient shorthand. It refers only, of course, to academic ability. But our ability/capability space is multi-dimensional, and it is unlikely that these children are at 'the bottom' on all counts. However, in school work, they were slow to begin with, and have now become conditioned to being slow, in the bottom group, and failing. Slow learning often has psychological and social origins. A well-chosen educational program can lead them through to a success; this can affect their self-perception and self-confidence; and this in turn can lead to further successes. Thus, the slow learner may not be forever condemned to plodding through remedial programs: a few (computer-originated) successes may see him or her back in the 'normal' student group. A dramatic growth in both skills and motivation has been observed in learning-disabled students as a result of work with Logo. This may be the first situation in which they take the initiative, compared to their usual dependent condition. For the first time, the focus is on their capabilities, rather than on their needs, and the students develop an intelligent self-image as they learn to teach a 'dumb' computer.

The teaching is done by the children, with the computer as learner.

8.3.2   Writing

Lally and Macleod (1982) have developed computer-based writing exercises in which letters of the alphabet are displayed on a screen (Fig. 8.1). The student presses down on the screen with a digitizer pen and moves the pen along the guidelines within an accuracy defined by the cursor box size. As students track successfully, the thin guideline changes into a thicker path. If the student starts at the wrong end of a stroke, lifts the pen or moves the cursor box too far off the guideline, path-filling stops and a small blinking spot calls attention to the point where the pen should be.

Students track various letters of the alphabet during training sessions. In some letters only portions of the outline are visible. Getting students to track incomplete stimuli encourages them to think about what they are doing and to predict letter shapes from

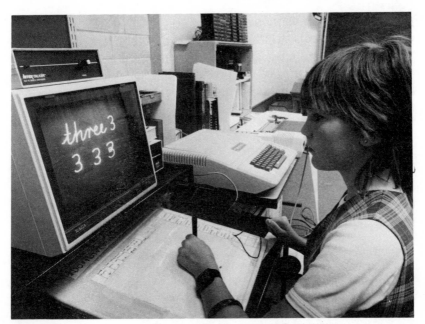

Fig. 8.1

memory. Together with the use of a variable size cursor box, this procedure allows the amount of support given by the computer to be reduced as the student's competence grows. A large cursor box is used with children of lower ability. Gross motor movements resulting from their attempts to approximate letter shapes cause the computer to produce well-formed model letter shapes. This procedure reinforces the appearance of the desired product rather than students' possibly ill-formed attempts. As students' skill improves, the cursor box is gradually reduced so that their movements are shaped to become more and more like those required to produce the desired model letters without computer support. Speed and accuracy of tracking are displayed at the end of each exercise: most students are intensely interested in their performance and see reductions in cursor box size as a mark of achievement.

These exercises enable students to be accurate but active learners. They are given external support appropriate to their growing competence in the skill and informed quickly of any errors (thus localizing the consequences of wrong choices and interrupting development of erroneous patterns). The exercises impart a much greater degree of control over the handwriting process than is possible with conventional techniques, and at the same time encourage students to think about what they are doing. The procedure adopted emphasizes the process used in handwriting as well as the appearance of the product. This exercise is effective in improving handwriting skills both with intellectually handicapped schoolchildren and with nonretarded children who have a specific learning difficulty.

8.3.3   Reading

Lally and Macleod (1982) have also developed a reading program, to teach students to recognize a beginner's reading vocabulary of 105 words.

"During exercise sessions, overlays of sixteen words are placed over a matrix of 16 large buttons. Twelve different overlays are used to present the training words. Each overlay has versions with the same words in different positions to avoid responses being based on sound–position associations.

The computer gives instructions such as 'Press *was*'. If the student responds correctly, a light under the appropriate word flashes and the computer says the word three times. If the student presses the wrong word, say, '*saw*' instead of '*was*', then the computer responds with 'You got *saw*, try again, press *was*'. If the student has not responded after five seconds, or has already made more than one error, the light under the correct word begins to flash. When the student presses this word after prompting, the machine says 'Right, but try again, Press *was*'. The same word is presented until the student responds correctly within the given time interval. Presentation of new words occurs only after correct responses so that the learner is not swamped with a large number of different and unknown words, but rather deals with a small subset of words until these are correctly recognized, causing the subset to gradually increase until it reaches sixteen. At the end of each set of sixteen trials, the computer gives verbal results to the student.

Intellectually handicapped students who received five hours of computer- assisted instruction with the above exercise over a period of four weeks showed an increase in the number of words correctly recognized from an average of 39 to 69. Of great interest was the fact that this improvement was maintained a half year later (an average of 71 words being recognized), even though no further computer-based training took place."

Other reading programs have been developed especially for dyslexics, emphasizing the left to right development of words (Pollard 1983).

8.3.4   Arithmetic

Lally and Macleod (1982) report on programs to teach number concepts (by the display of two rows of squares with equal or unequal numbers of squares) and spatial concepts (by reference to the relative location of buttons in an 8×8 square array).

In summary, the important aim for any level of student is to construct a learning environment which challenges a child's current (incorrect) world model, but which the child can perceive as a variant on this, not one which is totally unrelated.

We shall return to this topic in Chapter 12 in connection with the learning of programming.

In connection with the more severely mentally retarded, Williams *et al* (1982) observe that the literature is meagre. They refer to 25 reports, all of which tend to be positive but vague. The general lack of reading skills in this group is a problem. Pictures are essential, and hence a videodisc (which can store a large amount of pictorial information) is useful.

8.4   THE GIFTED CHILD

The obvious way to help the gifted child is to set higher level work. If a 'grade 4' child is too advanced for 'grade 4' mathematics, then give him or her 'grade 6,7, ...' mathematics. While the teacher would find it very difficult to spread his or her teaching so widely, the assistance of a computer allows the child to proceed at a more appropriate pace. There are, however, at least two difficulties with this obvious solution, which relate to the style and context of education.

8.4.1   Style of education

The gifted child is not just ahead of his or her age level, but is usually also much quicker at the work s/he does, grasping ideas, perceiving connections and appreciating consequences, more rapidly than average. Thus, material designed for the average grade 6,7 ... may not be quite right for the gifted grade 4. It is characteristic of this type of child that we cannot predict just what they will be capable of doing. (It can even occur that the most intelligent child in the class is also the slowest.) Therefore, specially designed teaching material is required, and this material must provide a flexible learning environment. This environment should foster the use of divergent thinking; take the student close to the frontier of the subject at hand; and facilitate performance evaluation. The computer affords the best means of providing such an environment (Kolstad & Lidtee 1981), giving students opportunities to extend themselves in an unstructured and unlimited way. With computer assistance, gifted children have composed music, produced creative art work, solved complex problems, and created fantasy and other simulation games.

This brings us to the topic of learning to program, to which we shall return in Chapter 12. However, it is worth commenting that the Logo language was designed to have 'no ceiling', that is, to permit the expression of indefinitely complex ideas. Logo therefore provides an appropriate environment, and students can use it to write games and CAL material. The former capitalizes on their typical interest in games playing, but leads them into the study of advanced data structures and algorithm design. Contests develop within groups of students to write an unbeatable game. Writing CAL material makes use of their school experience and gives them the chance to set up an environment for others. However, the gifted child is quickly ready to progress from a simple computer system to a larger, more complicated one, and/or to more theoretical studies.

8.4.2   Context of education

The second difficulty with the obvious solution (of simply giving grade 7 material to grade 4) relates to the context of education. Whereas mathematics usually is, and science can be, taught as an abstract or technical system, subjects such as history, English, geography and religion are almost unintelligible if shorn of their social context. However, the grade 4 child, even the gifted child, is not sufficiently mature to handle the social questions raised in grade 10 history. In fact, many of the social problems raised in schools are altogether out of place there, for any child, because it is impossible to appreciate their significance until one has acquired more maturity and experience of living and working with people. Thus, ways must be found of extending gifted children academically, without isolating them from their peers. The extension activities must not rely on a higher level of social maturity that is inappropriate and not beneficial to the child.

Finally, just as the slow learner has needs other than the specific topics, so does the gifted child. The latter, having experienced success in this academic area, may become immersed therein to avoid failure in other areas — including social contact. This can be overcome in a number of ways. The group research project, the computer-based simulation for a group of children, the activity of tutoring weaker students: all these can help to remove the social barriers erected by many bright children.

8.5   PHYSICAL ABILITY

Moving outside the 'normal' classroom, we consider those with a physical handicap of some level of severity. The blind, or partially sighted; the deaf, or partially deaf; the deaf and dumb; the quadriplegic; the cerebral palsied; the spastic. Computers are useful in work with the handicapped, because this work is labour intensive, and there are few trained personnel. However, these students may be as disabled in their use of computer as in other ways, and so computer-based learning often depends on the provision of interesting and expensive peripherals. The deaf comprise the largest group to benefit from computer technology (Williams *et al* 1982), although there is very little material that is specific to the use of the deaf (or perhaps because of this fact, as it enables the deaf to take advantage of generally available materials). The blind, on the other hand, have received little benefit so far.

Given the appropriate prosthesis, there is no reason why the handicapped should not participate in education, including computer education, just like anyone else. There is often a blurring of the distinction between 'computers for the disabled' and 'computer education for the disabled'. Goldenberg (1979), for instance, is talking about education as enabling communication so that children can learn. However, as we observe at the end of the chapter, as the necessary technological advances take place, it is possible to distinguish the computer as prosthesis from the computer as educator.

8.5.1   Computer 'spectacles'

One common instance of artificial assistance for a bodily function is the use of spectacles to correct visual defects. We can draw comparisons and contrasts with the prosthetic use of special computer peripherals for overcoming other handicaps. Firstly, just as there is no one lens design that will suit everyone, so each individual needs a personalized computer system. Secondly, there is a range of visual abilities considered 'normal' and similarly a range of physical abilities considered normal. Thirdly, glasses are socially acceptable. While someone who can see only 3 or 4 yards is clearly handicapped, we tend not to think of them as such, because the handicap is overcome by means of glasses, and glasses themselves are (paradoxically) accepted as 'normal'. Hearing aids and wheelchairs, however, are not seen as 'normal', although they are increasingly being accepted as such. Perhaps, as computers radically extend the capabilities of those we now call 'handicapped', we shall no longer see them as such, but regard the person and computer as a whole, just as we already do with spectacles. By providing support to a system which exists but cannot stand alone, glasses restore essentially normal status to a person who would be severely disabled without them. Fourthly, again we have a contrast, in that unlike spectacles computers are not restricted to one medium, but can accept almost any input and produce almost any output. In order to do this, special input and output devices are built, and special software to control them is designed.

8.6   COMMUNICATING WITH THE COMPUTER

There are many ways for people to input data to a computer, and many ways for the computer to produce its output (Sections 14.3–7). However, most input devices involve manual dexterity and all output devices require the exercise of one of the senses (usually sight). Special devices for the handicapped must be designed with the specific handicap in mind.

8.6.1   Input devices

1   Unary devices. A variety of devices that offer a single switch or key to be controlled by the chin, a toe, a finger, a puff of air, or some other single movement (Fig. 8.2). Clearly, this permits only a one-bit input signal, and if the user is not to simply communicate in morse code, something must be done to enhance the speed of communication. One approach is to provide a list (menu) of possible commands on the screen, with a cursor moving past them. When it reaches the desired menu item, the user presses the key. This has been used to enable children to construct a sentence, which is then spoken by the computer (Cohen 1982).

Fig. 8.2

2   Limb path movement. Some people are capable only of making a movement which does not terminate precisely enough for the above, but which can be monitored to give an adequate interpretation of the desired input. If this is used in the context of drawing on a graphics tablet, the person's motor control often improves as a result of the noise-filtered feedback (Goldenberg 1979; cf. Lally & Macleod 1982).

3   Myoelectric signals. If the movement of a muscle is neither strong enough nor accurate enough, the neural signal to the muscle can be monitored, and used to control the computer.

4   Eye-tracking devices. Eye position can be monitored, so if gaze control can be reliably maintained, it can be used as an input signal. However, this obviates eye contact during communication, and forces eye movement to be related to the screen menu scan, rather than to the spirit and flow of the communication.

5   Voice input. Input devices exist that will recognize up to a hundred words spoken by a particular individual. In fact, these need not be words in the usual sense, but any vocal sounds, so the user must simply be able reliably to produce a few vocal sounds. Again, as with limb movement, the positive and useful employment of a person's rudimentary speech capability is likely to lead to an improvement and extension of that capability (Goldenberg 1979).

8.6.2   Variety

There is less variety in output than in input devices, and all require the user to be able to see, hear or touch. Some devices are designed to communicate back to the handicapped user (examples are braille printers for the blind and large character screen displays for the partially sighted), while some are designed to communicate with other people on the user's behalf (these include voice synthesizers for the dumb). Clearly, voice synthesizers are also useful for the blind user.

8.7   CATCHING UP

The handicapped need not only special peripherals, but also access to normal standard software (Vanderheiden 1982). It has been observed that as the developing countries use modern technology, the underdeveloped countries are falling further behind, despite special assistance. In analogous fashion, 'normal' people are using computers to enhance their learning, employment etc., and handicapped people are only using them to bring them up to 'normal'. Thus the handicapped are not reaping the general benefits of computers, and are still behind the non-handicapped. The problem is that the software controlling the special peripherals is often incompatible with the standard software. The latter is written on the assumption of full system availability, and may destroy values vital to the peripheral handling programs. This suggests that one should build (special purpose) prosthetic computer systems, and design them to be connected to a standard system (or preferably several standard systems). Returning to the spectacle analogy: the short-sighted wishing to use a computer do not wire their eyes to the machine; they don the separate special purpose prosthetic spectacles, and then look at any standard system. The same approach is now feasible with the computer prosthesis, because the microcomputer is small enough (Feldman 1983). To be of real assistance to the handicapped person, the prosthetic computer should not only match the particular disability, but provide the Smalltalk/Macintosh style facility to switch easily between tasks, patching results from one package into another, and passing from program to program without losing the user's place in any of them.

This physical separation of the two logical functions being performed by the computer clarifies the real needs of the handicapped. So many of our communication modes are conditioned by normal capabilities, that we seek to train the handicapped to use them, or isomorphic replacements. For example, teaching the deaf to speak, and down-playing the value of sign language. Of course, the normal person cannot use sign language, so speech is needed to avoid being cut off from communication with normal people. However, this approach is like straining to walk instead of accepting (and improving on) the wheelchair. The handicapped may be more capable of handling a different modality, and should not have the 'normal' modes forced on them. If they can use their preferred mode, and have the computer both understand it and translate it into normal communication as desired, then their learning problem is eased.

The ability to use standard software will open the way for the handicapped to train as programmers. With increasing amounts of work being done at home, and the increasing amount of information processing activity, there is scope for great increases in gainful employment for the handicapped.

Chapter Nine   Courseware design

If any man wishes to write a clear style, let him first be clear in his thoughts
                                        J.W. von Goethe (1749–1832)

9.1   DEVELOPING CAL SOFTWARE

Teachers may buy text books and project material or write their own, and the same is true of computer-based educational material. However, producing a CAL program needs significant expertise in computer programming and ample time to devote to the programming task, either or both of which a teacher may lack. Conversely a professional programmer may not have the necessary educational expertise. Fortunately, we can divide the development of CAL courseware into two parts, namely specification, which requires educational expertise, and programming, which requires programming expertise. These tasks may be undertaken by a teacher and programmer, respectively, provided that they liaise closely to ensure that what is produced is what was wanted (Section 9.1.1). Alternatively, both tasks may be carried out by a single teacher/ programmer, provided that s/he has enough time (Section 9.1.2). We consider the specification, design and evaluation of CAL material in this chapter, and programming in the next.

9.1.1   Separate programmer and teacher

If a program is to be written by a specialist programmer, a teacher must be closely involved. One suggestion is to establish a writing team, involving perhaps three subject specialists (including at least one serving teacher), one instructional designer, and one programmer. Watson (1982) says "although ... difficult to organize, the active involvement of serving teachers in the writing of material provides much more spin-off to a project than any initial proposal would suggest". She points out that despite the excellent work done so far in the Computers in the Curriculum Project (see Appendix), its CAL material is still seen as an exceptional contribution to the curriculum. Furthermore, the educational validity of many CAL programs is highly questionable. These defects may be overcome by the integrated development of CAL material at the same time as curriculum innovation and development. This may be achieved by the attachment of one or more programmers to the curriculum development team. Clearly, it is helpful if these programmers have a teaching background; conversely, although the others in the group need not know how to program, they should have some understanding of the computer's capabilities, strengths and weaknesses, and of the precision of specification required.

One advantage of having a separate programmer is that s/he can quickly implement either a section of the material requested, or a first approximation to it. Such a first approximation is called a prototype. Prototyping is a useful technique in the production of any software: seeing the implementation of what, in theory, seemed a good idea, can often lead to a drastic re-thinking. Iterations of this step also engender in the teachers in the group the necessary computer understanding referred to above. A second advantage is that the teachers have access to students who can test the successive prototypes. A third advantage is that a permanent curriculum development group can embark on long term commitments. It can seek out and establish links with teachers who have ideas for programs; then write, test (fully) and document the resulting programs, including repeated consultations with the teachers, and extensive classroom trials; arrange the production of quantities of

these materials in print and on disc; and establish retailing or other circulation mechanisms.

Disadvantages of this approach are that it needs organization and finance. A teacher could not afford to employ a programmer to develop a CAL idea. Most schools could not afford this, either. Therefore the Department of Education, or some other centrally funded agency, must establish a writing group, by employing a programmer (or programmers) and relieving selected teachers of some teaching duties.

Some education authorities try to do it more cheaply by finding a teacher with computing expertise, and relieving him or her of all teaching duties. Perhaps surprisingly, this is not an ideal solution. The teacher seconded to programming can quickly begin to respond more readily to programming imperatives than to educational ones, and can get out of touch with the realities of classroom teaching and organization.

9.1.2   Teacher/programmer

Suppose, then, we decide not to separate the teacher and programmer functions, but to find a teacher with a high level of expertise in program development through computing training or extensive experience. Unfortunately, it takes a long time to produce good CAL programs: about 100 hours of work to produce 1 hour of CAL material is the oft-quoted figure. Putting it another way, this represents working full time through one of the short vacations of the academic year to produce 1 hour of lesson material. Compare this with the generally accepted average ratio of 5 to 1 for the preparation of an 'ordinary' lesson. With a class of 30 students, this results in 0.2 teacher preparation hours per student hour. Furthermore, the lesson may be re-usable for at least 1 more year. If 1 hour of CAL takes 100 hours to prepare, 500 students must use it to get the teacher/student time ratio down to 0.2. It is probably impossible to use it for anything like this number of students before the lesson is obsolete (unless it is sold commercially, and not just used in the teacher's own school). In making this comparison, it is worth noting that in an ordinary lesson 'student hours' are not individual, while in a CAL lesson they are not personal.

Why does it take so long to produce CAL courseware? Firstly, producing any well-designed, correct program is a time-consuming business, and producing good interactive programs that can respond sensibly and usefully to all inputs is particularly difficult. Secondly, the time is analogous to that required by a teacher to convert his or her personal teaching notes into a text book: terminology must be changed from idiosyncratic to standard; ideas normally carried mentally from year to year must be made explicit; and as far as possible the book must be made to stand alone, as the teacher will not be there to augment it.

At present, since there is little good courseware available, there is a strong tendency (and need) for people to produce their own. As soon as they do however, others, also feeling the lack, seek a copy, and the writer feels obliged to spend the necessary time (as in writing a text) to make it usable without the writer's presence.

Looking ahead, as computer assistance is integrated into the educational process the distinction between generally available material, the production of which involves a large amount of effort, and locally written material which can function only in the context of the particular writer, will become clearer. Furthermore, just as texts cannot fully replace the teacher's own notes, so, ultimately, commercially available courseware will not fully replace the local *ad hoc* material. Indeed, the occasional bug which necessitates evasive action by the student, or a recovery procedure by the teacher, can be most instructive about computers: the students realize at first hand that computers do only what they are told, and that the quality of a computerized process depends in part on the standard of the program, which has been written by a person.

The teacher tempted to take advantage of a readily available microcomputer should note these comments from a professional programmer with a large insurance company: "User attitudes to micros have in general been enthusiastic. At first users are quite prepared to develop and control their own systems. They start becoming disenchanted when programming takes longer than two weeks, when systems become too bulky to handle or when the system simply fails. Having developed their systems, users want and expect to hand over control and maintenance to someone else".

9.1.3   Use of in-service courses as writing workshops

Shaw (1982) has creatively incorporated the advantages of having a group of people producing courseware into a time that teachers have already decided to allocate to computing, namely an in-service introduction to computing. "To provide in-service courses without recognition of their value in generating ideas for software is to waste valuable opportunities for taking the state of CBL (Computer-Based Learning) ahead with maximum impetus" (Shaw 1982). The essential observation is that in instructing about computer use, one must take some specific example(s). Often these are fairly trivial, mainly because problem solution by computer needs a knowledge of the problem area also (as indicated at the beginning of this chapter), and the instructor normally has a heterogeneous group of learners, with no common non-computing expertise. However, the teacher in-service instructor has a homogeneous group of learners (provided s/he emphasises educational rather than subject area aspects). This permits the exemplification of the whole process of specification, design and implementation of a significant computer program for the presentation of CAL. On the subject of in-service courses, the following appropriate slip of the pen occurred in a recent university essay: "If teachers need to go away to undertake computing courses, time release and renumeration will have to be arranged."

9.2   EDUCATIONAL DESIGN CRITERIA

Assuming that a teacher has decided to write a CAL program, what considerations should s/he bear in mind? For at least three reasons, the most important ones are the educational ones. The main reason, of course, is that the design of any educational material should start at this point. The computer should be used creatively, or it may be irrelevant. The second reason is that, as the teacher is moving into unfamiliar territory (with CAL), it is reassuring to start with familiar topics. Thirdly, the answers to the educational questions often suggest a good approach to the programming activity, which is a significant help to the novice CAL programmer. Shaw (1982) observes that teacher hesitancy about program specification was dissipated once answers were found to questions such as: What is the purpose of this unit (aims and objectives)? Why use a computer (CAL) approach? What is the scope of the unit? What problem situations or questions will be presented to the student? What will the student do in response to these? What will the computer do in reply to the student's response? How will the computer be instructed to respond (i.e. what is the mathematical model, data base or source of data)? What will the student do with the information generated by the computer? Furthermore, the process of finding answers effectively produced outline specifications for programs.

Watson (1982) points out that no unit in the Computers in the Curriculum Project was developed before key questions were asked, including: What are the teaching objectives? What background curriculum material has to be understood before the program can be used adequately? What learning framework can the unit provide and how may it be organized? What understanding would you expect from the students after using the unit? How adequately could such understanding be subsequently tested?

Gare (1982) has produced a comprehensive checklist for the educational design criteria which should be taken into account. These give rise to programming considerations, which is the correct direction of development. The following list is based on Gare's.

Sections A and B form the basis for deciding whether to develop the program, and, if so, they guide that development.

A. Identify the curriculum area and audience.
   1. General subject area.
   2. Curriculum area.
   3. Intended audience.

B. Analyse the task.
   1. Purpose of program.
   2. Educational objectives.
   3. Necessary prerequisite knowledge.
   4. Materials and techniques currently employed in teaching this topic. This will give ideas on presentation, and assist in documenting the program, and hence enable other teachers to recognize whether and where the program will fit into their teaching.
   5. Specific contribution(s) to be made by the computer.

Sections C, D and E identify the particular computer characteristics which will provide and enhance the desired teaching methodology. They begin to move into the sphere of programming considerations.

C. Determine the instructional strategy.
   1. Program type — drill and practice, tutorial, simulation, game, tool, diagnostic testing, 'electronic blackboard' (i.e. replacing and extending blackboard or overhead projector use).

2. Teacher use — introducing a topic, problem-solving, reinforcement, extension, revision.

3. Student use — alone, small groups (competitively or co-operatively), class, own time.

4. Type of use — substitute, alternative, supplementary, remedial.

5. Expectation — deductive or inductive reasoning.

D. Determine the mode and style of interaction.

1. Student input — keyboard, voice, paddles, graphics tablet, light pen (see Chapter 14).

2. Computer output — animation, colour, three-dimensional representation, sound.

3. Assistance — hints, help routines, repetition.

4. Program 'personality' — encouraging, humorous, neutral (if this exists!).

5. Program type — only run to completion or abort, results at any interim stage, stop and continue later.

6. Other student activities — discussion, research, paper work.

E. Formulate evaluation procedures (if appropriate)

1. Difficulty — random, hierarchical, elective branching.

2. Evaluation — none, right/wrong, right/wrong after several attempts, right/wrong subject to time limit, number correct/ incorrect, completion/non-completion.

3. Report to student— type: score, comment

        — medium: screen, sound, printout

        — format: text, numbers, pictures

        — frequency: end of question, end

source is recorded in order to safeguard the author or distributor with respect to copyright. The statement regarding author/source should appear on all program documentation notes.

3   Program description. The description (which need not be the same for student's, teacher's or technical notes) states the purpose of the program in enough detail to enable the student to appreciate the intent of the program.

4   Background. A general background to the subject content, possibly referring the student to a specific text book or other sources of information.

5   Prerequisites for use. The hardware and software which must be available, and the preliminary or concurrent research work or data collection which must be carried out.

6   Objectives. These should be stated clearly.

7   Operating instructions. Complete instructions on how to use the computer program, including switching on, inserting discs, how to seek help, and how to stop the program. Self-contained input instructions, including examples where appropriate.

8   Sample run. Where possible a complete sample run of the program should be included in the notes although it may not be possible to include a sample run of a program which involves interactive graphics.

9   Additional references.

10   Supplementary exercises and suggestions for further study.

9.3.2   Teacher's notes

1 Program name and file name.

2 Author/source.

3 System and language. These notes specify the program language, the computer system to be used and any peripherals or other resources necessary. A basic system is considered to consist of a CPU and keyboard, together with a video or TV screen. If a printer or other extra hardware is necessary it must be specified under this heading.

4 Package contents list. This informs the teacher of the other notes or resources associated with the package.

5 Subject. The school subject or subjects for which the package has been approved.

6 Level. The examination level(s) or appropriate school year(s).

7 Educational need. The particular educational need which led to the production of the package is explained, and the instructional strategy described.

8 Background. This information gives a general background to the subject content, and may refer the teacher to other sources of information.

9 Package objectives. The objectives of the package should be stated.

10 Program description. The description (which need not be the same for student's, teacher's or technical notes) states the purpose of the program in enough detail to enable the teacher to judge whether the package may be of relevance to a particular class.

11 Pre-knowledge. Any necessary pupil pre-knowledge.

12 Suggested teaching plan/presentation. Recommendations regarding an introductory talk, a classroom management plan, or any other relevant information.

13 Measuring pupil achievement. A description (with suitable material if necessary) of how the teacher can assess pupil achievement of the objectives.

14 Suggested follow-up. Recommendations to the teacher regarding follow-up investigations.

15 Appendices. Appendices, including such items as external data and references, may be included if necessary.

9.3.3   Technical notes

1 Program name and file name.
2 Author/source.
3 System and language.
4 Formulae or principles used. Where a program uses formulae or specific principles to arrive at a value, this information must be included in the notes.
5 List of variables. A list of all input, output and temporary variables.
6 Program structure. Where possible, program structure notes or diagrams should be presented.
7 Listing. A complete listing of the programs and subprograms.
8 Appendices.

All such documentation should be written according to accepted rules for good writing. The clearest writing uses simple sentences, as far as possible, to convey information more easily. This is important for instruction manuals. Measurements of the reading age of the adult population show that the average is 15 years.

Complicated writing, common in science and technology, can be measured in a number of ways, of which the Flesch formula (Flesch, 1948) is probably the best known. The formula is:

$$\text{Reading ease} = 206.835 - 0.846s - 1.015w$$

where s is the number of syllables per 100 words, and w is the number of words per sentence. A passage with a score of 100 is understood easily, while one with a score of zero is practically unreadable. Forty is difficult, and 65 is standard.

9.4   COURSEWARE EVALUATION

9.4.1   Testing, selecting, assessing

The term 'courseware evaluation' refers to three quite different processes. However, since a lot of actions are common to the three processes, the distinction often becomes blurred.

Software testing

When any program is written, it must be tested. This testing is carried out in a number of stages (e.g. Woodhouse *et al* 1984).

1   The program components (subprograms or modules) are exercised using test data designed by the programmer. This is to ensure that the individual programming statements have the desired effects.

2   The program or program suite as a whole is exercised on test data provided by the system designer (who may be the same person as the programmer). This is to check that the whole program works together correctly.

3   The program is run on actual data provided by the user. Such data are likely to contain combinations not thought of by the designer, and hence provide further testing of the program.

4   If the program is to replace some existing system, the two are run in parallel for a while, and the two sets of results compared before finally changing over to the new system.

Stages 1 and 2 are directly applicable to CAL programs. Stage 3, however, is very time-consuming for interactive programs. Successive user inputs depend on previous outputs, and hence the testing really needs someone to sit at a terminal and work through the program. At this point it is convenient to ask some students to do this, making it clear to them that the program is under development, bugs may be expected and a status report would be appreciated. Students in a higher form than that for which the program is intended may be better able to explore bugs and their pattern of occurrence, and to cope with documentation which may be minimal at this stage.

Stage 4 involves what is called (in that horrid educational verb) 'trialling', or 'piloting', and is closely related to prototyping (horrid computing verb!). Total parallelism is impossible to achieve — the same person cannot be taught the same thing twice *ab initio*. Parallel running is sometimes achieved by using the new material in one class and the formerly used material in another. Sometimes this causes too much antagonism (from the class using existing material, and from their parents), and a skewed result (from the Hawthorn effect on the other class). In any case, it is still not the same as the introduction of, say, a new payroll system. Given certain input data on hours worked, wage rates and tax rates, there is just one correct answer for the wages and taxes payable. The purpose of the parallel run is to use the old system to calculate the correct answer as a check that the new system has also produced the correct answer. Teaching, however, has no single 'correct answer' but specified objectives, and what we want to know is whether these have been achieved. Answering this question is not testing the correctness of the software alone, but assessing the appropriateness of the courseware as a whole. This activity, which could be called formative evaluation, shades into the third process which falls under this heading of 'courseware evaluation' (and which we shall call 'assessment').

Courseware selection

Teachers have built up a lot of expertise in the selection of textbooks. From the plethora of texts available, we home in on the desired area, the desired approach, and finally a suitable text. This process may involve a lot of work. We read publishers' blurbs, authors' summaries, impartial reviews, and chapter titles; read the preface and skim the contents; look at type, layout, pictures, diagrams; check the index; read a few sections for language level and expression; pose a few questions and see if the book can answer them. Eventually, we decide 'yes' to one or two books, and 'no' to a large number. This process, if named at all, is called 'selection'. With the increasing availability of CAL material, a teacher who wishes to use some to support a course must go through a similar process, and this process is currently known as 'evaluation'. We suggest that for educational consistency, we should move towards the use of the term 'selection' in this area, also.

At present, few teachers know on what basis to select software: What to look for and how to find it. We shall suggest some criteria in Chapter 14 and refer to various lists of 'evaluation (sic) criteria' that have been published. The reason for the use of the term evaluation for this process, is because it shades into the third process, which properly deserves that name.

Courseware assessment

A major theme of this book in general, and this chapter in particular, is the primacy of educational considerations. After the introduction of any new curriculum, method or technology, its use should be carefully monitored, its effects checked, its performance evaluated, and all this compared with the stated aims and objectives. CAL courseware should not be exempt from this process. In line with current educational usage, this is what should be called 'evaluation'.

In selection, we ask the question 'Does the stated aim of the package correspond with what I want to do?' In evaluation, we ask the question 'Does the package achieve its stated aim?' The dividing line between selection and evaluation is not clearcut because selection should be based on as much information as possible, and this information is not complete until one can assess the results of using the material. Many lists of evaluation criteria (so-called) are principally selection criteria, with a smattering of evaluation (assessment) criteria. Microsift (1982), for example, is a 'structured format for evaluating and selecting courseware', and the phase which is described as evaluation 'may or may not include observation of student use of the package'. A check list of 21 items is given, two of which ('The package achieves its defined purpose' and 'The program is reliable in normal use') can hardly be answered without a full assessment (evaluation). Some of the others would also need class-room use to provide a definite answer, while the rest can reasonably be categorized as 'selection criteria', in our terms.

Similarly, Foulis (1982) suggests eleven questions to ask of a CAL package, one of which (Is the package robust enough to survive rough treatment?) is an assessment question, and a couple of others are borderline, while most relate to selection.

In summary, then, we have

1   software testing, by programmers, during development;
2   courseware selection, by teachers before purchase; and
3   courseware assessment or evaluation, (i) by programmers during development; and (ii) by teachers after use.

9.4.2   Courseware modification

Teacher evaluation may well suggest modification of some parts of the CAL package. This may be the software, but could equally well be parts of the associated documentation, such as aims, types of usage, etc. In theory, if the developers have carried out a full evaluation during development, no amendments should arise as a result of evaluative comments from teachers. In practice, however, all software is seen as subject to constant change. A system is investigated and a new (computer-based) procedure is implemented: but now this is a system, which may be subject to further investigation and introduction of another procedure; and so on. The phrase 'system life cycle' was coined to make explicit the on-going nature of the system development process (which stems essentially from the lack of clairvoyance on the part of system developers). Often system developers try to foresee some of the likely modifications which teachers may wish to make and build in the ability for customization of the courseware (Section 10.4). Clearly, there are narrow limits to what is possible in this direction.

Chapter Ten   Writing computer
                                   assisted learning software

My English text is chaste, and all licentious passages are left in the decent obscurity of a learned language   Edward Gibbon (1737–1794)

10.1   THE PROGRAMMING TASK

In Chapter 9 we indicated the two spheres of expertise which must come together in the production of CAL material, and then described activities related to the educational sphere. This chapter covers programming aspects, and may be omitted on a first reading by a teacher who has no programming expertise and is not currently contemplating writing CAL software. Since this chapter is about the writing of programs for student use, the term 'user' usually denotes a student or students.

10.2   WRITING INTERACTIVE PROGRAMS

A program is interactive (or dialogue or conversational) if, firstly, it involves a high proportion of input to and output from the computer, throughout the program, in contrast to a program that has input only at or near the the beginning, and output only at or near the end; and, secondly, later inputs depend on earlier outputs. Most CAL programs must be interactive, for this is the most significant instructional characteristic of the computer. The computer should rarely be used as an automated page turner, or blackboard look alike. (The term 'electronic blackboard' denotes not a simple blackboard replacement, but the use of the computer's capabilities to present normal blackboard material more flexibly. For example, drawing successive parts of a diagram, and then rotating it to give a three-dimensional effect.)

The user must be able to communicate easily with the computer program; and the form of the output which the program produces for the user must be convenient and easy to understand. This is true for all programs, but perhaps especially for interactive ones in which the user is conducting a dialogue with the program. Some critical points for consideration are as follows.

10.2.1   Prompts

An indication that the program wants a response from the user is called a prompt. These must always be clear and explicit. If a student is unsure what to do s/he will quickly lose interest (probably after pressing a random selection of keys). As far as possible, the same (or similar) prompt format should be used throughout a program. The aim of the program is for the student to learn a topic, and the mechanics should be as unobtrusive as possible. For a similar reason, do not offer unnecessary choices: "Press space bar to continue", is better than "Press any key to continue".

10.2.2   User responses

This brings us to the responses required of the student. These should be short, to minimize errors arising from mis-typing (unless the purpose of the program requires longer responses). To this end, a lot of user responses are coded, the program offering a range of responses (a menu), with the desired response to be indicated by typing a single letter or digit (or touching the menu item on the screen with a finger, light pen or cursor). However, Want (1982) suggests that this gives "too high a priority to speed and ignores the central purpose of the unit — learning. From this point of view, the typing of keywords closely related to a topic seems more useful than typing 1,2 or 3 chosen from a menu". He suggests the hypothesis "that the use of keywords provides a reinforcement of ideas which may well be embodied in such keywords as reflection, volume, sheer, dilute, heat." Want discusses in detail the use of keywords as a means of shortening and standardizing user input, without going to the anonymity of single character coding. Suggestions include predefined system keywords (preferably standardized over a suite of related programs); provision for user-defined keywords; and default numeric values to simplify re-runs of simulation and calculation programs by minimizing the number of values the user must provide each time. Keywords with their key board orientation, are now less common as increasing use of the mouse (Chapter 14) permits a more screen-oriented interaction.

As a further aid to error-free input, the program should check (validate) all input, and accept only that which is of an appropriate form and value. Any other input should give a warning message and the opportunity for the user to try again. If the required input is currently displayed (on the screen), it is reasonable to repeat this procedure until the correct input is provided. Otherwise, the program should take some well-defined alternative action after a specified number of tries. Another refinement is to ask the user to confirm a response which, while legal, is surprising (like a very high price, low temperature or small population).

The responses required should be consistent, with similar prompts expecting similar responses. For example, responses should either always or never need to be terminated by pressing the return key. If it is necessary to have a mixture of these forms, the different responses should be logical and consistent. For example, all coded, one-character input, and only such, might be accepted without termination by the return key.

10.2.3   System responses (to user input)

Again, the prime requirement is that these be clear and intelligible. We have already implicitly mentioned a class of responses, namely error messages. These must be well-located, so as to draw the user's attention to the place where the error has occurred; be precise, so as to indicate what error has occurred; and be explicit as to the remedial action to take. In fact, there is a nice philosophical point as to when an error has occurred. Let us suppose that the program has just prompted 'press space bar to continue' and the user presses some other key.

1   The program, receiving unexpected input, produces nonsensical actions, or aborts. The user is clearly at fault and has made an error, but equally clearly, the program should be written to avoid this sort of response.
2   The program is designed to print 'no: press space bar'. An error has occurred, and an error message has been produced.
3   The program is designed to ignore any other key stroke. In a sense, no error is possible!

Programs should be written to take the worst the user can throw at them and still keep smiling

Programs should be written to absorb the worst the user can throw at them and still come up smiling. This requirement embodies a lot of the time it takes to write CAL programs.

System responses should certainly not be condemning (destroying the user's self-confidence and self-image). But neither should they be patronizing (a danger if the 'encouraging' option is chosen at D4 in Section 9.2) nor slick (a danger if the 'humorous' option is chosen). What seemed clever or funny to the author on one occasion can be merely tedious to the user, especially when seen a hundred times. An equally difficult problem is to regulate the length and detail of the system's responses. At the beginning of a physics simulation, the message:

"With the configuration and values you have chosen,

the pressure is — and the temperature is — "

might be appropriate. However, after the third or fourth successive run, it would become tedious, and

"pressure — ; temperature — "

would be more acceptable. One solution is to indicate the full or short responses, and then allow the user to select which s/he prefers. A trivial example of this is the standard initial game message:

"Do you want to see the rules? Y/N"

This is a particular instance of the general problem of trying to say the same basic thing over and over again but in different ways to avoid boredom.

Realize that the most carefully written program will sometimes miss the significance of the student's input. Realize, too, that the dialogue is not written principally for the good student, who needs little assistance in learning, but for the weaker student. This means that far more (execution) time will be spent in the non-main line sequences, and the author will therefore devote more of the programming to devising and coding responses to wrong answers, than to the main line material (cf. Bork, pp. 15–52, *in* Taylor 1980).

The system should always indicate its status to the user. Like a silent companion, a screen that fails to tell the user that the system is processing is very hard to get along with. One program produces the screen message 'I'm looking! I'm looking!' during a file search.

10.2.4   Screen layouts

This refers to what is displayed on the screen of the microprocessor or terminal. There are a few simple rules for good design:

1   be consistent from one screen to the next;
2   arrange statements in the same order as actions to be carried out;
3   avoid excessive abbreviation;
4   use spacing generously and wisely;
5   allow adjustment of the level of helpful prompting information to the level wanted by the operator;
6   do not clutter the screen with too much information, or too great a variety of symbols, colour, or scripts or inverse colour blocks;

7 do not overuse the facility for blinking, as it may reduce concentration. If a blink is used, it should be at the rate of 3–5 per second.

When using colour:

1 be consistent;
2 never use more than seven colours; try to use fewer than five;
3 avoid bad colour combinations of neighbouring red/green and yellow/blue;
4 avoid red or green at the periphery;
5 dark lettering on a light background is preferable for prolonged work.

The dilemma of the screen as a window on a larger picture is that while it conceals unwanted information, it can also hide wanted information. Current spreadsheet programs (*Visicalc*, etc.) allow scrolling over a large worksheet.

10.3   PROGRAMMING LANGUAGES

10.3.1   Language characteristics

Programming languages are designed to control the processing of data, and so must include instructions to

1 input and store data of numeric and other types;
2 output stored data of various types;
3 assign values to specified data items;
4 execute instructions in a sequence determined by the current values of data items.

In practice, of course, most languages provide sophisticated forms of these instructions to increase the ease and applicability of the language.

Some problems require the frequent execution of particular operations. For example, business processing involves many references to files, and records in files; information retrieval involves detecting whether one or more of a set of specified words occurs in a given text. Therefore some languages include instructions which enable the user to specify conveniently the operations in one (or more) such category. Such languages are called special-purpose languages. Cobol facilitates file handling, and so is a special-purpose commercial language; Snobol permits easy specification of pattern matching for information retrieval or language translation; Simula provides facilities for writing simulation programs. In contrast to such languages, one which provides no such special facilities is called a general purpose language. PL/1, Fortran, Basic and Pascal are often included in this category (although Fortran is also described as a special-purpose language for numerical calculation; and Basic and Pascal were specially designed for people to learn programming).

Two special-purpose languages designed specifically for writing CAL programs (or lessons) are Pilot and Tutor. Languages designed for this purpose are called author languages. As already observed, when using a CAL program, the user expects to be in frequent communication with the computer, usually via a VDU (visual display unit). Therefore, author languages facilitate graphical output, and make the action of many statements conditional on the user's most recent input.

If a special-purpose language contains instructions of types 1–4 above, of course, it can be used for general processing — albeit possibly with difficulty. Cobol and Snobol can be used for general processing (and the former often is). Gaelic, a special-purpose language designed for describing the shapes of integrated circuits, cannot be used to solve other problems. Conversely, a general purpose language can be used for a special application, albeit possibly with difficulty: random file processing in Pascal and pattern matching in Fortran cannot be done easily. Often, however, the only language known to the prospective author and accessible on the available computer is a general purpose one, so it is pressed into service for whatever problem is in hand. It is because Basic is so widely known and available that it has been used in a lot of inappropriate circumstances.

All the languages mentioned in this section are called third generation languages. Fourth generation languages are designed to help the person with problem expertise but little programming knowledge to write the problem specifications (Chapter 9) in a formal way, so that the computer can then build an appropriate program. Unfortunately, all current fourth generation languages (Linc, Focus, Ramis, Total, etc.) are special-purpose commercial languages. Prolog (the only fifth generation language) is a special-purpose language for building and using data bases of a wide variety of forms. We shall say more about languages generally in Chapter 12. For the moment, we concentrate on author languages.

10.3.2   Author languages

In the sphere of author languages, Pilot can be used for general processing (and has been canvassed as a preferable alternative to Basic). Tutor can also be used thus, but Planit and Decal would be much more difficult, while Mentor cannot be so used at all. (These languages are discussed below.) Conversely, Basic, Fortran, Logo and Pascal are all languages which were not designed with CAL in mind, but which have been used for authoring. In fact, most CAL programs have actually been written in a general purpose language. It is a matter of heated debate which type of language to use, and then which language to use within the type.

10.3.3   Pilot

Pilot (Programmed Inquiry, Learning Or Teaching) was developed from 1968 onwards by John Starkweather at the San Francisco Medical Centre, University of California (Tatnall 1982). The original version (Core Pilot or Pilot 73) incorporated eight operations which had been identified as comprising the bulk of CAL material, and was free of the assumptions on teaching philosophies (largely oriented towards drill and practice) which had been built into most CAL languages. Later a standard Pilot (Common Pilot) was developed. This is now available on several mainframe computers (including the DEC VAX) and several microcomputers (including the Apple and Atari, and CP/M systems). Common Pilot has two modes (student/ lesson and teacher/author). It is built upon 13 simple instructions; has very extensive pattern matching facilities; flexible graphics with a picture naming facility; crude subprogram and looping capabilities; and a useful (but reactionary!) indirect execution facility. It has a staccato feel to it, unlike the flow of a language (such as Pascal) with flexible block and control structures. Pilot is the most commonly used author language.

A Pilot instruction has the form

label op-code modifiers conditioners relational-expression:
   text.

The op-codes are as follows:

Code	Name	Action
PR:	Problem	mark the start of a problem group and set options
R:	Remark	self-document a program. These instructions are ignored at execution
T:	Type	display text to the student
:		continuation of a Type instruction
A:	Accept	receive student answer
M:	Match	compare student answer
J:	Jump	branch forward or backward
U:	Use	call an internal subprogram
E:	End	terminate a (sub)program
C:	Compute	execute an instruction in a Basic-like language (or, in some implementations, a certain general-purpose language)
D:	Dimension	allot array space
XI:	Execute Indirect	execute the instruction contained in a string
FI:	File Input	read a record from disk storage
FO:	File Output	write a record to disk storage
G:	Graphics	display point and vector graphics

Labels are optional; the use of the text field depends on the particular operation.

Modifiers change some detail of the normal execution of an op-code. For example: type, but do not go to the next line; match, but allow spelling errors; accept, but only a single character.

Conditioners cause an instruction to be executed only if the condition is met. For example: type, but only if the student's input matches a specified value; type, but only after a specified number of input tries.

An instruction containing a relational expression is executed only if the value of the expression is true.

Apple Pilot handles four separate types of files concurrently (text, graphics, characters, sound), and hence makes frequent accesses to disc, which makes programs quite slow both to develop and use. Copilot, developed by B. Keepes at the South Australian College of Advanced Education, was designed to be simple and cheap, and is probably of most use at primary level. Superpilot (see Thornburg 1982b) is designed to be as powerful as Pilot, but easier to use.

10.3.4   Tutor (Sherwood 1977)

In 1967, Paul Tenszar, then a graduate zoology student, at the University of Illinois, originated the Tutor language in response to the difficulty of authoring on the existing PLATO III system. In 1970, the Computer-based Education Research Laboratory (CERL) began implementing PLATO IV, and concurrently developed Tutor to its present form. PLATO, and hence Tutor, run on large Control Data computers.

The use of Tutor requires a special terminal with a small number of special purpose keys, and preferably a touch-sensitive screen. The language is therefore screen-oriented, with text and pictures able to be located anywhere on the screen. There are built-in graphics facilities for drawing circles, boxes and vectors, and the user can also plot any desired shapes involving straight lines and segments of circles. The language itself requires very little mathematical or computing ability at first, but has very extensive facilities for the more advanced user. Lessons are structured into units, which are very flexible in internal form, and can be linked into intricate sequences.

Users may define subroutines, with parameters, and iterations may be specified. Since subroutines of calculations can be performed conditionally, Tutor can be used for general programming, although not very easily.

Here is a short segment of Tutor code (after Sherwood 1977).

Instructions		Explanatory comments.
unit	geometry	$$ unit name
at	1812	$$ specifies a screen co-ordinate...
write	what is this figure?	$$ ... at which to display this line
draw	510; 1510; 1540; 510	$$ Draws a triangle with the indicated co-ordinates
arrow	2015	$$ Draws the Tutor arrowhead. This divides the display statements from the response handling statements.
specs	okcaps	$$ Capital letters acceptable.
answer	<it, is, a> (right, rt) <angled> triangle	
		$$ <...> denotes optional and (...) alternate strings in the student's response. If the response matches, the next statements down to 'wrong' are executed.
write	Exactly right	$$ Displayed below the student's response. 'ok' follows the response.
wrong	<it, is, a> triangle	$$ If the response matches this, the statements down to next 'wrong' are executed 'no' follows the response.
at	1605	
write	Please be more specific. It has a special angle.	
draw	1410; 1412; 1512	$$ Draws the box on the right angle.
wrong	<it, is, a> square	
nextnow	treview	$$ The only key that will have any effect is the 'next' key and this

transfers control to a unit called
treview, without deleting the
current screen.
One result of running this code is shown in Fig. 10.1.

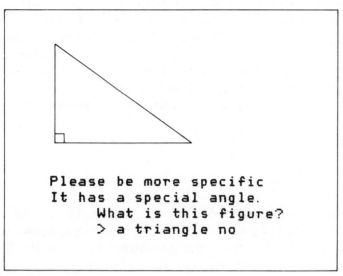

Fig. 10.1

In 1970, Tutor and Coursewriter (an IBM machine specific language) were the two most commonly used languages for authoring. In 1976, Tutor and the general purpose languages Basic and APL were most used. MODCOMP computers use Tutor in their 'SIMPLER' CAL system. Control Data are now emphasizing their stand-alone Author and Delivery System for Control Data microsystems. Authoring package modules ('models') are provided, which guide the author by prompting for responses in a structured form. The models include: interactive training (ITM), which comes closest to offering the facilities of Tutor: drill and practice (DPM); certification testing (CTM), a restricted DPM; tutorial lesson (TLM); situation (not system) simulation (SSM), a multiple level tutorial-type model. This is to Tutor rather what Author is to Mentor.

Plato CAL material (although not yet the authoring facility) is becoming available on Apples.

10.3.5   Other author languages

Planit

Programmed LANguage for Interactive Teaching, is an early author language, more recently adopted by Prime Computer (Frye 1981). The lesson script (CAL program) must be grouped in frames, which may be of Question, Multiple-Choice, Conditional Question, Decision or Programming type. Planit has extensive calculation, but no graphical facilities. It is a complete writing, saving and editing system. However, the lesson format is much more restricted than that of Tutor, and it would be impossible to implement more than CAI.

Decal (DEC 1977)

The Digital Equipment CAI Author Language is more flexible and easier to use than Planit. Like Planit, it has its own associated editor, but no graphics facilities. Since it embodies Basic, the BC (Branch conditional) command transfers control to any specified segment, and the V (evaluate) command evaluates any Basic assignment statement, one could write a general program in Decal, but only with difficulty (and clumsily).

There is a facility for communication from the student to the author, and facilities for author inspection of performance reports, including unanticipated responses, and the students' comments. These can help the student to feel in control of the learning activity, provided the comments are acted on (or at least responded to).

Mentor

The Mentor language (Sussex *et al* 1982) was developed at the University of Melbourne to support the teaching of Russian. It is specialized for drill and practice work on a DEC VAX computer with terminals, and could not be used for general programming. It is written in Fortran 77 and Pascal. The menu-driven Author program can be used to prompt the author to supply text, questions, answers, etc., which Author builds into a Mentor program (i.e. lesson).

Just as with most special-purpose areas, the available author languages span a fairly wide spectrum. At one extreme is Pilot, which is a true programming language. At the other extreme are precisely tailored languages like Mentor. However, there is no standard, high level, machine independent, complex CAL language, combining authoring aids, calculational mode and graphics capabilities, and new designs are produced quite frequently with the aim of rectifying this.

10.3.6   General purpose languages

In Chapter 3, we identified several facets of CAL, of which CAI was only one. However, many author languages are directed towards this form (Tutor, Planit, Decal) or even to the drill and practice subsection of it (Mentor, and, to a certain extent, Planit). Even Pilot is lacking when it comes to writing modelling and simulation programs, as such problems require the full capabilities of a powerful general purpose language, for both algorithm and data structure representation. (We do not consider using a simulation language, as they are not readily available for microprocessors.) Short et al (1982), for example, compare the relative performances of Pascal and Pilot in writing a CAL program which is heavily based on information retrieval and hierarchical (tree-structured) data. While Pascal lacks Pilot's convenience for programming interactive dialogues, appropriate Pascal procedures can be written without too much difficulty (provided the Pascal implementation has reasonable string-handling facilities). Conversely, however, Pilot's representation of all but the simplest data structures is crude, difficult, slow, and obscure. The authors conclude that innovative applications of CAL are likely to require the power of a general programming language. It is noteworthy that Conduit programs are almost all in Fortran or Basic. MECC (Minnesota Educational Computing Consortium) programs are mainly in Basic, which is also the language used in the Chelsea Computers in the Curriculum Project. (See the Appendix for references to these organizations.) Basic is the general-purpose language with the best interactive and string-handling facilities, but it lacks Pascal's data structuring capability, most versions lack the facility for distinct parameterized subroutines, and the simpler versions lack flexible conditional and iteration statements. It is, of course, widely known and available on most machines. As Logo is gaining ground as a school language, it is beginning to share these two advantages and has therefore been used for CAL. Its text handling, pattern matching and subroutining capabilities are good, but its data structures lack variety. Fortran has better structure than Basic, and is also widely available.

10.4   OTHER PROGRAMMING CONSIDERATIONS

10.4.1   Modules

We cannot in this text pursue program design considerations that are not specific to CAL programs. A general programming text, such as Bishop (1982) (for Basic), Dromey (1982) (for Pascal, and more generally) or Woodhouse *et al* (1984) (non-language specific), should be consulted for this purpose. All programs should be developed in accordance with the state of the art of software engineering at the time of writing. It is worth mentioning one aspect of software engineering or structured programming, namely the use of modules. The division of a program into separate, self-contained modules, each representing a logical subtask of the problem, and having a minimum of communication with the rest of the program, has a number of advantages. These include: (i) A reduction in the amount the programmer must bear in mind at one time. This results in fewer errors, faster error detection and more reliable error correction. (ii) Program adaptability, to take advantage of new computer facilities or peripherals, to incorporate a new, faster, implementation of a function, or to respond to a change in specification. (iii) Program modifiability, to permit positive responses to teacher evaluation (Section 9.4) and/or to permit teachers to incorporate personal amendments into the program.

This third advantage is the reason for our mentioning modules here. CAL courseware should support the teacher, and not require the adoption of an unaccustomed teaching style (Lewis & Want 1981). Teachers are used to adapting text books and other curriculum material, and will be able to do likewise with the documentation of the CAL package (Section 9.3). Such adaptation could be futile, however, unless the software can be correspondingly amended. The software design should, if possible, allow the teacher some control over the way students use the programs, or the route they take through them. One example of this is the use of keywords

(Section 10.2.2). A program might have a predefined set of keywords (primary keywords) which invoke specified sequences of program modules. In addition, the program may permit the user to specify new (secondary) keywords to refer to other sequences of program modules. This requires the teacher to be told about the modules and their function, and the program to be able to incorporate the teacher-defined keywords and treat them just like the programmer-defined keywords. The program *Route* (Chapter 6) permits the costs of freeway construction to be changed. The documentation indicates the line numbers of statements to be changed and the appropriate new statements to include.

10.4.2   Computer capabilities

Some factors which can only finally be answered after the program is written, but to which approximate answers should be sought as soon as possible are: Will the program fit in the available memory? What are the memory implications of a static background, plotting or drawing, animated shapes? What are the memory and time implications of any special peripherals (sound synthesizer, light pen, etc.: see Chapter 14)? How many pictures are required? How much text is required? Are utilities, to do text and graphics, for example, required, available, and small enough? Is the animation rapid enough? Can program segments be loaded from disc quickly enough not to make the user impatient? Remember, too, the absolute necessity of documentation (Section 9.3).

Any modifications not explicitly permitted by the documentation should only be attempted by someone with a high level of programming competence. Even an apparently minor change to a program can have far-reaching, unforeseen consequences.

PART II

LEARNING ABOUT COMPUTERS

Chapter Eleven   **Computer courses**

No-one, not even the most experienced and eminent teacher, the most knowledgeable educationalist, or the most perceptive psychologist, has the faintest idea what the best methods of teaching are C. Evans (1931–1979)

11.1   SOME QUESTIONS

Teaching is not a static activity. Topics and methods are continually changing, and the last 30 years have been a time of particularly extensive change. Mathematics teaching now makes explicit the underlying abstract structures; science teaching has incorporated investigative study, to exemplify authentic experimental work; history teaching refers to original documents and uses historical research techniques; geography and other subjects have been incorporated into a unified 'social studies' approach. Against this shifting backdrop, computing has appeared. In response to this, a niche has frequently been carved out of 'mathematics' or 'elective' lessons, for the teaching of programming. However, as the disciplines of computer science, computer engineering and computer technology, and the penetration of society by computer applications, are growing by leaps and bounds, there is increasing pressure on the school curriculum to change and expand to take account of this growth. How should this be done?

1   What should be taught? Programming is the usual first answer to this, but is this appropriate, and what else should be included?

2   Why should it be taught? What are the objectives of a computer course? Is giving the student "confidence and competence in mastering our computer-based society" (Woodhouse 1983) adequate? And, anyway, how can we do this? Educational theory requires the second question to be answered first, but it is impossible to decide why something should be taught until one knows what the something is. In practice, discussions about 'why do we teach subject X?' refer, not to an abstract notion of what X entails, but to existing (or proposed) courses. For a new subject, these questions should be considered together. A tentative answer to one forms a basis for answering the other, and vice versa, and this process may be repeated until a satisfactory conclusion is reached.

3   At what level should it be taught? Thirty years ago, set theory was a university mathematics topic; 20 years ago it was an explicit primary school topic; now it is an explicit secondary school topic, but primary school teachers realize that it is implicit in much of their teaching. Computer programming was an elective at university 25 years ago, and at secondary school 10 years ago, and is now taught in some primary schools. Is there a 'right' level, or does it not matter?

4   How should it be taught? As a separate subject, as part of social studies (or similar), or by 'osmosis' through the use of the computer in CAL? The downward migration of courses makes it clear that we are in the midst of rapid change. It is not yet clear, however, what the final situation will be. At present, we are busily introducing new computing courses. It may be that very soon we shall be phasing them out, as appropriate work on (and with) computers is incorporated into other subjects (Woodhouse 1984).

5   What should be displaced to introduce it? See Section 11.10 for some comments on this.

The opening paragraph of this chapter reminds us that we have no firm answers to these questions, even for subjects that have been with us for hundreds of years. It is not surprising that we have no firm answers in computing, where both the subject matter and the implementations of it are changing rapidly. Therefore, what we say in these chapters is based on the current state of knowledge and will become obsolete in a few years time. The problem is compounded by the different levels of development reached in different places, differences which are observable even within a small geographical area. So, a secondary school has input from primary schools with vastly different computing programmes; and a university has some freshmen with no contact with computers, others who have made it a subject of special study at school, and others who have already written and sold programs commercially. In such a situation, there are no easy answers. However, the only lifeline is to remember that we are in the business of education, and to keep educational considerations paramount (just as with software design: Chapter 9). In this way, the rationale for a course provides an enduring skeleton, even if the means of fleshing it out change from time to time. An *ad hoc* course based on 'what is available cheaply now' may lose all meaning when that particular machine is superseded.

It is incontrovertible that the part played by computers in society is already very significant, and will become even more so. We may take this as our point of departure, and ensure that our educational design is appropriate for this situation.

Part II (Chapters 11 and 12) relates to teaching about computers, and hence assumes a greater knowledge of computers than is the case in Parts I and III. However, other teachers are encouraged to read it, as much of it is intelligible without this knowledge.

11.2   WHAT IS COMPUTER SCIENCE?

11.2.1   Scope

There is yet another question which must precede 'what should be taught?', and that is 'what is there to teach?' One cannot make good decisions on curriculum design without considering the context of the course, including both the scope of the subject itself, and its relation with other subjects. It is a failure to realize (or act on) this that leads to the proliferation of isolated 'computer programming' courses in schools, often given by someone whose only knowledge of computing is that one language. Let us first, therefore, describe the subject known variously as computer science, information science or electronic data processing, from which topics are to be selected for inclusion in school courses.

11.2.2   Information

Computer science is about information and the ways in which information may be represented, arranged, stored, processed and referred to when required. Information is to computer science what energy is to physics, namely the underlying physical quantity whose study provides the raison d'être for the discipline. In fact, some people prefer the term 'information science' to 'computer science'. Nonetheless, the term 'computer science' is more common, because information processing depends so heavily on the computer (as astronomy does on the telescope, for example). While there are, of course, many other means of processing information, only the computer can do so much so quickly. Without the computer we would not be able to process enough information for it to be a significant phenomenon. Without the computer, we should have had to find ways of organizing society that are less information-intensive, and contemporary society would be quite different. The French have coined the term 'informatics' (informatique) to denote this subject in which the study of information and the study of computers are intertwined. Another common term is 'electronic data processing' (EDP), which embodies the three ideas of the computer (electronic), the information (data) and the processing. We associate information and data because data are the basic symbols (letters, digits etc.) by means of which information is represented. Conversely, information is the meaning attached to data.

We often attach meaning to data by grouping them in particular ways. Three letters; c,a,t, become a word 'cat', with a certain meaning; five digits and a symbol: 8,5,0,0,0,$, become a number '$85000' with a certain meaning; a lot of names and numbers become a file of student records, or a university data base. All such groupings are called data structures and each has its own characteristics and meaning.

This is not the extent of the hierarchy, however, for knowledge is at a higher level again. Knowledge arises from the careful comparison and combination of information. A fourth level, the application of knowledge, characterizes human activity, and is sometimes classed as wisdom, sometimes as intelligence. We know a lot about the representation and processing of data and information, but not so much about the representation of knowledge. Knowledge engineering and the development of expert systems (Sections 2.7 and 4.5) is one of the most exciting current research areas in computer science.

Computer science, then, is about data or information, and the patterns or structures in which it occurs or can be arranged.

11.2.3   Algorithms

Computer science is also about algorithms that specify the processing of data. An algorithm (see Woodhouse *et al* 1984) is a finite procedure, or sequence of specified actions, for carrying out some task. We may have an algorithm that sorts a list of names into alphabetical order; or one that calculates wages payable and tax deductible. In each case some information is being processed by the manipulation of the data which represent it. In computer science we analyze existing algorithms and design new ones; develop methods for expressing complex algorithms; prove that algorithms are correct; and compare algorithms, both empirically and theoretically, on the basis of the length of time it would take a computer to carry them out, and the amount of computer storage required for the data they process. Since an algorithm is a method or procedure for solving a particular problem, computer science involves the analysis of problems and the synthesis and evaluation of problem solutions.

11.2.4   Computers

Computer science is also about the computers that process the data according to the algorithms. The machine itself, the hardware, must be built, and this involves logical design and physical construction of the processor, the store, and the peripherals (cf. Chapter 14). Then it must be maintained and operated. The computer is built to process data, and this processing is controlled by expressing algorithms in computer programs, collectively known as software. Programming languages must be designed, and then programs must be designed, from the most complicated suite of programs for controlling the launching of a space rocket to a program to add two numbers together. Then these programs must be corrected if errors show themselves, and modified to do new tasks (this is called program maintenance).

11.2.5   A course

The last three sections outline the area of computer science. Whole components of tertiary study have been covered in one word, while others are totally unmentioned. However, there should be enough to indicate the scope of computer science, and to show that it is possible to select many different subsets of this material, for study at a variety of depths, to meet different educational requirements.

11.3   WHAT SHOULD BE TAUGHT, AND WHY?

Some reasons suggested for school computer courses are:

1 preparation for employment;
2 preparation for higher education;
3 self-development of the student;
4 education for a computer-based society;
5 to consider the multifarious applications of computers;
6 to teach computer use (i.e. operation)
7 to teach computer use (i.e. programming).

Clearly these reasons are neither exhaustive nor distinct. The first four are probably the major reasons; 4 includes 5; 2 includes 6; and 7 may be part of any of 1–4.

11.3.1   Employment

To implement this aim, it is necessary to identify what typical employers want of their new employees. Key punch operators are still required, although less so than before. An appropriate course could be combined with a typing course. Conversely, the call for word processor operators is increasing rapidly. Again, the skill could be taught in the context of a typing course, or learned 'incidentally' if word processing is used in, for example, essay composition.

Apart from these two rather specific skills, however, employers who require employees with computing knowledge usually need far more (or far more specific) knowledge than can reasonably be covered at school. To become a computer engineer or designer, one needs at least a tertiary course in electronic engineering and computer design; to become a computer programmer it is almost essential to pursue a tertiary course in systems, data structures and programming. Technicians able to diagnose and rectify faults in, for example, peripheral devices, are usually employed by the manufacturer and trained on their employer's specific equipment. A school or vocational college could hardly afford the range of equipment necessary to offer meaningful courses. Similarly, computer operators are trained on whatever machine their employer uses. Finally, employers often prefer to train an existing employee, anyway.

Thus, it is difficult for schools to offer specific preparation for employment. Apart from one or two small specific topics, the best approach is to provide a general preparation in the context of computer literacy (Section 11.6) or computer studies (Section 11.7). The latter can include descriptions of various jobs in which people make significant use of computers, and also careers in computing.

11.3.2   Higher education

An upper school (HSC or A level) course can be seen as preparatory for higher education in at least three ways, namely (i) providing specific topic prerequisites; (ii) enabling an adequate level of achievement; (iii) introducing advanced study techniques. To meet (i), just as with preparation for employment, it is necessary to identify the entry requirements of the destination, in this case a tertiary institution. At present, the overlap between various schools' computer courses is so small that most tertiary institutions cannot reasonably require any computing knowledge. This is gradually changing, however, and some institutions 'stream' their student intake on the basis of students' previous computing work; while others are requiring previous study of computer science. We shall consider upper school computer science courses in Sections 11.7 and 11.8.

Considerations relevant to (ii) and (iii) are not peculiar to computing, so we shall not pursue these points.

11.3.3   Self-development

There is another reason for study, particularly at upper school level, and that is an interest in the subject itself. If a subject is studied for its own sake, it is particularly important to capture the flavour and characteristics of the subject. As Section 11.2 shows, for computer science this involves the study of information and algorithms, and the processing of the former by a computer, under the direction of the latter. These must therefore be the emphases of any course under this heading. This point will be emphasized in the discussion of specialist computing courses in Sections 11.7 and 11.8.

11.3.4   Society

In school, we should be educating children to take their place in society (whether to operate within that society or to change it). Since computers are an integral part of the mechanisms upon which contemporary society is built, they must feature in such an education. A balanced course requires some study of algorithms and data (but not to the same depth as in Section 11.3.3); first hand experience of computer use; a survey of a small number of well chosen applications; and a consideration of the implications for people and society of these applications. The term 'computer literacy' has been coined to describe this approach, which we shall discuss in the next section. Clearly, someone may study 'for self-development' under this fourth heading also.

11.4   EDUCATION FOR SOCIETY: WHAT SHOULD BE TAUGHT?

Despite the wide and increasing influence of computers in society, it is not obvious how much we all need to know about them. After all, electricity is vital to western society, but few of us know more about it than how to turn knobs and flick switches — yet this does not give us all a sense of insecurity or inferiority. The principal difference is that all but the oldest members of our society have grown up with electricity, and we are comfortable with its use and our dependence on it. A similar comment applies to the central role played by the motor vehicle and our lack of general school courses on car driving or vehicle maintenance. (There are a few such courses, but they are not suggested as being essential for all.) With the computer, however, there are few adequate adult role models for computer understanding and use, and so an explicit educational programme is required. This situation, however, will be of short duration. Within a decade, all such general computer education will come via parents, personal computer ownership, and integrated courses. These courses will spread computer studies across the disciplines, just as contemporary aspects of motor transport, such as assembly line working conditions, motorways and urban sprawl, buying a car, industry protection, pollution and excursions by motor vehicle are covered in social science, geography, consumer education, economics, chemistry and physics courses.

At present, however, it is appropriate to have some specific courses, and as individual teachers have accepted that children need to know about computers, the number of courses on 'computer programming in Basic' has proliferated. There is obviously merit in teaching students to program: to return to the vehicular analogy, one could describe how it is possible to travel at 100kph, but this could still seem like fantasy to someone who had not experienced driving a car. So, most people need to program to appreciate fully that the computer can work at high speed, that it can produce erroneous results (when programs are incorrect), and that jolly or admonitory messages originate with the programmer, and are not evidence of the computer's humour or perspicacity.

Unfortunately, the short programming course has significant disadvantages.Some students are turned on by the activity of programming, but become bad programmers because few programming principles are presented. While the teacher is encouraging the weaker students, this type of student becomes largely self-taught, either within the classroom or in an extra-curricular context. Conversely, the short course may be of no lasting benefit to the uninterested student, who will soon forget what was learned. In fact, some students are actively put off by the necessary precision, and some by the well-organized logical thought required to produce a solution to a problem. Furthermore, an understanding of the computer's place in society is not achieved by the study of syntactic details. Programming is an intricate activity, and such study may be counter-productive, leaving those students who have been bored and/or frustrated by the course more baffled by and apprehensive of the computer-based society than they were before. Those who fail may perceive themselves as social misfits if society really is dependent on computers.

The shortcomings in a programming course for an introduction to the place of computers in society being recognized, the idea grew that what was required was not such detailed 'technical' knowledge, but a more general 'awareness' of computers. McDougall (1980) defined computer awareness as the possession of sufficient knowledge to enable informed discussion to take place on the basis of what is seen or heard about computers. This involves familiarity with computing processes; knowledge of computing technology and its use; and an insight into the implications of computing technology for society and the individual.

The following objectives for a computer awareness course for Forms 3 and 4, based on this definition, were developed by the Computer Studies Curriculum Committee (1983):

1   To give students an appreciation of the computer's role both in society as a tool of business, commerce and industry, and in recreation.
2   To discuss many of the issues of concern raised by the introduction of computers and their widespread use in our society.
3   To give students opportunities to work with a computer: (a) interactively with prepared programs, and (b) using simple programs prepared by students themselves.
4   To introduce students to the components of a computer system and to some of the terminology used in computing.
5   To show the computer as a development in the history of information processing and computation.

The course to achieve these objectives is structured as follows:

Computer Applications and Implications	(40%)
Using a Computer	(30%)
Components of a Computer	(20%)

History of Computers   (10%)

involving 40 hours of instruction.

In practice, many computer awareness courses have been composed mainly of superficial generalizations, and almost all have lacked an adequate emphasis on the essential linking concept of data. All students need to understand the concept of data and be aware of its ubiquity They should realize that the ubiquity and versatility of the computer is due not to intelligence but to its capability to process data. For example, a hospital computer can help with the vastly different functions of disease diagnosis, blood sample analysis, patient monitoring, and accounts production, to the extent that each of these functions involves data, albeit of various types and structures. While a knowledge of algorithm design is less important under this heading than in Section 11.3.3, a balanced course does require some appreciation of problem-solving (algorithm design).

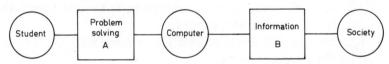

Fig. 11.1

The student devises problem solutions, which are carried out by a computer (Fig. 11.1). In doing so, the computer manipulates information, upon which society is based. We can now see that both awareness and programming courses fail through breaking this chain: the former omits box A, while the latter omits box B. Neither, therefore, can give the student confidence and competence in mastering our computer-based society. The situation is even worse if the awareness course does not make clear the centrality of data and information (and thus barely deals with box B), or the programming course emphasizes syntactic detail rather than problem-solving (and hence fails to show how programming and box A are related) (Woodhouse 1983). For real student understanding of computers, the two courses should be integrated. Such an integrated course is now usually called computer literacy. Luehrmann (1980) maintains that neither computer awareness nor use of CAL is sufficient, and that learning to program the computer is essential, because "it is intellectually improper to inculcate beliefs and values about a subject that do not arise out of direct experience with the content of that subject."

11.5   LEVELS

The discussion to this point has suggested that we teach computer literacy (as a preparation for life in our society), computer studies (with a practical/employment orientation) and computer science (with a theoretical/ tertiary orientation). This leads to the following sequence, in which implications from Chapter 7 have also been included. The sequence is expressed in terms of 13 levels, referred to as preparatory, and years 1–12. The Australian preparatory grade corresponds to the American kindergarten; primary school corresponds to the UK infant and junior schools; in the UK, secondary school normally encompasses seven levels rather than six.

1   Primary school
(i) Preparatory grade, year 1. Concrete activities, perhaps with robot turtle. Playing and exploring.
(ii) Years 1 and 2. Word processing, perhaps with the teacher doing the keyboard work.
(iii) Years 2 and 3. Adventure games, to associate computer use with an enjoyable activity, and encourage creativity.
(iv) Year 2 onwards. Team projects and goal-oriented projects, involving co-operation and planning.
(v) Year 3 onwards. Word processing as a general tool (see Chapter 4), with the children doing more keyboarding.
(vi) Years 5 and 6. Information handling (Chapter 4).
(vii) Years 5 and 6. Logo (Chapter 5), for the study of algorithms, problem solving and programming, and the unfettered exploration of computer use.
2   Secondary school
CAL relevant to different subjects should be used throughout as appropriate.
(i) Years 9 and 10. Computer literacy (section 11.6)
(ii) Year 5. Computer studies (section 11.7)
(iii) Year 6. Computer science (section 11.8)

The existence of computer literacy as an identifiably separate course in Years 9 and/or 10 should be only a transient phenomenon.

In the next section we describe such a course, but suggest that as soon as possible the subject matter be integrated into the rest of the curriculum through Years 7–10 (7–11 in the UK).

Specialist computer study should be restricted to Years 11 and 12 (Years 12 and 13 in the UK), as the material suggested in Section 11.6 is as much on computers as need be covered by all students. Specific study of computers can thus be a matter of choice in the later year(s), whatever the reason for the choice (cf. Section 11.3).

11.6   COMPUTER LITERACY

11.6.1   Literacy

Watt (1980) defines computer literacy as a collection of skills, values, and relationships that allows a person to function comfortably as a productive citizen of a computer-oriented society. He identifies four areas, namely the ability to: (i) control and program a computer to achieve a variety of goals; (ii) use pre-programmed computer applications in a variety of contexts; (iii) understand the growing economic, social, and psychological impact of computers on individuals, groups and society; (iv) make use of computer-related ideas for information retrieval, communication, and problem solving.

The word literate means 'able to read and write', and 'learned'. The word numerate was coined by analogy with the first meaning to denote a command of numerical skills. The term computer literate has clearly arrived in the same way. Some people stress the concept of 'functional literacy' (e.g. Lawless 1982), and set the standard so low that it borders on illiteracy! We should prefer, however, to pick up the second meaning of literate, and maintain that no-one today can claim to be literate who does not have the basic facility with computers that we describe in this section and Section 11.4. Adopting this view, the qualifier 'computer' is unnecessary, and we are simply describing one aspect of literacy. Essentially, literacy denotes the ability to operate independently in one's environment. Thus, other aspects of literacy are reading, writing, numeracy, elementary creativity, and some political and environmental understanding and ability. Hade (1982) considers in some detail the necessary meaning of literacy in an information society, and identifies textual, aural, visual and computer literacy, in each of which areas it is necessary to be able to understand, convert, evaluate and create messages. Just as literacy in the traditional sense is not restricted to particular courses, but is part of the fabric of our society, so this must be the case for 'computer literacy', also.

11.6.2   Topics

As indicated in Section 11.2, and reiterated in the last section, the centrality of information to our society, and the computer's role as information processor, are vital features, and must be grasped by the students.

Description of data flows in a manual system can lead to the concept of data flow through a computer system. The major components of a computer system should be identified together with their purpose and operation and interconnection. This should include some coverage of peripherals.

Then there is an enormous number of topics which are suitable for study. These include employment, privacy, crime, electronic funds transfer, point of sale terminals and direct debit networks, airline booking systems, air traffic control, medical uses, machine intelligence, and, of course, use in schools. The one essential is to deal with a few of these topics in some depth, rather than with a lot of them at the level of 'and the computer is used here, too'. The 'wedge' approach (Woodhouse *et al* 1984) helps to maintain perspective. (Computer literacy is like a round layer cake, cut into wedges, with each wedge an application and each layer an implication.)

Computer structure and peripherals can be described in more detail, and the students shown how to operate them, just before coming to programming. The course should involve about 40 class hours.

11.6.3   Programming

There are essentially two reasons for learning to program in a computer literacy course. The first is for students to appreciate that the computer is not intelligent, but is logical. One cannot say 'you know what I mean' because the machine does not! In many spheres, potential ambiguities are resolved by context — often a context as wide as our whole knowledge of the person with whom we are communicating. When communicating with a machine, however, we must be much more stringent with our logic, and the way people become aware of logical steps is by inputting illogical ones and noting the nonsensical results. Thus, we are not teaching an ability (programming) so much as something negative (the nature and limitations of computers).

The second reason is to gain an understanding of and ability at problem-solving. We are now more than ever aware of the impossibility of students learning all they need to know before they leave school. 'Continuing education' and 'job training' are rapidly becoming accepted features of our society. One of the major emphases of primary and secondary school education, therefore, must be to prepare students for a wide variety of potential experiences. One aspect of this is to develop general problem-solving skills, rather than merely skills in solving particular problems. Systematic problem-solving includes a number of processes, many of them iterative.

   (i) (a) Appreciation of the problem.

      (b) The need to make assumptions about its meaning.

      (c) Validation of these assumptions.

      (d) Firm specification of the problem.

  (ii) (a) Simplification to manageable form.

      (b) Acceptability of simplified problem.

 (iii) (a) Understanding the basic quantities (data) involved.

      (b) Recognizing the inherent structure of the data.

      (c) Representation of the data in an appropriate form.

 (iv) (a) Recognizing the overall structure of an algorithm to solve the problem, and its natural subsections or modules (the 'divide and rule' approach).

      (b) Successive refinement of the necessary solution steps (top-down development).

      (c) Identification of separate sub-problems for solution (bottom-up development).

      (d) Intelligible expression of the solution algorithm (in pseudocode form, for example).

  (v) Evaluation of the trial solution, and a return to (i) if the result is not acceptable.

Just as in mathematics, if our aim is to teach the concept of proof, our objectives must include specific proofs, but these must not assume the major importance. So here, we must keep the problem-solving in mind, and not replace it by a set of objectives that involve a host of syntactic and mechanical detail. It is far less important to be able to write Pascal code or Basic code than to understand the principles of developing a program. Notice that coding does not appear in the above description of problem-solving: it is important to see programming in a particular computer language as a means to an end, rather than an end in itself. We would not attach as much importance to programming at this level as does Luehrmann. It is just the link between a problem to be solved and a machine that can solve it. With this emphasis, the skills and knowledge acquired in this context can then be transferred to other contexts (Section 3.4), so the student should be able to apply his or her competence in problem-solving to other subjects (just as mathematics is a tool for other activities).

In view of our comments in Section 11.4 on the possible bad effects of teaching programming, we suggest that it not be formally assessed. Algorithm design could be assessed, using criteria of correctness, and evidence of understanding and use of the processes indicated above. With programming, pressure to produce a solution simply leads some students to frustration, and the temptation to copy others' code. Even if the copying is not deliberate, small amounts of assistance from different people can soon result in an acceptable program, which is not really the student's own work. It is more important that a student has really done a little than apparently done a lot.

Another reason for this suggestion is the vastly different rates of learning programming. While one child cannot handle the first program, another will work from the manual and overtake the teacher's programming skills. If the latter happens, do not be afraid to admit the gaps in your knowledge, and be prepared to ask the advanced student for specific information and advice. This, after all, is what co-operative learning should be all about.

11.6.4   Classroom organization and method

Computer use need not feature in the early part of a computer literacy course. It is helpful to start with the students' current knowledge, using discussions, essays, short projects, etc., to open up the topic, followed by deeper study, research, visits and computer use. The following suggestions are based on Gare (1982).

Thinking/talking

1   Have the students write down what they know about computers, and use this as a basis for discussion.
2   Ask the students each to find out one use of computers.
3   Discuss computer assistance: automatic tellers, automatic petrol pumps, point of sale terminals, etc.
4   Discuss the future of schools, work and shopping in the light of computer networks.
5   Invite a visitor to speak or lead a debate.
6   Show videotapes or films.

Moving/doing

1   Each student draws a map of how to get between two points in the school and another student tries to follow it.
2   In pairs, one student describes how to solve a numerical problem while the other wields a pen and paper.
3   In pairs, one student specifies Logo-like instructions to guide the other around obstacles in the room.
4   Now try to follow similar instructions to draw a line on squared graph paper.
5   Role plays of situations discussed in 1.

Programming

1   Introduce a computer game or simulation, which the students play.
2   If the Logo language is available, using the turtle implement similar activities to 3 and 4 in Moving/doing.
3   Otherwise, choose a simple program in Pascal or structured Basic for the students to run.
4   Work through the program, showing which statements have which effect.
5   Ask the students to suggest simple modifications and show how to implement these.
6   Have the students exercise the program on various data.
7   Set a simple problem, and introduce the steps in problem-solving.

8   Iterate 7 as desired to cover the aspects of algorithm design for a variety of problems.

Thinking/writing

1   Write a story on a computer topic.
2   Design a computer advertisement.
3   Write a poem. The following poem was written by a Year 11 student (Lamb 1983).

Help! It's a computer.

That's a computer sitting there.
Like a snake waiting for me to step on it,
Waiting to bite me.
Fifty three keys, gleaming white, like teeth.
The screen watching me like one horrific eye,
Watching its prey, waiting for the right moment.
And it's more intelligent than me.

I take my life into my own hands,
I press a key.
'Syntax error'.
It bit me,
I'm dead.

Hold on,
I'm not really dead.
It didn't bite.
And look: It didn't understand.
It's thick,
It can't do anything by itself.
It's totally helpless; it couldn't hurt a flea.

I rebel,
Using a switch at the back.
'Click.'
It's dead,
I killed it.

The computer literacy course may be taught by one teacher; or by several teachers under a single co-ordinator. The latter can be more difficult administratively, but should help the integration of computing into other subjects. Remember that, as a separate course, computer literacy should disappear within 5 years.

11.6.5   Resources

It is a good idea to cut out any relevant newspaper cuttings both as sources of information to stay up to date; and as sources of misinformation to start discussions. You will often find it useful to have enough cuttings to give one to each pair of students as a basis for some of the work suggested in Section 11.6.4.

Ensure that you practise the use of any hardware or software before introducing it to students. Remember, too, that while some children cannot wait to get their hands on the machine, others are more reticent and must be patiently encouraged.

11.6.6   Conclusion

The emphasis of the computer literacy course is on the application of computers (to other disciplines), the implications of computers (for other areas) and the programming of computers (to solve problems in other subjects). This outward orientation can best be achieved by integrating this work on computers with the work in other subjects, and should be spread over Years 7–10. For example, in geography lessons students use CAL to learn geographical topics, are informed how geographers use computers, and consider the computer's applications to and implications for those things that geographers study. This should include explicit consideration of geographical data: its structure and typical processing required. This approach is then repeated for all subjects of study. Furthermore, the introduction of increasingly flexible, user driven and widely used CAL reduces the need for an explicit programming component, as students experience significant computer use via CAL. If explicit work is required on computer structure and operation, or problem-solving and programming, this could be taken separately outside the aegis of any other subjects.

11.7   COMPUTER STUDIES

In this section and the next we draw heavily on Atkins and Oski (1982), and Computer Studies Curriculum Committee (1983 b and c), which contain excellent suggestions on teaching methods.

11.7.1   Prerequisites

In the first section of this chapter, we mentioned the rapid changes in curriculum content at various levels. At present, a Year 11 computer studies course might have to start from scratch, while in five years time it might have the sort of basis implied by the sequence in Section 11.5. We shall assume that situation has been reached, as this assumption allows us to give the fullest possible coverage. If this situation does not obtain, some (or all) of the material we suggest for computer literacy must move into computer studies, with material from the latter then going into Year 12 computer science.

11.7.2   Orientation

This course should have a practical orientation, with students becoming aware of computing as practised in the world outside the classroom. Manipulating turtles, hacking over-long Basic programs, and superficial brushes with applications are inadequate for this.

11.7.3   Topics, methods and assessment

A course length of about 120 hours, spread over the whole year, is envisaged. For each topic, the suggested proportion of time to be spent on it is indicated. A wide variety of lesson types and teaching techniques may be used, including formal lessons, practical work, films, excursions, small groups, individual worksheets, projects, reading assignments, field studies, class presentations, visitors and visits. A particular problem is of access to the computer. Often this means planning for one small group to be using the computer in any one session, with groups rotating between activities. This in turn means having all activities planned at the start of a unit. Furthermore, different worksheets will be needed if several different computers are used (McDougall 1981).

History of computers (5%)

This should not be exhaustive, nor should it be a superficial history of machines. Its purpose is to set the computer in a long term historical context, so that it is seen as the latest in man's attempts to collect and handle increasingly complicated information; and to set the microcomputer in a shorter term historical context, so that it is seen as one of the latest manifestations of the rapidity of technological change.

Essays are an obvious assessment method, together with projects involving the study of a person, computer company, programming language development etc.

Algorithms and modelling (10%)

This builds on and formalizes earlier work, covering the problem-solving processes, tools and techniques listed in Section 11.6.3, with emphasis on clarity of expression, quality of documentation, correctness of the pseudocode algorithm, and recognition of what constitutes a good solution. The concept of a model should be introduced, with examples of models used in different disciplines. Models used in real-life applications should be discussed, and algorithm design then shown to be equivalent to model-building (cf. Chapters 5 and 6).

Assessment is based on algorithms produced, which should exhibit all the above qualities and not solely correctness.

Programming and operating (10%)

This is the natural extension of the previous topic, and of the introductory work in computer literacy. Using an appropriate language, algorithms are implemented, preferably involving the (simplified) real-life models introduced in the previous topic. A short time should also be spent on a contrasting language (e.g. Basic/ Prolog, Logo/Pascal, Logo/Cobol) to show the possibility of an entirely different form of language. For economy of student effort, the second language should be chosen with the needs of the other curriculum subjects in mind. Business studies, for example, would benefit from a knowledge of Cobol, but would not be assisted by a study of Fortran.

This topic should also include any necessary revision of the structure and use of the computer and its peripherals.

Computer systems (10%)

Concepts of hardware and software; analogue and digital computers; control unit and arithmetic unit; RAM and ROM; floppy and hard discs; special purpose peripherals; high and low level languages; microcomputers and mainframes; real-time and batch processing; ASCII and other codes.

The approach here could involve more advanced use of the school computer system (disc copying, file transfer, backup), videotapes of different devices and their uses; visiting speakers, and visits to installations.

Assessment could compare advantages and disadvantages of various devices and procedures.

Careers with computers (5%)

Careers that computers have opened up should be described (operator, programmer, analyst, engineer, salesman, etc.), together with some jobs that have changed significantly as a result of computer use (assembly line work, secretarial work, factory control, etc.) Well-planned site visits, preferably including discussions with workers, should be followed by in-depth reports (covering, for example, the type of company, computer, peripherals, software, personnel, costs, and main computer use). This topic may be integrated with the work on Computer systems and Business studies.

Business studies (30%)

Concept of a system: the accounting system and subsystems such as payroll, debtors, creditors, stock. Structure of an organization, role of management, use of documents, data flow, communication methods. This can be introduced via a simple case study such as a petrol station or greengrocers.

Systems analysis, design and implementation. Considerations, constraints, costs, benefits. User involvement. System life cycle and prototyping (cf. Chapters 9 and 10).

Business programming: use of packages; development of a program; development of a suite of programs.

Assessment can include tests, completion of organization charts, system identification etc. for a particular system; program modification and possibly development.

Current computer applications (10%)

Current computer usage. Robots and their present and potential use. Computer assisted design and manufacturing. Videotex. Electronics in the office. Local area networks. Missile guidance systems. Developments during the past year, and trends for the immediate future.

The emphasis should be on coverage of a few topics in depth; covering for example, the reasons for the application, concomitant planned changes in the organization, unexpected effects, estimation of success or otherwise.

Trends for the future can partly be determined from the press, and could be the subject of an on-going class project. From news items and advertisements identify usages that are interesting but impractical, likely soon to become obsolete, or of long-term value; evaluate writers' biases, and try to characterize the views of various political parties and other bodies.

Effects of computers (10%)

Work: employment created, unemployment created, job satisfaction, work ethic, rate of change, leisure, position of unions, employers and government.

Privacy: meaning, rights, efficiency, data protection, legislation.

Crime and security: type, incidence and extent of computer crime. Computer use in law enforcement. Legal developments to take account of computers: copyright, evidence, theft. Possibility for disaster resulting from computer failure.

Benefits of computers: computer as a tool; harnessing its power, positive attitudes.

Useful methods here include videos, interviews, visits, debates, stories, role plays and surveys.

Word processing (10%)

This is a practical unit, covering creating, storing, retrieving, editing and printing documents through the medium of an actual word processing package. Distinction between editing (getting it right) and text formatting (making it look nice). Students should suggest desirable enhancements to the available package, and, conversely, consider what would be the minimum useful package. A mini-editor program implementing four or five commands could be written.

11.8   COMPUTER SCIENCE

11.8.1   Prerequisite and orientation

The prerequisite is 'Computer Studies', and the orientation is theoretical. This provides a balance over the two years, which is useful for employment and appropriate educationally: both in its own right, and as an introduction to the style and content of tertiary study.

11.8.2   Topics, methods and assessment

A course length of about 120 hours, spread through the academic year, is envisaged. The proportion of time suggested for each topic is indicated. The total exceeds 100%, and hence provides some choice. The choice may best be effected by omitting whole topics. Woodhouse *et al* (1984) is a good resource for this course. Just as with computer literacy (and computer studies) different topics can be taken by different teachers.

Data structures (20%)

Data has been emphasized throughout the study of computers, and here the abstract underlying structure is studied. This may include multi-dimensional arrays, stacks, queues, lists, linked lists and binary trees; file structures: serial, random and indexed sequential. Operations on these data structures as appropriate, including:

creation; addition, amendment and deletion of elements; sequential file updating; hashing methods. Searching: linear and binary search. Sorting: selection, insertion and merge sorts, and a faster random-access method. Although this course is more theoretical, all the structures and operations covered should be introduced by genuine examples of their actual use. Methods of implementing the structures, and algorithms to implement the operations should be studied and programmed under the heading of the programming topic.

Assessment should be via examinations, projects on uses of the various structures, and program implementations.

Data bases and files (10%)

This overlaps the first topic, and could be incorporated in it. However, the structure and use of a data base is somewhat different from the other structures (except files) and so there is merit in treating it separately.

Definition and use of data bases and data banks, and their relation to files. Examples of data bases such as the library or the school record system. Commercial data bases and access thereto. Creation of a data base, including data validation. Data fields, records and transactions: sorting, editing, reporting. Retrieving elements: planning a search strategy and constructing the appropriate boolean search functions. Restructuring the data base: file linking, indexing and merging. File security: transaction logging and backup.

The data base administrator. Application, potential and problems of data bases.

Practical experience must be included. This could be via a data base package, or use of the Prolog language (see Chapter 12).

Computer languages (10%)

A comparative study of the features of at least three contrasting high level programming languages (not including the main language used in the programming topic) covering methods of defining data, control structures, and suitability for various classes of problems. If possible, one of the languages should be a special purpose language, such as one designed specially for graphics, symbolic algebra, machine tool control or CAL.

This topic could be project oriented, with the contrasting language aspects covered in classes and private reading. Then, singly or in groups, students could identify some of the differences, their reasons and their effects.

Machine code (10%)

The study of machine code shows how programs are actually presented to a computer, and that there are certain features of any computer that are inaccessible from a high-level language. Examples of the latter are precise screen handling facilities, and other graphical and sound manipulations. As with the first computer language learned further down the school, the presentation should begin with small, complete programs, continue with students' modifying, and correcting these, and conclude with the students' developing simple programs of their own. An assembly language or an artificial machine language may be used for simplicity, provided it illustrates the points above.

Simulation and games programs (10%)

This is a type of program with which the student is now very familiar as a user. Again it would be possible to start with an existing program and modify it. The theoretical background includes the meaning of simulation, choosing a topic and establishing a model, and the use of random numbers. Practical considerations for the student in writing a simulation include the role of the computer, forms of user interaction, screen designs and speed.

System software (10%)

Operating system: batch, interactive, single and multi-user. Translators: compilers, assemblers, interpreters. Editors and other system utilitiies. The student should appreciate the role of the operating system in computer use, the different programs in charge of the computer at any time, and software as tools for general use. This appreciation should be based on experiments with available systems.

Artificial intelligence (10%)

Definitions of intelligence, and the study of computer programs said to exhibit intelligence (such as *Eliza, Shrdlu,* chess-playing and poetry writing programs; see Sections 2.7 and 4.5). Robotics; self-modifying computers; talking computers. Implications of AI for the future: Will intelligent machines be unpredictable? Does it matter whether a computer is intelligent? What will be the impact on society? The students should write a simple interactive intelligent program.

Computer logic (10%)

Switching theory, based on boolean algebra; truth tables. Basic logic gates, and simple combinational algebra. Flip-flops and sequential circuits: counters, shift registers and adders. Buses. Structure of a microprocessor.

This topic can be assessed by the design and implementation of circuits to perform simple functions, such as electronic voting, or an electronic combination lock.

Telecommunications (10%)

Data communications: mail, telephone, telex, radio, videotex, facsimile; local and international networks, transmission media, satellites, uses. Acoustic couplers and modems. Policies of the relevant government or private authority; facilities available; costs. Problems of integrity, reliability and security. Role of international standards. Impact of our increased communication capability on society: the paperless office, the child-less school, the car-less road.

Security (5%)

Computer security and misuse: crimes towards or by means of the computer. Security measures for protection of hardware and software against accidental and deliberate misuse. Difficulties of detection or prevention (Parker 1976).

Computers in literature (5%)

Study the changing perception of computers as indicated in novels. Read a number of extracts from novels, and in each case consider the context of writing, the age in which the action is set and the attitude propounded. Where possible, compare fact and fiction. Define science fiction, and discuss its place as pure fiction, social statement, non-threatening exploration of new ideas, predicting the future (Mowshowitz 1977 and a host of others, such as Toffler, Asimov, Clarke, Orwell, Verne, Wells, etc.). It may be preferable to include this in the literature curriculum (see Section 11.9.1).

Programming (20%)

Further development of problem-solving and programming skills should continue to emphasize principles of structured programming (software engineering). The problem and program topics should be drawn from the rest of the course.

11.9   ALL FOR ONE, AND ONE FOR ALL

11.9.1   One for all

Computing is a service subject, and the computer is a tool. Simulations, spreadsheets, word processors, data bases and CAL generally are used in science, economics, English, history and so on. In each of these cases, all that should be taught (about the computer) is enough to use the tool. This can most conveniently be done within the other subject, and the subject's content and method should be adapted to take account of both the availability of computers in school and the use of computers by practitioners in the subject area (Section 11.6.6). This sort of work, of course, will be one of the biggest steps towards generating (computer) literacy.

11.9.2   All for one

Computing is a served subject, and needs principles which are distinctly mathematical, physical, linguistic, psychological, etc. Just as the mathematician teaches mathematics for physics and economics, so s/he should teach mathematics for computer science, and similarly with the other disciplines (although there will always be demarcation disputes). Psychology can raise questions of cognition; philosophy of being; linguistics of grammatical structures; and physics of electronic designs. However, at school level, mathematics is the main contributor (Woodhouse 1982). Useful topics are binary arithmetic (fractions as well as integers), base conversions, floating point arithmetic, use of a finite set of numbers, coding theory generally, concepts of variables and values, algebraic structures (matrices etc.), boolean algebra and set theory, probability, and the concept and generation of random numbers.

11.10   FITTING COMPUTING INTO THE CURRICULUM

We are hesitant to suggest which subjects be displaced to accommodate the new computer work. One problem is that the designers and proponents of any new subject are expected to answer a lot of educational questions that are assumed or semi-ignored in respect of exisiting subjects. Changes in content or method of a subject are normally made against a larger background of unchanging assumptions about that subject. Even such drastic changes as the new mathematics or Nuffield physics leave a lot unchanged. Furthermore, such changes usually actually arise as an outworking of new educational ideas, so the educational questions are implicitly answered already.

Educational theory is, unfortunately, a difficult entity with which to work, and theoreticians often worry about the questions they have asked and the answers they have obtained. As theories are developed it is natural to want to test them and implement them, as one might with a new theory in chemistry. The problem with testing is that this will affect the education of individual children — probably for the worse, if the theory is ill-conceived, and possibly for the worse anyway, for a host of uncontrollable reasons. The problem with implementation is that educational practice cannot be changed rapidly: a lead time of 5 years would be a minimum, to allow for the ideas to be accepted, teachers to be trained, and these teachers to develop new curricula. Practical teaching therefore tends to continue without major change, simply leaning towards the current theory at any time. A new subject, on the other hand, has to exhibit its total agreement with current theory, in order to be acceptable. Some subjects remain in the curriculum merely 'because they are there' already, while a new subject must justify its introduction.

Note, however, that computer use or computer courses are no guarantee of an educational advance. CAL can reinforce existing methods, or even revert to outdated ones; and computer courses can be as dreary or irrelevant as any other subject can. This is why we have emphasized the need to set the educational priorities first.

11.11   FORWARD PLANNING

In planning a course outline, the teacher should look well ahead. The crucial question is not 'what can I introduce next year?' but 'how should all the courses look in 5–10 years time?' (cf. Woodhouse 1984).

As implied earlier, computer study has migrated (or, is migrating) downwards from tertiary to secondary to primary level. Since an introduction to computers contains some fairly obvious topics (like elementary computer structure, electronic representation of data and concepts of programming) these topics first appeared in upper tertiary syllabi, then in first year tertiary, then in upper secondary, and so on down. In fact, this downward migration is happening so rapidly, that at present these topics are simultaneously in the recommended curricula in Victoria for each of the final three years of secondary school, and the first year of university.

Such a downward migration is an educational disaster, as everything gets changed simultaneously, with enormous increases in pressure on resources (both human and physical) and a danger of losing sight of the educational goals. Suppose that topics A,B,C and D are not currently taught, but that ultimately they should be taught in Years 9, 10, 11 and 12 respectively. Initially, we change the Year 12 syllabus to include topic A. Such a change involves much extra work for the teaching staff. Subsequently, we introduce topic A to Year 11. This implies not one lot of extra work, but three:

introducing topic A in Year 11; in the same year, teaching topic A in both Years 11 and 12 simultaneously; and, in the following year, introducing topic B in Year 12. When topic A moves to Year 10, we have one year of teaching A to Years 10 and 11, and one of teaching B to 11 and 12, before introducing C; and so on. This whole process becomes a major disaster for 5–10 years, which will be compounded by staff turnover and the need to amend the syllabi for A, B, C and D to take account of advances in knowledge and technology.

It is far better to aim directly for the ultimate desired pattern by first changing the Year 9 syllabus to incorporate topic A. The subsequent introduction of topic B to Year 10 then involves only a similar lot of extra work, since the changes are confined to one form, with all the other forms covering topics that have already been taught at those levels (at least once). Similar comments apply to the subsequent introduction of C and D to Years 11 and 12. Furthermore, the level of extra work is such that it may be feasible to carry out these changes in successive years. Thus, the change will be completed in only 4 years, giving much less time for staff changes and for changes in subject matter.

The first solution is often adopted through a lack of advance planning. Sometimes, however, the second solution is actively rejected for the more creditable reason that all those who pass through the school just ahead of the wave of change will not be taught these topics that we have now decided are desirable. However, it is better to implement the second solution and simultaneously to have a short, special course (e.g. 'Introduction to topic A') in Year 12, than to retreat to the first solution. This not only involves less work than solution 1, in which almost the whole educational enterprise is in flux simultaneously; it also keeps separate the solutions to two separate educational problems, relating to long-term curriculum changes and short-term emergency provisions, respectively.

Chapter Twelve

Computer languages

An individual may speak and read a dozen languages, and yet be an exceedingly poor creature   George Borrow (1803–1881)

12.1 CRITERIA FOR LANGUAGE CHOICE

We have suggested in Chapter 11 that competence in programming should be seen as an integral part of learning about computers at all levels. This requires the selection of a particular language(s). In this chapter, we survey some computer languages which are canvassed as appropriate for school computing, and suggest which could be used at which level. The treatment of the various languages is unequal, because of their large differences in form, application and utility.

Firstly, we suggest some criteria upon which to base the choice (Woodhouse 1983).

1 Availability of a system for running programs (availability).
2 Teacher knowledge (tuition).
3 Ease of teaching and learning (simplicity).
4 Language structure for problem-solving (structure).
5 Utility of the language (utility).
6 Appropriateness for the course or level (appropriateness).

12.1.1 System availability

In view of the reasons we have suggested for learning programming, the ability to run programs is very important. Many of us have gone through a phase of teaching programming using a computer at a distant location. Mark sense cards, prepared by students, were gathered by the long-suffering teacher, and taken or posted to the computer centre. The students got a turnround time of at best a couple of days, and at worst over a week. Turnround time is the time between submitting a program to be run and receiving the results. This is close to zero when using a VDU or feeding your own cards through a card reader. The longer the turnround time, the more difficult it is to maintain one's train of thought in developing the program. A distant system is therefore unsatisfactory (unless the school has on-line terminals connected to it).

Availability also includes how many computers (or terminals) are in the school, how accessible they are, and how much time each student may spend on them. Only if the purpose of teaching the language can be achieved without executing programs does this criterion become unimportant.

12.1.2   Teacher knowledge

The typical current situation is that a particular teacher is enthusiastic about teaching programming and knows a particular language. It is natural to wish to teach this language. However, the language — perhaps Fortran learned in the context of a university science course — is not necessarily the most appropriate one for the students, who have a different reason for learning programming. Furthermore, since one's second and subsequent programming languages are much easier to learn than the first, the teacher should not shrink from selecting an unknown language if it is highly satisfactory on other grounds. Once chosen, the language should be studied for a while before embarking on teaching. Programming is one topic in which it is very difficult to stay 'a page ahead of the students'. At a very early stage, students can ask questions which can only be answered satisfactorily from a knowledge of the language as a whole.

12.1.3   Ease of teaching and learning

The language should be capable of being easily learned (for the students' benefit) and easily taught (for the teacher's). In addition to the structure of the language itself, the language environment is very important in facilitating the learning process. Program writing, running, editing and storing facilities should be available, and be able to be invoked through the medium of simple and obvious instructions.

12.1.4   Language structure for problem-solving

The language chosen should be such as to facilitate the achievement of any specific goals which have been established. In our case, the main aims are to direct the computer in the manipulation of data, and to practise problem-solving techniques. Referring to Section 11.6.3, we see that systematic problem-solving involves the control of detail, and its organization into steps and levels, so that the solver can also keep sight of the overall goal. The next section (Section 12.2) is devoted to elaborating this criterion for language choice.

12.1.5   Utility of the language

Some weight may also be given to the value of the language to the student after he leaves school. This would suggest that commercial languages (such as Cobol, RPG or PL/1) be considered, or possibly scientific languages (such as Fortran). It would also suggest rejection of the intricate language APL, and of Basic and Pascal which are principally designed for teaching purposes. These considerations, however, may be incompatible with other criteria.

12.1.6   Appropriateness for the level

Criteria 4 and 5 have touched on this. Under this heading we include appropriateness for goals other than learning problem solving or preparing for employment, and appropriateness for the various stages of learning through the primary and secondary years.

These six criteria are not all of the same type. The first two are situation dependent: a new system can be bought, and an unknown language can be learned. The third is more fixed: it is possible to obtain some improvement through the adoption of different teaching methods and the creation of different learning situations, but APL and Cobol are clearly more difficult than Logo or Basic, for example. The fourth is an absolute and depends on the language itself; the fifth varies from time to time, but again is not under the teacher's control; while the sixth is only under the teacher's control in that aims can be changed.

Teachers should also be aware that most languages come in different dialects. Although Pascal, for example, should be identical on different machines, in practice the different versions may be slightly different. This variability is most noticeable with Logo (some versions of Logo offer only the turtle graphics part) and Basic.

12.2   STRUCTURED PROGRAMMING

12.2.1   What is a structured program?

In the 1950s and 1960s, serious difficulties were encountered in the writing of very large programs. One reason for this was the lack of a theory of programming. Large programs were written using *ad hoc* extensions of methods (intellectual, technical and organizational) that had worked with small programs. The resulting programs took far longer to write, ran much more slowly, and contained many more errors than expected. (Amateur programmers often have a similar experience in trying to push Basic beyond its capacity: see Section 12.3.1.) At the end of the 1960s, E.W. Dijkstra drew attention to this, and suggested that, because of our inability to hold a lot of complicated processes in mind at once, we should establish a 'discipline of programming' (Dijkstra 1976). Program design has now come to be seen as an engineering activity, like bridge design, and is called software engineering. The aim of software engineering is to design well-structured programs. A program is called well-structured (or just, 'structured') if it exhibits the following characteristics.

Data

1 The algorithm and the data it processes are clearly distinguished, and each is fully described.
2 Natural representations are used for the data of the problem.
3 The intelligibility of the program is enhanced by the use of mnemonic variable names.

Algorithm

4 In expressing the algorithm as a program, the program layout corresponds closely to the algorithmic sequence.
5 The program can be understood in stages: broad outlines first, with successively finer details later, as and when desired ('top-down').
6 This understanding is enhanced by the subdivision of the statements of the program into paragraphs, connected by a small number of instructions called control statements.

A program which is structured can be understood more easily, both by the original programmer and others; can more easily be proved to be correct; can more easily be corrected; and is generally completed more quickly, as the testing and debugging stage is considerably shorter than with the *ad hoc* program. On the debit side, it may take more storage space and/or computer time to run.

12.2.2   What is a structured language?

Whether a program is structured depends, *inter alia*, on the language in which it is written. It is possible to write unstructured programs in any language, but not possible to write structured programs in every language. In order to permit the writing of structured programs, a language must possess the following facilities.

Data

1 The language provides a variety of data structures, which are clearly distinguishable from the algorithm describing the operations on them (cf. item 1 above).

2 Data is of various types: integers, non-integers and characters, for example. Furthermore, data of these various types can be grouped in many ways, into sets, matrices, lists, records and files, for example. All languages provide facilities for handling some of these types and structures. Some languages, such as Pascal, Logo and PL/1, also permit the programmer to define further types as appropriate for the problem (cf. 2 above). Logo provides fewer basic types than does Pascal, and most data structures must be constructed from lists.

3 Clarity is aided also by the availability of longer names for variables (cf. 3 above). Names such as X or X3 are more abstract, and hence difficult to keep track of, than names such as RATIO or MAXWAGE. Continuous reference to the program documentation is necessary to check what names like X or X3 represent, while 'RATIO' carries an indication of its meaning in its name. The program becomes more readable, and hence simpler for the original author, and later readers, to understand.

Algorithm

1 Subprograms. A device is needed for distinguishing and naming separately identifiable sections of the program, and this can be done in Logo, Fortran, Pascal and Forth (cf. 5 and 6 above). Such subprograms are variously known as procedures, modules or subroutines. A subprogram should be self-contained, with one entry point and one exit point. It should be designed to do a specific job, invoked by reference to its name, and receiving information from, and passing back information to, the calling program by means of well defined variables (parameters of the subprogram). Other variables used by the subprogram should be confined within it (these are called local variables), so that there is no chance of accidentally changing the values of identically named variables in the main program. (A global variable is one which the subprogram inherits from the main program.) If all these conditions are satisfied the subprogram is a 'black box' which can be used without knowledge of its mode of operation. This encourages the 'divide and rule' approach (modular programming) mentioned in Section 11.6.3, which helps to make up for our inability to hold a lot of processes in mind at once. It also assists in top-down program writing and understanding. Such modules can also be used by different programs, thus avoiding duplication of effort.

2 Blocks. In the English language, we group letters into words, words into sentences, and sentences into paragraphs. In Basic, we group letters and digits into variables and numbers, and variables and numbers into statements, but there is nothing corresponding to the paragraph. The same is true of Fortran and RPG. In Pascal and PL/1, the analogue of the paragraph is the block or compound statement, which comprises a group of statements encompassed by the words 'begin...end', which act like brackets. The block is used like an English paragraph, to group self-contained ideas and enhance intelligibility (cf. 6 above). Obviously, a language with procedures but no block facility can give a name to the group of statements and invoke them as desired.

3 Control statements. These are needed to organize the blocks and/or procedures into the desired algorithm (cf. 4 and 6 above). Given a few appropriate control structures, a programmer can produce a problem solution which is readable and relatively easy to update. Further, practice with a programming language which contains the right concepts explicitly in its syntax and vocabulary will tend to inculcate those concepts into the user's thought processes and habits of problem analysis and programming. Unlike Pascal, many high-level languages are deficient to some extent in this area, and some structures have to be simulated using the GOTO statement. While it is possible for experts to use the GOTO statement carefully in a disciplined context, there is abundant evidence that this does not normally happen. On the contrary, many unstructured programs are difficult to read and the writing of such programs is frequently of little or no educational benefit (Atherton 1981).

12.3   SOME PROGRAMMING LANGUAGES

12.3.1   Basic

We must begin with this, as it is the most widely used

microcomputer language. [Quotations in this section are from Kurtz (1978)]. Basic (Beginners' All-purpose Symbolic Instruction Code) was designed at Dartmouth College in the early 1960s by J.G. Kemeny and T.E. Kurtz. It was directed at liberal arts students who 'would balk at the seemingly pointless detail of Fortran, Algol or assembly language'. Basic was designed to be easy to learn, and easy to use from a terminal. While these are commendable aims, they encourage the user to sit at the computer and ask 'what can I do with it?' It is because the answers to this question can be trivial and/or inappropriate that we have emphasized the need to start with educational questions. After all, who actually needs the computer to print 'HELLO'?

Ease of use was achieved by interweaving Basic and its operating system, and using short common English words (RUN, SAVE, BYE) as system commands. Ease of learning was achieved in a number of ways: removing distinctions, such as between integer and real numbers; omitting the concept of type; providing defaults (for dimensions, output formats, etc.); simplifying the handling of strings of characters (words, names, etc) so that problems involving letters and words can be done easily, and programs need not all be mathematical; simplifying the conversion between numeric and string forms; allowing only short names for variables; making the editing process very simple; and producing intelligible error messages, relating to the Basic code. Thus, simple programs can be written quickly.

However, Basic offers only clumsy alternation and iteration statements, while its subroutine facility is minimal. A subroutine in Basic is not named; it is called by referring to a line number. Because the start of a subroutine is not defined, any statement can be the target of a GOSUB statement and so the system cannot detect an erroneous call. Problems arise in using the same subroutine in different contexts because it would often be necessary to change both variable names and line numbers. A programmer would not always find this worthwhile and the opportunity to use safe, well-tested modules as part of a new program is lost. Furthermore, through its ease of editing, Basic also encourages the 'suck-it-and-see' style of programming: if the program does not work, change a line and see what happens. A related bad practice is to write a large program by making *ad hoc* extensions to a smaller one. It is because the results of this approach are programs that still contain errors and yet are almost impossible to correct that we have emphasized the need to start with well-organized algorithm design. As the Alvey Report (1982) said: "just providing schools with microcomputers... will merely produce a generation of poor Basic programmers". M. Tucker, director of the USA Project on Information Technology and Education, says that "Basic is a poorly constructed language: it teaches kids to think crooked, if at all". Kurtz says "some of us have learned how to use GOSUB with discipline, but Basic itself remains laissez-faire on this issue"; and admits "that GOTO has an attractive simplicity for novices, but should be discarded at an early stage in favour of structured constructs; that multi-character identifiers are less limited; and that graphical output is needed".

Basic offers only a small number of facilities, and hence an interpreter (or compiler) to process Basic programs is relatively small and easy to write. The four features (ease of learning, terminal use, small interpreters, simple interpreter) brought Basic to the fore with the proliferation of microcomputers, with their keyboards and small stores, intended for novice computer users. A large body of Basic knowledge and an enormous library of Basic programs were built up, providing two good reasons for not now abandoning Basic. A third reason is that many games programs are written in Basic. These provide a good starting point for language description and the improvement of existing programs, as recommended for the introduction to programming in the computer literacy course. A fourth reason is that vast strides have been made in developing Basic. In the above, we have been referring to standard or minimal Basic. Some versions of Basic differ from this more than they do from other languages bearing different names. Microsoft Basic is one such. In fact, "rather than being a single language with dialects, Basic is really a class of languages, all with a common core".

The recommendations on Basic are therefore:

1 It may be used as described above in the Computer Literacy course.
2 Try to choose a structured Basic.
3 Use the language carefully, and the GOTO statement sparingly, so as to write structured programs.
4 Set some exercises to bring out the weaknesses of the language, as well as those that bring out its strengths.

The usual way of teaching Basic is to have the students write

10 PRINT "HELLO"

and gradually add more statements (synthetic approach). Building on the sort of basis of computer use that we advocate, a better approach is to read and amend the code for a game which the students have played and enjoyed (analytic approach). Students could find the statements that draw a figure, play a tune or calculate the score, and replace them with statements of their own. This is especially meaningful if it is amending an aspect of the program which students have criticized. Try to ensure that the program to be studied is well-written.

12.3.2   Pascal

Like Basic, Pascal was designed to be easy to learn. However, designed (by N. Wirth) in about 1970, it embodies the more recent understanding of good techniques for algorithm design and expression (control structures, blocks, procedures), provides a wide range of data structures (arrays, records, files, sets, pointers), and permits the programmer to define further data structures. We can, for example, define a type

$$sex = (male, female)$$

and declare the variable 'worker' to be of type 'sex'. This then allows us to write

$$if\ worker = male$$
$$then...$$

which is clearer and more explicit than having to use integer coding and write, for example,

$$IF\ WORKER = 1\ THEN\ GO\ TO\ 560$$

This facility demands that the data to be used in a program be specified explicitly (declared). This explicit introduction of variables is often considered to be a defect, but it is in fact very valuable in de-bugging, in making programs safer, and in clarifying the programmer's intent in the program.

The main control structures parallel the flow diagram 'test and branch' (alternation) and the flow diagram loop (iteration or repetition). They are

Alternation

(a) if...then...else...
   for a two-way branch, as in

   if d>0
       then x := sqrt(d)
       else x := −sqrt(−d)

(Note the use of ":=" rather than "=" in the assignment statements. This avoids the confusion over such assignments as n = n + 1 being erroneously regarded by students as being an equality.)

(b) case...of...
   for a multi-way branch, as in

   case ch of
       I: insert;
       D: delete;
       T: type;
       otherwise error
   end

This means that if the variable ch has the value I, the machine carries out the process called 'insert', if ch = D, it does 'delete', etc.

Iteration

(a) repeat...until...
   which terminates on a condition tested at the end of the loop:

   repeat
       input;
       process;

```
          output
    until all input handled
(b) while...do...
    which terminates on a condition tested at the beginning of the
    loop:

    while not done do
      begin
        input;
        process;
        output
    end


(c) for...do...
    which terminates after a specified number of iterations

    for i: = 1 to n do
      begin
        input;
        process;
        output
    end
```

Pascal does not have Basic's simple facilities for string handling, editing or system control, nor Logo's ease of handling graphics or list structured data (although UCSD Pascal is a dialect which offers a Logo-like introduction to graphics and procedures at an early stage of learning the language). Pascal is strongly recommended for computer science, where data structures are being studied in depth. An approach to teaching Pascal is described by Woodhouse (1981). It is suggested that simple problems be introduced and solutions developed jointly with the class. The solutions are written in English, and gradually formalized into pseudocode (a sort of pidgin Pascal) and thence into correct Pascal. Procedures should be introduced early to assist in dividing problems into manageable parts. Only one alternation (if...then...else...) and one iteration (while...do...) statement need be introduced at first.

12.3.3   Logo (see Chapter 5)

Like Basic, and unlike Pascal, the language and operating system are integrated, so that one line of typing produces a miniature program.

Furthermore, Logo's emphasis is on graphics, and that one-line program may control a robot (turtle) on the ground or a representation of it on a VDU screen. The Logo learning environment has had significant impact on the education of exceptional students at both ends of the spectrum of ability. Logo's designer, S. Papert of MIT, aimed for a language with 'no threshold' (it is trivially easy to start using) and 'no ceiling' (the advanced user does not exhaust the language's potential).

Logo is being used for teaching introductory programming at all levels, from primary school to adult education. Wills (1980) lists features of the language which make it suitable for introductory programming.

1 a very simple starting level;

2 each of the commands produces a concrete, visible response;

3 it is non-threatening, due firstly to its emphasis on graphics rather than on overt mathematics, and secondly to its focus on the turtle; in Logo an unexpected result is not seen as a personal failure;

4 visible debugging;

5 because the language is user-defined, it becomes individually tailored to reflect the student's own interests and abilities; the vocabulary will only contain words with which she is familiar... therefore the language will be different for each individual;

6 because the user builds his or her own language, she also controls the level of complexity (Wills 1980).

A concrete visible response!

While the turtle graphics part of Logo and its value for introductory programming are widely recognized, the more advanced features of the language are less well known, as they have only recently become widely available. There are now full Logo implementations for the Apple, Texas Instruments 99/4A, Commodore 64, Atari, IBM PC, Sinclair Spectrum, RML-480Z and BBC Acorn. This means that students need not necessarily "grow out of" Logo, even if they have exhausted their interest in exploring and experimenting with the graphics commands, since the more advanced parts of the language embody many of the challenging concepts of modern computer science. Drawing on the work of Harvey (1982) let us examine some features of Logo that make it a suitable language for more advanced programming work.

Firstly, a Logo program can be built from subprograms or procedures, which have the following form. For clarity, we use the symbol '&' to indicate which lines are output by the computer. This symbol does not in fact appear when using Logo.

```
        TO PRINTSQUARE :X
        PRINT :X * :X
        END

        PRINTSQUARE 5
&       25
        TO SQUARE :X
        OUTPUT :X * :X
        END
        SQUARE 3

&       I DON'T KNOW WHAT TO DO WITH 9
        PRINT SQUARE 3
&       9
        PRINT (SQUARE 3) + (SQUARE 4)
&       25
        TO AVERAGE :X :Y
        OUTPUT (:X + :Y) / 2
        END
        PRINT SQUARE (AVERAGE 5 6)
&       30.25
```

OUTPUT makes a result available to another procedure, which can PRINT it or use it in some other way.

In Logo any procedure can use any other procedure as a subprocedure. This includes the possibility of a procedure using itself as a subprocedure; this is called recursion. Recursion allows a complicated problem to be described in terms of simpler versions of itself, and is therefore a very powerful problem solving tool. (All modern procedural languages allow recursion. Among widely used languages, only Fortran allows procedures but not recursion. Most versions of Basic have neither.) The following Logo procedure makes use of recursion. TYPE is like PRINT, but produces all the results on the same line; "/   causes a space to be output.

```
TO BACKWARDS :NUMBER
IF :NUMBER < 0 [STOP]
(TYPE :NUMBER "/   )
BACKWARDS :NUMBER — 1
END
```

This procedure could be used to count backwards from an input number:

```
      BACKWARDS 10
&      10 9 8 7 6 5 4 3 2 1 0
```

BACKWARDS has an input parameter named NUMBER (a variable). The first time BACKWARDS is called the value of NUMBER is 10. The IF statement fails and the value of NUMBER is printed (10). The last statement calls BACKWARDS again with a new input (10 − 1). However, this is not just a return to the beginning of BACKWARDS, but a call to a completely new copy of itself. The value of NUMBER is printed (9) and the process is repeated with a new value of NUMBER (9 − 1). Eventually BACKWARDS will be called with a negative value for NUMBER. This causes the IF statement to be successful and the procedure finishes.

Logo is a list processing language. Instead of the array familiar to users of Fortran and Basic, Logo uses a structure called a list as a means of grouping data together. Unlike arrays, lists are not necessarily fixed in size and they do not have to contain data of only one kind. The elements of a Logo list can be numbers, words and other lists, allowing a great deal of flexibility. Hierarchies (lists of lists) can be used to set up complex data structures. Examples of lists are

[THIS IS A LIST]
[THIS IS A LIST [AND AN EMBEDDED LIST]]

We pay for the list's flexibility and varying size when we seek a particular element in it. It is not possible to access the nth element directly as it would be with an array. Although this is slower for some classes of problem, the programming is not difficult or lengthy when recursion is used. It means that Logo is suitable for a great variety of projects which are not necessarily algebraic or mathematical, but are nevertheless interesting and non-trivial. Letters, words and sentences can be handled well by the list processing features, enabling interesting projects with English or foreign languages to be carried out.

Primitive operations FIRST, LAST, BUTFIRST and BUTLAST operate on list elements. LAST picks out the last element of a list; BUTLAST picks out all but the last element. Using these operations the following procedure reverses the contents of a list. [] denotes a list with no elements in it.

```
TO REVERSELIST :SENTENCE
IF :SENTENCE = [] [STOP]
(TYPE LAST :SENTENCE "/  )
REVERSELIST BUTLAST :SENTENCE
END
```

When the procedure is run,

REVERSELIST [THIS IS A TEST]

the computer will output

TEST A IS THIS

A small change to this procedure would enable the characters within a word to be reversed as well.

Logo is a derivative of Lisp, a major language in artificial intelligence research. The list processing features of Logo make available the ideas and concepts of artificial intelligence. Abelson (1982) develops game playing procedures and a knowledge data base in Logo. Sentence generation and poetry writing procedures such as those described in Section 5.3.2 demonstrate uses of lists in language processing.

An important feature of Logo is its extensibility. This means that when a procedure is defined in Logo it becomes another primitive construct of the language. This facility allows students to create new language features, enabling new higher level language constructs to be developed out of primitive commands. Thus desirable aspects of computer languages can not only be discussed but actively explored. For example, there are few iterative constructs in Logo, but they can easily be defined by using recursion. In this example (Abelson 1982) the RUN primitive executes the contents of the list that follows it. The values of ACTION and CONDITION contain one or more primitive commands or procedures.

```
TO WHILE :CONDITION :ACTION
IF NOT (RUN :CONDITION) [STOP]
RUN :ACTION
WHILE :CONDITION :ACTION
END
```

Other iteration constructs can easily be developed. The RUN primitive illustrates another aspect of Logo's ability to create new languages, namely that both program and data can be manipulated.

Naming is an important feature of Logo. We have seen that the titles given to procedures become new commands in the language. Names are also given to inputs for procedures, and to data items — numbers, words or lists. The following example shows how a list or its name can be printed.

```
        MAKE "MESSAGE [THREE BLIND MICE]
        PRINT :MESSAGE
&       THREE BLIND MICE
        PRINT "MESSAGE
&       MESSAGE
```

This idea can be extended to several levels of naming.

The concepts of local and global variables are made explicit in Logo, as they are in Pascal. Inputs to procedures are local variables, and have no value outside the procedure itself. Global variables are created using the MAKE statement, outside procedures, or inside provided the MAKE is not used on an input to the current procedure. A global variable is known to all procedures called by the procedure it is in.

A number of implementations of Logo provide the ability to create multiple graphics figures called sprites, which can be given shapes and moved around with commands similar to those of turtle graphics. In some cases the sprites can be programmed in parallel, with primitives for detecting collisions. Other implementations provide multiple turtles that can be programmed asynchronously; a turtle can be HATCHed and given a procedure to execute in parallel with other turtles. This software allows the exploration of multiple player games and parallel processes at a level of difficulty consistent with the ability of upper secondary students.

Logo is designed to make explicit fundamental ideas of computer science and problem solving. Unfortunately, its rapid development has led to the implementation of slightly different versions on different machines, and this causes problems with teaching materials. Another problem is that on 8-bit microcomputers with only 64 Kbytes of memory, Logo quickly uses up almost all the memory. This is not serious for the beginner writing small programs, but limits the teacher and upper year students. Furthermore, the full use of the list processing facilities requires detailed embedded recursive procedures. What might be better is a cross between Logo and Prolog (see the next section).

Logo will not replace vocational programming languages, for it is not a language for solving the problems of commerce and industry. It is, however, an excellent language for thinking, playing, learning and exploring a wide variety of advanced and relatively abstract ideas, as well as the simpler concrete world of the graphics turtle. Approaches to teaching Logo are discussed in Section 12.4.

12.3.4   Prolog (Ennals 1983)

This is the only other language that deserves serious consideration for general school use. As with Logo and Basic, the user is programming almost before s/he knows it. Prolog (Programming in Logic), designed in 1972 by A. Colmerauer at Marseilles, differs from all the other languages described here in that it is a descriptive, not imperative, language. (This makes it difficult to assess according to the criteria of Section 12.2.) A Prolog program comprises sentences which describe what we want, that is, how the output is related to the input, rather than sequences of instructions which tell the computer the necessary steps to carry out the task. This removes the distinction between data base and program, between data retrieval and computation. For example, we may input to the Prolog system simple sentences:

> Elizabeth mother Charles
> Philip father Charles
> Elizabeth mother Anne
> Philip father Anne
> Anne mother Peter

and compound sentences:
> x parent y if x mother y
> x parent y if x father y
> x grand-parent y
> > if x parent z and z parent y

which the system uses to augment its data base. Then questions produce a response based on these data. For example
> does (Elizabeth mother Charles)

produces
> Yes

while
> which (x parent Anne)

produces
> Answer is Elizabeth
> Answer is Philip
> No (more) answers.

Like Logo, Prolog offers a powerful list-processing capability, but crude alternation and iteration implemented as recursion. Prolog would be an excellent language to use as computer literacy is integrated into subject teaching. All subjects could use such a data structuring facility, with programming being learned almost incidentally. This is probably the best approach to learning to program in Prolog. Ennals describes the applicaton of Prolog in English, French, history, information retrieval, mathematics and science. Applying the computer to such a variety of subjects is an excellent way to appreciate its characteristics and capabilities. In any case, when the Japanese Fifth Generation Computer Project takes hold (Chapter 2), we may all be writing in Prolog! The invention of another language (called Turing) that also permits the user simply to write down what is to be done has just (1984) been announced at the University of Toronto. This approach emphasises clear thinking within a subject, rather than intruding extra levels of conceptual difficulty: the student is developing a specification, with the added advantage that it can be run as a program to test its correctness. Unlike earlier CAL, which either involved large systems (such as PLATO) or dated languages (such as Basic), Prolog is both widely available (and easy to use) on microcomputers, and closely bound up with the leading edge of computing research.

12.3.5   Forth (Brodie 1981)

Forth was designed by C. Moore during the 1960s as a real time programming language to control the movement of a telescope. It is a stack-oriented language using reverse polish notation. A stack is a linear storage, to or from which can be added or removed only the top element. Reverse polish notation, used in many calculators, has the operator last: 5 4 +, for example instead of 5 + 4. This is the first problem namely an unfamiliar notation; the second problem is that all constructs are forced into this reverse polish form, even those for which it is unnatural; thirdly, program debugging is very difficult, as it involves the programmer keeping track of what is where on the stack; fourthly, variable names can include punctuation marks, which looks strange.

On the other hand, Forth is fast, encourages extensive use of subprograms to build up programs, and permits use of the machine's facilities. In other words, it is rather close to machine code. Do not use it, except as a special project in the Computer Science course.

THAT'S DAPHNE — SHE'S VERY GOOD AT DE-BUGGING PROGRAMS!

12.3.6   Smalltalk (*Byte*, August 1981)

Smalltalk was developed by A. Kay at Xerox during the 1970s. The basic concept is the Dynabook: a computer system as easy to use as a book and notepad. To this end, one can work on several tasks at once, once, each contained in (separate or overlapping) windows on the VDU screen. This concept has been implemented in a form more accessible to schools in Apple's Lisa and Macintosh microcomputers. A Smalltalk program is structured, not in terms of data items with values, but in terms of objects which send and receive messages. This makes it particularly good for writing simulation programs.

12.3.7   Boxer

The concept of a total computational environment, begun in Basic and extended in Logo and then Smalltalk, is taken still further in Boxer, a language currently under development at MIT. Boxer will provide graphics, text editing and programming at a single level. Where Logo uses natural language associations for learnability,

Boxer uses spatial associations: the objects of the system are rectangular boxes, which are susceptible of varying interpretations and varying uses. The principles underlying Boxer are described by DiSessa (1982) and Abelson (1984).

12.3.8   Cobol

This is the most used commercial language. It has excellent facilities for describing data which is structured as files and records, and for handling large amounts of such data. With care, good programs can be written in Cobol, as it separates data and algorithm descriptions, permits looping and branching, and has a rudimentary subroutine facility. However, Cobol programs are very long, because they are designed to be readable by the non-programmer, and to be self-documenting. The only place for Cobol in the course would be in the business studies section of Computer Studies, but here it would be ideal.

12.3.9   Machine code or assembly language

These are called low-level languages. Machine code is a representation (in binary form) of the sequences of on/off electrical signals that drive the computer. Assembly language is a representation of machine code using decimal numbers and algebraic symbols to make it easier for people to understand, and to reduce the probability of writing bugs into programs. These languages are aligned towards the computer's structure, and not towards any particular type of problem. Assembly language could usefully be studied in the context of study of the computer's structure and operation (Computer Science).

Before choosing a language, look at the desirable features described in Section 12.2, and try to ensure that the language has these. Do not teach a multiplicity of languages for the sake of it. Nonetheless, by the end of Computer Studies, at least two, and by the end of Computer Science at least three different languages should have been covered, so that the students can understand that the same thing can be done in quite different ways.

12.4   APPROACHES TO TEACHING LOGO

A teacher develops a distinctive methodology for many reasons. These include particular curricular aims, different student audiences and the teacher's own model of the ways in which learning does or should take place in students. Already a considerable variety in approaches and strategies for teaching (or encouraging the learning of) Logo are being developed. No doubt more will appear as more teachers become experienced with the language.

Three such teaching approaches are described and compared below. Clearly these are not the only ways in which Logo might be learned; they are selected to illustrate possible differences, and to provide a framework within which to consider other teaching and learning approaches. The following are used as bases for comparison between the methods: the order in which students encounter parts of the language; the extent to which students using the approach work toward specific goals; and the amount of teacher intervention and of student autonomy implied by the approach, in initiating activities and in subsequent work.

12.4.1   Synthetic approach

In this approach the individual turtle commands, FORWARD, BACK, LEFT and RIGHT, are introduced first, usually in the context of controlling a robot turtle. Students explore and practise using these and other primitive commands for navigational and other turtle driving projects. Then students begin to plan outcomes for their turtle drawings. This usually involves using groups of primitive commands, and leads into the building of procedures and subprocedures which can be combined, built on and modified.

In the earliest Logo work, based at the Massachusetts Institute of Technology (Papert 1976; Papert 1977; Papert *et al* 1978), children were generally encouraged to explore individual projects, in a relatively unstructured way, with teachers available for consultation as needed. After an initial group introduction, individual children were shown further features of the language as they were needed for the tasks they were planning, so each developed his or her own personal Logo environment. This approach resulted in the production of some highly individual projects of enormous variety. These ranged from simple patterns to very complex drawings using turtle geometry; from simple sentences to story-writing or game-programming projects using the list processing features of the language (Watt 1979a). This work gave strong support to claims that Logo can provide versatile and highly personal learning experiences for children of a wide variety of abilities, backgrounds, interests and learning styles (Papert *et al* 1978; Watt 1979b; Overall *et al* 1981).

This synthetic approach, combining and building onto mastered primitive commands and concepts, is a clearly established methodology for teaching the language. Many books exemplifying this approach are available.

What assumptions about learners and learning are implied by this approach? There is an emphasis on not attempting too much at first, and on becoming confident with concepts at a very concrete level before attempting more abstract material. These techniques are particularly suitable for young, naïve or apprehensive learners.

In the very early stages the activities here are teacher initiated, but the method aims to give students confidence so that quite soon they should be able to explore more independently with little teacher intervention, until their planned projects require programming techniques or commands beyond their present level.

The approach is product oriented, in that it assumes students are motivated to achieve various planned ends as they program the turtle, whether these ends are navigational goals, designs or drawings.

This approach is not prescriptive, in that students are allowed to develop their own ways of grouping the primitives. The approach is thus designed to suit students of a variety of learning styles and preferences.

12.4.2   Analytic approach

Here complete procedures written in Logo are presented to the learner, to be read, typed into the computer and used, even if they are only partly understood at the time. The primitives and concepts of the language are encountered in the context of working procedures.

This teaching approach is documented in *Learning Logo*, versions of which have been written for several microcomputers (McDougall *et al* 1982; Adams *et al* 1983; McDougall *et al* 1984; Squires *et al* in press). "This book is written in such a way that at times you might be typing into the computer commands that you only partly understand. It is possible to use Logo procedures without completely understanding their details. In fact, experimenting with these pre-written procedures is a good way of learning how they work" (McDougall *et al* 1982).

The procedures presented are carefully chosen and deliberately ordered to illustrate particular concepts, increasing in complexity as the learner progresses. By reading, using, modifying and extending these procedures, the learner develops an understanding of the programming concepts embodied therein. The learning model assumed here bears some similarity to that occurring in natural language acquisition.

This approach differs from the synthetic one in that, to some extent, it 'throws the learner in at the deep end'. However, it shares with the synthetic approach the attributes of being product oriented, and of using projects initiated by the teacher at the outset while encouraging the student to explore and be independent as skills and understanding develop.

The analytic approach might be seen as more prescriptive than the synthetic one, as it deliberately uses procedures exhibiting good programming techniques or style. Logo itself is designed to encourage use of modularity and other good programming techniques, and this approach might almost be expected to preclude students writing any but well structured programs, although this is by no means certain.

12.4.3   Investigatory approach

An example of a quite different way of introducing Logo to children is provided in the "turtle humming" approach used by Nevile and Dowling (1983). The hums of A.A. Milne's Winnie-the-Pooh were fragments of melody which "came suddenly into his head"; similarly a turtle hum is a fragment of turtle path which is not particularly planned or designed. The user enters a hum-call such as FD 25 RT 37 FD 26 LT 74, to set the turtle 'humming'. Hums can be successfully called without previous planning, and without any understanding of the likely outcome in visual form — the hum might create a recognisable shape, a fancy squiggle or merely a line. Only the simplest vocabulary (RT, LT and FD) and the most elementary keyboard skills are needed.

Once the learner is familiar with the primitive commands and the entering of hum-calls, these are used to explore concepts such as similarity, reflection, repetition, rotation and reversal. A hum-call can be repeated by simply re-typing it. It can be repeated with an extra turn first, and if this is done several times the initial shape will be rotated about its starting point. If the hum is retyped with left and right turns exchanged the shape will be reflected, and so on.

While it might be argued that turtle humming does not teach programming as such, children using this approach are using the computer as a tool for independent exploration and experimentation, and the learning of Logo occurs concurrently.

Turtle humming, like the synthetic approach, is a bottom-up method, beginning with concrete, low level, single command activities, and building on these. However, there is a major contrast between these two bottom-up methods. While in the synthetic approach the student directs the turtle with particular navigational, design or drawing goals in mind, this is not the case in turtle humming. In most turtle humming work the learner need have no idea or plan for the outcome to be produced by the turtle commands being entered. "There are no wrong hum-calls, so the children cannot experience failure" (Nevile & Dowling 1983).

Turtle humming probably has learners working independently sooner than is the case with the two methods described previously, since exploration can begin with so little prerequisite knowledge. Nevile clearly believes that teacher intervention in Logo learning should be relatively limited:

> "When children are let free to control the Turtle, even in the most restrictive way, they cannot produce pictures which do not in some way reflect themselves. Tidy minds make tidy pictures, scatty minds make scatty pictures, inability to conserve length makes funny images, etc. The children see direct representations of their actions, and the teachers see them too. The mind-mirroring of the computer is an aid to understanding at both levels: the teacher's understanding the children and the children understanding their work. If the children were told in advance to draw a square, and taught how to do it, what learning could really take place at either level? I suggest that one cannot be empowered and directed at once." (Nevile 1984).

12.4.4   Discussion

Which then is the best approach to Logo teaching for a particular teacher to use? The answer, as is so often the case in education, is that it depends. In situations where students' confidence, motivation and variety of learning styles are important, teachers might use techniques from the synthetic approach. If good programming style and efficiency of learning are desirable, then the analytic approach might be valuable. For development of an investigative style of working, the turtle humming approach has much to offer. And clearly the three methodologies described are not the only possible approaches to teaching and learning Logo. More and different approaches are being developed as more teachers are becoming familiar with and using Logo, and choosing or devising teaching methods which match their models of learning processes in their students.

12.5   LEARNING PROGRAMMING

12.5.1   Structured learning

It is easy to pick up a golf club and hack at a ball. This is the necessary starting point for the game, to get a feel for the club, the swing, striking the ball, etc. Some people, with a natural flair for it, even make respectable scores in this way. However, no-one seriously suggests that really good golf can be played without study, coaching and discipline. The computing beginner who has learned some Basic, Logo, or whatever, is like the hacker: s/he has a feel for using the language, and some people can write quite complicated programs. However, really good programming needs study, coaching and discipline. Programs to solve real-life problems are usually long and complicated, and cannot be produced by ad hoc extensions of short, simple programs. Over the last 15 years, techniques and tools have been developed to enable large programs to be designed and written successfully. The techniques include top-down programming, data driven programming, use of subprograms, and full documentation; while the tools include pseudocode, modules, compilers, editors and data base systems. (Some of these have been described in Section 12.2.) The computing student should start to learn some of these tools and techniques, and to this end s/he should not simply be allowed to go on 'playing', whether in Basic or Logo. Eventually, when s/he has a good command of the language components, his or her learning of programming must take a more structured form.

12.5.2   The bright child

The teacher will often encounter a student who takes home the computer manuals, and soon knows more about the machine and its languages than anyone else — including the teacher. Do not worry about this: admit where your knowledge is lacking and seek the student's advice when appropriate. When possible, use him or her as a tutor for the other students. His or her expertise on the machine may arise from introversion, so a tutoring activity in this area of great expertise is doubly valuable, as s/he should be learning to communicate concepts. The student should not be allowed to skimp other subjects, nor hog the computer when others should be using it. S/He should be channelled into good practices, and guided towards learning more theory than the other students by good references for further study.

12.5.3   The slow learner

For the child with difficulty in learning to program, language choice is very important. As a matter of observation, few children have trouble with Logo (cf. section 12.3.3). Papert claims that "kids of all ages can learn to program". You must provide concrete techniques, such as physical models of computers, using identifier names on boxes with pieces of paper inside bearing the current identifier values (see, for example, the Scottish Computer Project).

12.5.4   Games

Games can be valuable for learning, and computer programming has been called the best computer game of all (Malone 1981). The player receives frequent performance feedback; the game can be played at different levels of difficulty; there are obvious goals (whether the program works) and more can be generated (speed, size and writing time of the program, for example); and there is often more than an element of the unexpected.

PART III PRACTICAL CONSIDERATIONS

Chapter Thirteen

Other uses for computers in schools

Tis not enough to help the feeble up, but to support him after   W. Shakespeare
(1564–1616)

13.1   THE COMPUTER AS SUPPORTING ACTOR

So far we have considered two aspects of the computer's involvement in school activities, namely a vehicle for teaching (Part I) and an object of teaching (Part II). The computer can also be used in other capacities to support these major activities. Such support roles include computer managed learning, administration, library services, and the computer club.

13.2   COMPUTER MANAGED LEARNING (cf. Section 2.2.1).

13.2.1   Computer managed learning or instruction (CML, CMI) refers to classroom management systems that use computers to help teachers to organize and manage teaching and record-keeping for classes. *Prima facie*, this seems quite distinct from CAL, and initially it was. However, the flexible role of testing has led to some merging of the CML/CAL activities.

Teachers have always kept records, including, for example, objectives, lesson plans, assignments, marks, progress reports and attendance. However, with increased emphasis on individualization of instruction, reporting to parents, and accountability to the community, the amount of record keeping and reporting has increased significantly. The computer can be used to alleviate this.

13.2.2   Computer based testing (CBT)

We first consider the use of the computer to ease the burden of test preparation, administration and marking. This can be done centrally or locally.

Centralized CBT

A commercial or department of education testing service prepares tests on specific subject areas, and distributes them to schools. These tests involve multi-choice questions. The answer sheets or cards are returned to the centre, where they are optically read, scored by comparison with the correct results and a specified marking scheme, and the results analysed. The analyses can take many forms, including defining 'good', 'average' and 'poor' students in terms of performance on the whole test, and then analysing each question to determine whether significantly more good students than poor students answered it correctly.

Such analyses help in the design of future tests, indicating which questions should be omitted as too easy, too hard or too confusing.

Such tests are often used as part of a standardized summative evaluation operation, and so, although the results are sent to the respective school(s), the teacher(s) may not see them. It would be more difficult to construct generally useful tests relating to intermediate stages of a course. Even if this were done, the results might not be available quickly enough for the teacher to take them into account in deciding on the next stage.

Distributed CBT

The advent of smaller computers, the consequent spread of these into schools, and the development of test scoring and analysis programs for them, now allows individual schools to devise, use, mark and analyse their own tests locally. These need not be used only at the end of a course, as the individual teacher can set questions which are relevant to the particular point reached by a particular class. Moreover, the results are likely to be available immediately, and the teacher can use them to decide whether to move on to the next topic, skip ahead, revise the existing topic, or recapitulate earlier work. Furthermore, these decisions can be made for the whole class, or for individual students. If this decision process is coded as a computer program, and the computer itself is used to prescribe further (individual or group) instruction on the basis of the test results, then we have shaded over into CML.

13.2.3   Computer managed learning

This can take a variety of forms, depending essentially on the role played by testing.

Testing based: off-line

Tests are set (manually or automatically), and the computer scores them and, on the basis of the result, prescribes what learning activity should take place next. This prescription is the computer output, and the teacher or student must then act on it by consulting the specified text, invoking the specified CAL lesson, carrying out the specified research project, or whatever.

Testing based: on-line

Tests are set (manually or automatically), and stored in the computer. Students take the test via a terminal, and the scoring and analysis are performed immediately. Again, the next lesson is determined on the basis of the result.

This concept can be taken even further: instead of producing the next lesson on the basis of the result on the last test, the system could produce the next question on the basis of the response to the last question. This comes close to drill and practice in appearance, but is intended to permit the individual student to pursue an appropriate testing sequence, and may result in his having to answer fewer questions, as the machine may be able to select those questions which will give the most information on the student.

In either case, if the CML system incorporates CAL programs the student can be offered an appropriate CAL lesson immediately on completion of the test. Thus the testing becomes less summative and more formative.

Non-testing based: control of instructional sequence

The teacher devises a large number of student assignments, and specifies the appropriate assignments, sequence, tests, etc. for each student. (This is very time-consuming.) Students are then directed through the individualized sequence, while the machine records their performance. The teacher can review the record at the end of the day and revise the specifications for the morrow.

This provides a closer approach to individualized instruction than ordinary CAL because of the human intervention. The teacher is relieved of marking, but experiences no reduction in amount of work — just a replacement of some activities by others.

Non-testing based: record keeping

In this model, no attempt is made to integrate students' activities with computer use. The teacher simply uses the computer as a recording device for the sort of information mentioned in Section 13.2.1. This should only be done if it simplifies access to this information, eases the production of term reports, and so on.

13.2.4   Conclusion

Few schools make heavy use of CML. It needs a relatively large machine, and significant staff commitment in order to work properly. Software is not widely available, and much of what exists is of poor quality. Some teachers have pressed ordinary commercial data-base management programs into service, because in CML we are keeping an 'inventory' of academic performance, so an inventory program can be used. CML is based on behaviourist assumptions, and may reduce teacher–pupil contact if taken to extremes. It may involve the teacher in an inordinate amount of data entry work.

However, if done properly, it can have great benefit, and many people feel that the greatest benefit comes from the planning which precedes implementation. CML needs subject matter to be analysed and sequenced, and academic objectives clearly identified. It also forces teachers and administrators to examine existing practices and clarify goals, lines of communication, and the relation between the different instructional and administrative activities that comprise the total educational effort.

As with many computer applications, the data recorded in CML for one purpose can also be used for other purposes. Records of students' performances can be used as a basis for careers and further education counselling; and can be summarized into reports from the school to government bodies on subjects studied, pass rates, and so on. We should be aware that there is a question of privacy here. Student records may contain subjective comments; they may relate to home background; they may reflect on the quality of teaching. This makes them very sensitive, and only to be disseminated with caution, and for purposes expressly stated in advance.

13.3   ADMINISTRATION

Computers are used in many commercial organizations to process information relating to staff, salaries, accounts, orders, resource management, and so on, and a school is an organization that involves all these functions in support of its primary educational goals. Thus, most of the problems are not specifically educational, but general organizational and hence general systems analysis and design principles apply. Therefore we do not cover the topic in detail here.

13.3.1   Distinction of functions

When large computers were first built, they were so expensive that no organization could afford one unless it was used by several departments. Departments often found it irksome to be forced into an inappropriate style of information handling. The advent of the cheap minicomputer in the 1960s was greeted with delight by such departments and other small organizations which were then able to afford their own processing equipment, and set up a system fitted to their use. In an analogous development, when individual teachers first became aware of the educational possibilities of computers, the machines were too expensive for most schools to buy for only CAL, or only learning to program. Most cases for purchase of a school computer therefore emphasized its versatility, and suggested that it could be used for school record keeping and timetable construction as well. Unfortunately, when a computer was bought, the enthusiastic teacher was then expected to be the school's systems analyst, systems designer, programmer and operator — unpaid, of course! Furthermore, the CAL and administrative uses do not fit well on the same machine. There can be contention for time of use; problems of student access to sensitive information; and serious differences between the optimal system for the two purposes. Therefore, the ever decreasing cost of microcomputers is a source of great delight, as schools can now afford to buy different machines for different purposes. The teacher should not be expected to be competent to investigate and specify requirements for an administration computer (although s/he may be able to offer helpful comments).

13.3.2   Characteristics of school administration

The clearly defined hierarchical structure typical of most business organizations does not exist. The line between administrative and non-administrative activities is not sharply defined, and school members assume multiple roles. Thus, one cannot readily equate certain administrative functions with the job titles of personnel. Administrative functions are performed by the school principal (and any deputy or vice-principals), the bursar, the subject and level co-ordinators, teachers, secretarial and clerical staff, the canteen manager, the school council and certain members of the local community. An administrative system should help all these people to manage the school's resources (human, physical and financial) as effectively as possible.

Administrative applications can be classed into three main sub-systems:

1 student administration;
2 financial administration; and
3 administration of (non-human) resources;

but with overlap and interaction between them.

Student administration

This will require the recording of personal and family data, academic data (class, subjects, assessments), and possibly library data (books borrowed). These must all be updated as appropriate.

Financial administration

The principal and/or bursar must keep track of funds under various headings. The official account (for maintenance, administration, etc.), bookshop account, external account (funds for excursions, etc.), general account (funds from parents), canteen account, and possibly others. Reports must be produced as appropriate, and the records must assist forward budgeting.

Resource administration

To manage buildings, furniture, and equipment requires catalogues of books and other teaching resources, inventories of furniture and fittings, lists of equipment and consumables. The financial and resource administration tasks will be greater in a private school than in a government school of the same size, as many of the relevant functions for the latter are carried out by the central education authority; the private school will therefore require a more extensive program. There will, of course, also be other differences between schools, so each school contemplating administrative computer use should ensure that the proposed system will fulfil its needs.

One critical aspect of resource administration is the production of a teaching timetable. This, of course refers to human resources also, and to the control of students, so as an application it does not fit neatly under any of our three headings. This is because, of all our administrative tasks, it is least like a general commercial application. It is a very important part of school administration. While the curriculum is a statement of aims, it is the timetable which determines what is actually possible. Timetable construction is a very complicated problem (Johnstone 1985), and the best that has been achieved to date is to use the computer as a rapid and effective timetabler's aid, not a replacement for the human.

13.4   THE LIBRARY

Computer use in the library is a very interesting topic, as it falls into both the administrative and educational categories. The former includes cataloguing, circulation and all the librarian's other housekeeping functions. The latter is changing and growing rapidly, in line with changing views on the role of education. Where once it was possible to learn a trade at school and practise it the rest of one's life, now it is estimated that an individual will need to re-train completely every ten years. In such circumstances, it becomes at least as important to know how to find things out as to know the things themselves: access is more important than facts. The library is the major resource centre in which one practises 'finding things out' in this way. Therefore, its place in the educational process is much more akin to the science laboratory, where one puts theoretical concepts into practice, than to the counselling centre, which one attends for ancillary advice, when necessary.

Looking to the near future, therefore, lessons on information retrieval and library usage should be an explicit part of the curriculum. This should be a transient stage, however, like explicit classes on computer literacy. By the end of the decade, these concepts should be explicitly included in the syllabi of the various subjects. Thus, there is a clear affinity between computing and librarianship. The one relates to the representation and processing of information; the other to the classification and retrieval of information; and both should be integral parts of the education of all children beginning no later than lower secondary level. Computers, as information processors, are now widely used in libraries for information storage and retrieval. Therefore, the lessons on information retrieval must refer to information retrieval by computer.

13.4.1   Housekeeping

Many of the library's organizational tasks can be speeded up through use of a computer.

Circulation

An automated circulation system keeps track of who has which book at any time (Fig. 13.1). This permits recall and bespeaking to be implemented. Use of bar coded labels for both books and borrowers' cards permits automated charging and discharging (cf. Section 14.5.4). The system can simplify renewal procedures, the notification of overdue borrowers, and the production of regular statistical reports on frequency of use, etc. The Tasmanian State Library runs an on-line circulation system, and a number of school libraries are linked to it, and share the data base.

Cataloguing

This is a very time-consuming business. Automated catalogue creation enables the librarian to type in the catalogue information once only, and the machine then produces a spine label and a catalogue card or microfiche. It also keeps track of multiple copies and produces appropriate 'see' and 'see also' entries. Library networks now exist that eliminate the first stage (of information

Fig. 13.1

input) by making this available on request. TASCIS for example (Tasmanian Schools' Cataloguing Information Service) supplies catalogue cards via school terminals, on request.

Enquiries

The user formerly inspected a card file for information on a library's holdings. Most libraries have now changed to COM — Computer

Output on Microfiche — catalogues, and the user employs a microfiche-reader to consult the catalogue. If the catalogue is stored in a computer, an on-line enquiry system can be implemented, allowing the user to search for books by author, subject, title, etc. from a computer terminal. This is the subject of the next section. If the circulation system is also accessible, the user can also determine who has the book.

Authority control

Formats can be specified, and the computer-based system can monitor all usage and ensure that these are adhered to in the style of entry. Global changes can be made when it is decided to change a preferred term, for example, the replacement of 'woman' by 'women', or of 'force and energy' (a physics-oriented flavour) by 'energy resources'. Preferred terms must keep up with people's normal terminology if users are to be able to find what they want. A global change of typed cards is impossibly time-consuming, and most libraries have to compromise, by having an entry such as 'before (date) see 'woman'; after (date) see 'women' '.

Patron information

This might include the borrowing periods for various classes of user.

Acquisition

Order production, selection lists, etc. can be produced as in other commercial systems.

Serials control

Ordering, monitoring the payment of subscriptions, and monitoring arrivals are all actions susceptible to some computer-based support.

Many ready-made computer packages are available to perform one or more of these functions. Costs range from $2000 for an Apple-based system to $120 000 for a VAX-based system, and even higher. Clearly the facilities provided will vary greatly. Before buying anything, a prospective purchaser should see the desired system in operation, handling at least as many books, borrowers, etc. as it would be expected to manage at the purchaser's library.

13.4.2   Educational aspects

There are at least three educational reasons for computer use in school libraries.

Finding information

Students must learn how to plan a search strategy, possibly involving the use of Boolean descriptors to specify the subjects of interest [see, for example, Woodhouse *et al* (1984)]. This involves formulating an hypothesis, translating it into a suitable computer request and analysing the result; then continuing the search, or reformulating the hypothesis and repeating the process. It is important that at this learning stage the student be successful a lot of the time, to encourage greater use of the library and independent attempts to access information. However, the more information accumulates, the more difficult it is to maintain an adequate access and reference system. In a card catalogue, a lot of work is involved in producing 6–8 cards for various cross-references. With a computer-based system, however, it is easy to add a lot of description. This is doubly valuable in the educational context, as it not only conduces to the retrieval of the desired information, but also to positive associations in the student's mind with the information retrieval process. Rowbottom *et al* (1983) describe the Schools Information Retrieval Project which was designed precisely to investigate the requirements (hardware, software, personnel, and staff training) and the likely benefits to students of information retrieval activities. They report very positive results.

System familiarity

Most libraries are now based on COM catalogues, and use KWIC and KWOC listings (Keyword In/Out of Context). Students should therefore be familiar with such systems before they leave school.

On-line data base

Because large quantities of information can only be stored on computer if they are to be conveniently accessible (not to mention the inability of forests to grow fast enough to supply paper for the increasing number of books and journals!), much information is available only by computer from computer data bases. This applies particularly to the most recent information. Current educational practices are such that it is important to give senior students, particularly in the social and natural sciences, access to contemporary information. Therefore, access to these data bases results in the student acquiring both necessary information and valuable experience.

On-line data bases are prepared and updated by various organizations. So that no one user has to negotiate with each organization, information retrieval services or data base vendors do this, and then provide access to many different data bases. In Australia, for example, Ausinet is a data base organization which provides access to 30 data bases, including Australian Business Index, Australian Education Index, Australian Science Index, and Australian Public Affairs Information Service. Anyone of these can be accessed via the telephone system from anywhere in Australia, for the cost of a local call. The procedure is either to make the call and then connect the telephone to one's computer terminal; or to have the terminal and telephone permanently connected. Thus, Ausinet allows the telephone network to act as a nationwide computer network. It costs $25 per month to subscribe to Ausinet, while the cost of using any of the data bases ranges from $30 to $100 per hour.

A national computer network is only part of an international network, accessible from Australia via OTC's Midas service, a satellite communication system between Australia and the USA. Dialog and Orbit are two Californian data base services which may be accessed in this way. Orbit supports about 70 data bases, while Dialog supports about 200, including ERIC (Educational Resource Information Centre), Magazine Index (an index of 400 popular American magazines), Social Scisearch (an index to the literature of many social sciences, including economics, history, law, geography, political science and psychology) and Medline (index to medical literature). Clearly, access to such information is vitally important to teachers as well as students. When using Midas to search for information in an overseas data base, the initial telephone call to Midas is free; using Midas costs about $30 per hour ($12 connect fee plus a charge per character transmitted); and the connect time to the data base is of the order of $100 per hour, which is shared between Dialog and the data base producer/owner.

The Source, owned by Readers' Digest, and Micronet are two single data base services, containing a wide range of information. For example, all UPI journalist reports are held on The Source. The Australian version of The Source is called The Australian Beginning. The Videotex system [see, for example, Woodhouse et al (1984)] is another computer-based information-providing network, offering much current information. Versions of Videotex are available in Britain, Australia, Canada and France. Even if the information itself is not of great use in school, experience with Videotex would be helpful, since it is in quite wide use as a business system.

To use the services of an information network, it is necessary to have a computer or computer terminal; a modem (modulator/demodulator) or acoustic coupler to connect the computer to the telephone network, converting computer signals to telephone signals and vice versa; and, if using a computer rather than a terminal, a program to handle the communication activity.

13.4.3   The librarian

The increasing use of computers for library applications means that terminals should be stationed in the library. This in turn means that the librarian should be able to operate the computer and should understand its application to the library function. This implies a similar level of expertise to a subject teacher using the computer in his or her area. However, the affinity between computing and librarianship may result in pressure for the librarian to be a general consultant on all computing matters. As a school develops a significant computer facility, it will indeed need someone to fill the role of computer manager and resource person, but this should not necessarily be the librarian.

13.5   THE COMPUTER CLUB

It is a common experience that formal educational work in

computing raises many questions in the minds of lively students. Only a fraction of these can be covered in class, and in any case many of them are more appropriate to individual research and investigation. A good forum for such activities is an extra-curricular Computer Club. They can be carried out on an *ad hoc* and individual basis, of course. However, students' (and staff) time will be more effectively used and interest maintained longer if such activities and their results are shared. In some cases, a group of interested students will take the initiative, and in others a staff member will do it. In either case, activities should be dictated by student preference, with plenty of free time available to explore ideas and possibilities. The staff member may suggest projects, methods and references.

Clearly this is a very flexible and open-ended activity. It is mentioned here simply to draw it to your attention, and to observe that the computer's location and usage should permit this sort of unstructured activity.

Chapter Fourteen

Software and hardware selection

You pays your money and you takes your choice Punch

14.1 SYSTEM SELECTION

14.1.1 Selection committee

When a school embarks on computer use, it is concerned with what the computer can do, and this depends on the software. Software performance in turn depends on hardware capability, so in fact one must consider the total system — software and hardware, including the peripheral devices by means of which the user interacts with the machine. However, it is the software with which the user interacts, and so this should be the major emphasis in selecting a computer.

In Chapters 9, 10 and 11, we stressed the primacy of educational considerations in the design of courses and courseware. The same emphasis is necessary in the selection of computer systems, starting with a clear idea of what the computer is required to do. Before a computer is bought, careful thought should be given to the school's curriculum, as this is the context in which the computer is to be of service. While the use of a computer will suggest new ideas and methods, one should not re-model the whole curriculum just to fit the computer.

Initiatives for the purchase of a computer system are often taken by one enthusiastic teacher, who has an application in mind, convinces the principal, prepares a submission for funds, negotiates with suppliers, and then supervises the computer's use and operation. We shall describe a preferable — some would say idealistic — procedure. Although this ideal will not often be achieved, it is nonetheless a useful pattern.

1 Identifying what the computer is expected to do, and matching actual hardware and software to this, is a systems analysis and design process, and it would be valuable to obtain some informed assistance with it. Possible sources of such assistance are teachers, parents and

education department consultants. The first step, therefore, is for the principal to establish a small committee, consisting perhaps of the principal, two teachers, two parents and a departmental consultant. The principal would represent administrative computer applications, and consider the total impact on the school community. The teachers would be concerned with instructional computer use — CAL and computer studies; the parents would provide the (honorary) technical expertise in systems analysis and design, and computer capabilities; and the consultant would supply information on departmental policies and support, what other schools are doing, etc. Obviously, this structure would be varied, to include the librarian and/or bursar if appropriate, anyone else with particular expertise, and so on.

2 Now the committee seeks suggestions for computer use. A brainstorming atmosphere will encourage creative suggestions. To avoid this simply becoming a list of all possible computer applications in schools, a measure of personal commitment should be sought along with the suggestions. This may also provide an estimate of the staff time likely to be involved. Suggestions should indicate the purpose and the educational benefits expected. If the committee needs extra information, it may seek input from other relevant people, particularly staff, but possibly also the school council, and students. Conversely, it might be more appropriate to conduct a staff seminar to introduce the possibilities of computer use, rather than assuming staff knowledge and seeking their suggestions. Indeed, it may be necessary to buy or borrow a single, cheap system to give staff some experience and a chance to experiment before they are ready to make any suggestions.

3 Sort the amorphous mass of possible applications, using the headings we have introduced: CAL, by type and subject; computer studies; computer science (informatics); CML; library (housekeeping and information retrieval); administration (various categories).

4 Consider each of these proposals more critically, assessing the number of terminals or computers needed, hours of equipment use during a typical week, staff time involved, and student time involved. The proposals can then be gathered into groups, such that all applications in one group can use the same equipment, and can all be fitted into the week's timetable. Since it is unlikely to be possible (financially, organizationally or educationally) to implement all the

groups simultaneously, they should be ranked with regard to educational considerations. Such a list can form the basis of the school's long-term plan for integration of computers into the school's activities.

5   For each such group of applications (or, at least, the top few on the list) draw up precise specifications, and request a number of suppliers to propose a specific system (hardware and software) and its cost.

6   Re-examine the group ranking, and adjust it in the light of the information supplied by vendors, and other practical considerations (such as continuing staff availability etc.).

7   Check that there are good descriptions of how to operate the system, and local after sales service. Other desirable features are hardware expandability, and the existence of a lot of appropriate, high-quality software.

8   The most important factor is that the system should do what you want. Visit other schools, computer dealers, and exhibitions, and arrange demonstrations in order to try out and talk to owners of various systems. Ensure that you see your proposed system doing what you want it to do before you buy it, as reliably and rapidly as you want it to do it. This seems to preclude innovation, and so it does, but in practice most of our new departures are not as radically or totally new as we like to think. If you really are the very first, aim to get a special government innovation grant, or a special deal from the vendor as a 'demonstration site'. Similarly, it precludes buying new products, because these always have bugs. Do not confine your viewing to your proposed system: see also other systems doing similar things, as the comparison will help you to realize more precisely what you want.

We are describing a school-based approach to system selection, but there are other approaches. One is is district-based selection, with advantages of greater availability of special expertise, better purchase price, and a pool of software and advice. Disadvantages are compromises in selecting one type of machine for many situations, and diminished teacher control. An intermediate approach is for district selection and negotiation of a favourable price, with schools free to take advantage of this or not.

The next steps are to obtain funds for the system(s) at the top of the list, and plan for the implementation of the various activities.

These tasks, which may well be undertaken by different groups, are described in the next chapter.

14.1.2   Typical categories

Each school should go through the process of Section 14.1.1, not only to ensure that the final decisions are correct for that school, but also for the learning experience it provides. However, there is no need for each school to start out as if no such decisions had ever been taken before, and it may be helpful to have in mind certain typical categories of application, types of machine and costs involved. To this end, the following observations may be made.

If each school makes a totally independent decision in isolation, there is a proliferation of incompatible equipment. This prevents the sharing of experience and the transfer of programs and skills. Some schools make unsuitable choices, and others try to avoid this by doing nothing.

To avoid this fragmentation of effort, attempts are sometimes made (at education authority level) to find an all-purpose machine. This ensures compatibility between schools and so gives access to a wide range of software and experience. Furthermore, the authority can provide significant support. However, the only machines versatile enough to fit the bill are large, expensive, more complicated to operate than a microcomputer, and probably have less relevant software than the major microcomputers.

In 1982, the Victorian education department suggested an intermediate solution by grouping together application areas for which similar hardware specifications would be appropriate (cf. step 4 of Section 14.1.1). The three suggested categories were computer literacy, CAL, and computer science and administration. Allitt (1983) observes that, although these categories do combine the benefits of flexibility and standardization, they still imply that all school computing is of a general nature. In practice, however, the lack of teacher expertise makes it unnecessary in the short term to have equipment which can switch quickly from subject to subject; while the decreasing cost of special-purpose machines means that it is feasible to consider providing these as and when teachers are ready for them. Allitt identifies a number of specific areas for computer application in the immediate future.

1 Word processing, for vocational training and/or essay preparation. A good word processing package is required, and a class set of computers, but the equipment can be cheap, with monochrome screens.

2 Programming. Again a class set is required, with black and white screens, and one programming language (perhaps Logo).

3 Graphics. One machine, with colour and high resolution graphics, for demonstrations in graphic arts and technical drawing classes.

4 Administration. An industry standard machine, supporting a hard disc, four terminals, data base facilities, etc.

The special-purpose approach has a number of advantages. Hardware cost is reduced, software cost is reduced as little variety is required, equipment is used for 80% or more of the school week, a smaller number of operating skills is required, and the computer is more closely associated with educational aims and more easily integrated into the relevant teacher's sphere of competence.

Moving in the direction suggested by Allitt, the Victorian education department now recommends machines for specific purposes (word processing and Logo programming; computer science and commercial studies) as well as a general CAL machine.

14.1.3   Networks in the school

If it seems that more than one computer of the same type will be bought, one must consider whether they should be connected in a network. (Not all microprocessors can be so connected.) Advantages are that expensive equipment can be shared (one printer or one large disc for a dozen microcomputers); the teacher can supervise the students' work from his or her machine; and a single copy of a program on a disc at the master machine can be accessed from all the other machines, saving copying, and perhaps saving extra licence fees. Disadvantages are the need for the machines' use to be at best co-ordinated and at worst identical; the inability of some networked machines to function alone; the dependence of the whole network on the master machine; and the extra network driving software and hardware needed (these would be supplied by the microprocessor supplier).

14.1.4   Local area networks

Some manufacturers market connections and network interfaces which permit different makes of microcomputer to be linked, provided they are fairly close (up to a few hundred metres apart). Such general purpose connection systems are called local area networks (LANs) and the best-known is Ethernet. A LAN could be useful within one school, or to permit co-operation between neighbouring schools.

14.2   SOFTWARE SELECTION

Let us return to the selection process, in particular the selection of software. Although hardware choice is essentially an initial decision (apart from accessories, peripherals and other enhancements), we shall be constantly bombarded with further software for our system, and shall be constantly deciding whether — and if so, what — extra software should be bought. This is particularly the case if we buy a general purpose system. Even if we buy a system or systems with a special purpose in mind, however, we shall be constantly offered software that will extend its capabilities.

In this section, therefore, we give some guidelines for software selection, which should be used at initial purchase time and subsequently. They are particularly applicable to CAL software (or, more precisely, courseware) but may be applied, mutatis mutandis, to other software also. Teachers should become as adept at browsing through a piece of courseware and deciding on its educational merits and suitability as they now are at doing this with a proposed text book or video tape.

14.2.1   Selection criteria

Selection is the process of deciding how well a software package matches a set of pre-determined criteria. These criteria are of various types. Some permit objective decisions, but most are subjective; some apply to any package, while some depend on the type of package, or on the subject, or on the individual teacher. Each teacher should study lists of suggested criteria, and gradually develop a list that is best suited to his or her subject and teaching style. Many lists have been published; some long (Coburn *et al* 1982, chapter 5, Gore 1982, Microsift 1982), some medium (Foulis 1982), and some short (Preece & Squires 1984). (Remember that most use the term 'evaluation' rather than 'selection': see Section 9.4.1) Our suggested list is as follows. To avoid duplication, we refer the reader to Sections 9.2 and 10.2, where desirable characteristics of courseware are described in the context of writing it oneself.

Is CAL relevant and helpful to the proposed curriculum area and teaching strategy?

1   Is the material educationally valid?
2   Is the style of CAL appropriate?
3   Is the proposed learning experience the most appropriate for the subject matter?
4   Is the level of teacher involvement acceptable?
5   If the material is not locally produced, is it relevant to the local curriculum and are the idioms intelligible?
6   What prior knowledge is assumed?

Is the package correct?

1   Is the model valid and realistic?
2   Are the facts, graphs, grammar, etc. correct?
3   Is the material socially compatible with the school?

Is the computer used to best advantage?

1   Are graphics used, and used well? For example, are screen layouts attractive or cluttered; do the graphics enhance user interest or slow the process or distract; are the successive screens as static as pages of a book?
2   Are other facilities used, and used well? For example, joystick, paddle, mouse, voice input, sound output (see later sections of this chapter).
3   Is the approach motivating?

Is the computer's communication with the user helpful?

1 Does the package ask good questions?
2 Is the verbal complexity appropriate to the level of the student?
3 Is the feedback enough or excessive; helpful or threatening; encouraging or patronizing or self-consciously funny?
4 Are there 'help' routines or other user assistance?
5 Does the system tolerate user errors, such as pressing inappropriate keys? (This is called robustness.)
6 Are the responses fast enough?
7 Does the output disappear too soon?

Is the learner in control?

1 What is the sequence through the course, and can the learner vary it?*
2 Can the user review material?
3 Can the user skip passages?*
4 Can the prospective teacher browse through the course?
5 Are there different facilities to cater for the novice and the sophisticated user?
6 Is the machine as such unobtrusive?

What the learner is required to do should be simple and consistent; for example, always 'y' or 'YES' for an affirmative answer, but not sometimes one and sometimes the other; always press 'RETURN' after input or never, but not an arbitrary mixture.

Is there adequate documentation?

1 See Section 9.4 for a comprehensive list of what should be present.
2 Is it intelligible?
3 Is there adequate supplementary material?

Is the package flexible?

1 Can it be used in different areas?

2 Can the program be modified (cf. section 10.4)? Items 1 and 3 asterisked above are minor modifications; some packages permit the actual code to be modified to vary the form or content of the input and output, or to change the underlying mathematical model.

Administrative questions

1 Does the system keep a record of a student's progress and performance?
2 Who can inspect this record and how?
3 Will the program run on your computer? (Remember to check memory and peripheral requirements.) Will it run on other computers?
4 Is the cost of the package acceptable?
5 Have you seen it running?
6 Is there any after sales support?
7 Is it necessary to buy multiple copies for several computers?

Do not confine your attention to programs which are advertised as educational: many other programs, especially the better games, have great educational potential.

The reader should not feel daunted at the prospect of learning extensive new selection skills. Rawitsch (1983) points out that "evaluation of courseware need not be considered a mystical process, even by someone who is not versed in computer use. This is because many of the criteria used to judge courseware are identical to those one would use to judge any kind of instructional materials". In fact, probably 75% of courseware selection criteria are not computer-specific.

14.2.2   Finding software

You may learn of available software from a number of sources.

1 Your hardware supplier.
2 Publishers' catalogues: many book publishers now produce software.
3 Computer magazines, especially educational ones.
4 Other teachers: conferences, seminars and in-service courses are useful for this.
5 Education authority support services.

14.3   THE MACHINE–USER INTERFACE

No matter how powerful the computer, or how ingenious the program, the user's control of the computer and his or her extraction of the program's results is dependent on the available peripherals, that is the input and output devices.

For many years, people have communicated with computers via a typewriter-like keyboard. In many cases, this keyboard operated a machine which produced a particular pattern of holes (in a card or tape) in response to the striking of a particular key. The computer then 'read' the cards or tapes by means of a machine which sensed the patterns of holes and sent corresponding electrical signals to the computer. Sometimes the keyboard was attached directly to the computer, the striking of any key sending a corresponding electrical signal to the computer. The keyboard connected directly to the computer is still the most common means of inputting information to a computer. One concomitant of this is that a computer user should become a reasonably proficient typist. Many beginners are quite frustrated with their slow progress in learning to use the computer until they realize that in addition to learning to program etc., they are trying to learn incidentally a skill (typing) that is an explicit learning task for many people.

The machine's communication with the user has likewise been via the printed word, either by driving the print head of an electric typewriter, or by displaying the words on a television-like screen, or by driving a line printer to print characters a line at a time. These are still the most common means of outputting information from a computer.

However, it has now been recognized that people not only press typewriter-like keys and look at printed words and numbers, but also operate knobs and levers, draw, look at pictures, make use of colours, talk, listen and so on; and devices have been developed to permit the user to input to the computer in a variety of different ways; and to permit the computer to produce its output in a variety of different forms. Such a development is very good news for the teacher. The good teacher uses a variety of approaches to get his or her message over. Therefore, the increasing variety of input and output devices is extremely useful in permitting a range of computer-based approaches to a given problem, with increased convenience of use, enhancement in understanding, and reduction in boredom.

Humans communicate through their five senses. To the best of our knowledge, no computer communication involving scent or taste has occurred. However, the other three human senses have been involved, with the sense of sight being by far the most used. Sound has been used to a lesser extent, while touch has had minimal use. We shall deal with oral and aural communication later, and shall subsume touch under sight, for reasons that will become apparent.

14.4   COMPUTER GRAPHICS

One of the earliest developments was the use of the video screen, in place of a print head and paper, for computer output to a terminal. The resulting terminal, with keyboard and screen, is called a visual display terminal or unit (VDT or VDU). Its effect was to reduce the noise and eliminate the use of ribbon and waste of paper associated with the old teletypes. However, no use was made of the pictorial capabilities of the television-like screen. Gradually, however, this has changed, and now there is a wide variety of graphical input and output devices associated with VDUs.

14.4.1   The graphics screen

The image on a television screen is produced by an electron beam which lights small areas or dots on the screen. While the normal television screen can produce quite a detailed picture, more sophisticated terminals use a greater range of frequencies (20 MHz rather than 6 MHz) and can distinguish many more dots. They are said to have better resolution, and can display more detail in a picture. Some microcomputers relate graphics characters to keys, and allow a picture to be constructed by key strokes. However, in order to realize the full screen capability, the computer, which is outputting to the VDU, would have to be able to control the signal to each dot position. In practice, the average computer and screen can control the signal to individual groups of about four dots. This smallest individually lightable area is called a pixel (picture element). The control of pixels may be exercised by software or hardware. Many microcomputers set aside an area of memory, the values stored in which control the screen pattern directly. Such an area is called a memory map. For each pixel on the screen, it is possible to identify a particular bit (or group of bits) in the memory, whose current value (or values) determines the pixel's current brightness and, for a screen with the capability of displaying colours, its colour. To display a particular picture on the screen, a program is written to set the bits in the memory map to appropriate values, and then switch it into screen control. It may also be possible to build up different sets of values in different areas of store to represent different pictures. The screen can then display different pictures in succession quite rapidly if the program switches screen control between the different areas. Different screens have different numbers of pixels. Clearly, the more pixels on a screen, the better the screen resolution and the more precise the pictures which can be displayed. On the debit side, however, a larger memory area is required for the memory map, it takes longer to construct a picture, and may take longer to change pictures. The screen is also probably more expensive. Some microcomputers offer two (or more) graphics modes, usually known as low and high resolution graphics modes. These are usually in addition to text mode. If a coarse picture is adequate, low resolution may be used, and less memory is required.

Some computers use a programmable character generator for graphics work. This is a small amount (2–4 Kbytes) of read only memory (ROM) which maps key strokes or ASCII values to particular characters. Some microcomputers (or intelligent terminals) have several character generators, built-in or programmable, allowing the user to change character sets like the typist changes golf balls or daisy wheels.

14.4.2   The use of colour

Screens are either monochrome or coloured. Monochrome in fact means two colours: characters of one colour on a different background. While black on white is best for copy typing, green on white (greenscreen) is more legible, and amber on a dark background is easier on the eyes for long screen usage.

Much to be preferred, however, are screens and computers that permit the display of a variety of colours. Colour adds an extra dimension of interest to the screen, and hence to the use of the computer. "Students are bombarded daily by very high quality designs employing colour — television, magazines, etc. These materials, prepared by extremely competent industrial designers, constitute the 'background' world the student lives in. If the educational word presents a monochromatic view, it fails to compete for students' attention." [Bork, in Chapter 4 of Taylor (1980)]. Colour is almost essential to motivate student learning, whether in the use of videotapes or computers.

A second aspect of computer use is the search for reality. The world around us is coloured, technicolour replaced black and white films, and colour has replaced black and white television. Black and white pictures are an obviously artificial representation of the real world: it makes no sense to strive after extreme reality in our models (see Chapter 6) and then spoil it by presenting a monochrome end product. A tree in green and brown looks more tree-like than one in dark grey, and hence requires less effort on the student's part to identify it. While this seems trivial, it is important to minimize the irrelevant intellectual effort required of the user, so that his or her efforts may be concentrated on the heart of the topic(s) under consideration.

A third, and even more functional, aspect of colour is that it offers a further dimension of symbolism, and hence permits the presentation of more information. Maps can have differently coloured regions, height can be represented by colour, heat can be represented by colour, force can be represented by colour, and so on.

14.4.3   Animation

Other visual effects are possible, such as the flashing of a small section of the screen picture to draw attention to it. If a screen picture represents a game with players' tokens thereon, the token of the player who is to move next can be flashed. Another application is when the user is to type a response to the computer, and a marker can be flashed where the information will be displayed on the screen.

More ambitiously, animation of characters can be achieved by an extension of this concept. The BBC computer permits a lot of shapes to be drawn, and then switched on and off rapidly. If a similar shape is drawn in several different positions, and each one is switched on in turn, the appearance of motion is created. On the Apple, the user can create shape tables to describe the shape of a person, animal, car, etc. This can be displayed briefly in a chosen colour against a background picture, and then re-drawn in the background colour — effectively removing it. If this process is executed repeatedly, at successive locations, again movement is simulated.

Like colour, therefore, flashing can add an extra dimension of presentation of information.

14.4.4   Getting and changing pictures on the screen

As indicated above the basic way of doing this is to write programs, in appropriate languages, to control the computer's signals to the screen in the desired manner. However, not every potential user is willing or able to spend the amount of time necessary to gain an adequate understanding of the details of the computer's operation. In order to make the computer's graphical capability more widely and readily available, therefore, utility programs are written to permit the user to control the computer's pictorial display more easily. Such programs are often associated with special devices, such as joysticks, light pens and mice.

Manual operation of such devices can cause the contents of the screen to change, and a natural question is: 'How does this occur?' The first thing to realize is that any input device to a computer generates electrical signals, which are interpreted by the hardware (i.e. by the way the circuitry is designed) or by the software (i.e. by the running of a particular program). The latter is more common as it lends itself to greater flexibility. Each input or output device has a program associated with it. This program, called the device handler, has the task of interpreting the input signals appropriately (from an input device) or of sending the appropriate signals (to an output device).

Consider, for a moment, an electric typewriter. Pressing a key causes a current to flow in a particular circuit, which is so wired as to cause the corresponding letter to hit the paper. It would be just as easy to construct circuitry which caused the 'v' typeface to hit the paper when the 'w' key is pressed, although this would not be very useful (except possibly in the automatic implementation of a simple substitution cipher!)

However, most modern typewriters permit the head (ball, cup or wheel) to be changed, to allow the use of different alphabets or other special character sets. Therefore, sometimes pressing the 'w' key does not cause a 'w' to be printed. Such a change is caused by changing the hardware (namely the typehead).

In a similar manner, the striking of a 'w' on a terminal keyboard sends a signal to the terminal handler (program), which sets a value in the computer's memory (and also sends a signal to the screen to display a 'w'). When this value is sent, later, to a printer, via a printer handler, it causes a 'w' to be printed.

However, it is easy to think of circumstances under which we do not wish the pressing of the 'w' key to have the above effect. Let us suppose that the computer is to be used in learning about compass directions. To this end, a map is displayed on the screen (Fig. 14.1), and we wish the pressing of the 'w' key to cause a figure on the screen to move westward across the map. This may be achieved by replacing the terminal handler with a program which will receive the 'w' signal and then cause the desired effect. Another common example occurs in many computer games, where pressing the space bar causes an advance to the next stage of the game, rather than displaying a space character.

In summary, then, input and output devices are normally supervised by programs (handlers). By writing appropriate handlers, input from a device can be interpreted in a whole variety of ways, and output to a device can take a whole variety of forms.

Fig. 14.1

14.5   SCREEN-ORIENTED INPUT DEVICES

Of the devices described in this section, the light pen and touch panel offer direct screen control; that is, the user works directly with the screen. The other devices offer indirect screen control; that is, the user manipulates an object elsewhere, but this object is connected to the VDU and its manipulation produces an effect on the screen.

14.5.1   Paddle

A paddle has a knob which can be rotated to send a varying electrical signal to the computer. The paddle handler is usually designed to display a short line on the screen, and to move it around in response to the rotation of the knob. The line in question often represents a tennis racquet or other sporting implement, and this has given rise to the general term 'paddle' for both the screen line and its controller. Many games use two paddles, one for each of two contestants. In other cases, the two paddles are used to move a mark (usually a small rectangle, arrow, or cross) around the screen. (We shall use the general term cursor for such a mark.) One paddle controls its vertical movement, and the other its horizontal movement.

A paddle is usually provided with one or more buttons. Pressing a button sends a signal to the computer. Depending on the handler, the signal could be interpreted as 'fire a missile', 'hit the ball', 'enter the next dungeon', or 'put another window in the house plan on the screen, at the place currently marked by the cursor'.

14.5.2   Joystick

If you have ever tried to play the game of drawing a smooth curve by turning two knobs, each controlling movement in one direction, you will know how difficult it is. A joystick combines the two paddles into one device, to permit more accurate control. It is a vertical handle, which is set in a baseplate, and which can be leaned in any direction. In response to the changing signal, the handler causes the cursor to move in the corresponding direction on the screen. Many video games use joysticks, especially to control rocket ships and aeroplanes. Like the paddle, joysticks usually have buttons to signal when the cursor is at a particular point, and/or what action is to be taken there.

14.5.3   Mouse

A mouse is a small box with wheels or track balls underneath (Fig. 14.2). Rolling a mouse across a desk or other flat surface causes the cursor to move across the screen in the corresponding direction. Typically, the handler can record a movement by the mouse of as little as 0.1 mm. If the mouse reaches the edge of the desk before the cursor has moved far enough, one picks it up, moves it back, and rolls it again. Again, the mouse usually has buttons for sending signals, which are interpreted as specified by the handler (program). In practice, these devices normally come with a basic handler, and the provision for the user to extend it to determine just how the button-signals will be interpreted.

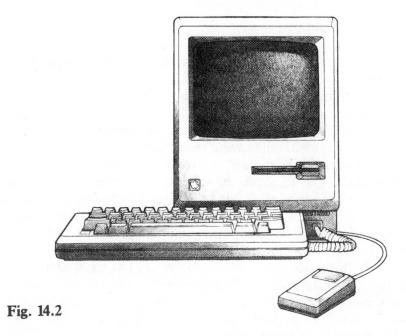

Fig. 14.2

An alternative mouse design does not have a moving wheel, but an optical sensor. This must be moved over a sheet of plastic on which a fine grid of lines is printed, and the mouse's movement is detected by its passage over the lines. Some mice have a built-in microprocessor, which significantly enhances their capabilities. Similar to the mouse, but less convenient, is the trackball which rolls around inside a container to move the cursor. Many keyboards have four arrow keys for moving a cursor around the screen (Fig 14.3). Clearly, the use of a joystick or mouse is much simpler than pressing these in the appropriate sequences.

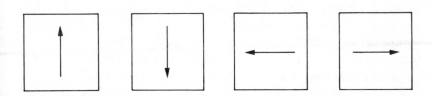

Fig. 14.3

14.5.4   Light pen

A light pen or wand is similar to a ball point pen in size and shape, but has a light detector in place of the ball. The light detector is activated by a switch on the side of the pen. This device uses the fact that the picture on a cathode ray screen is not permanent, but is constantly retraced, line by line, with each dot being switched on as required. If the wand is pointed at the screen, and detects a light in front of it, the moment when this happens is compared with the current position of the scanning dot, to obtain the screen co-ordinates of the place at which the wand is pointing. Many light pen handlers are designed to permit drawing: a cursor is displayed, and the light pen signals when it has been located. If the wand is now moved, while switched on, the cursor moves with the pen, leaving a track of lighted points behind it.

The light pen was a great innovation, but has a number of defects. It must be kept at right angles to and close to the screen, or the cursor can be left behind. Thus, it is obscuring the place at which one is 'drawing'. Furthermore, a screen is vertical, which is not a normal angle at which to draw.

The light pen is also used to input bar coded information. A bar code is a pattern of alternate black and white stripes of various widths. The pattern encodes certain information, such as product details (on supermarket merchandise), personal details (on an identity card) or bibliographic details (on a library book: see Section 13.4.1). A light pen passed over the bar code inputs the coded information to the computer, which deals with it appropriately.

14.5.5   Graphics tablet

To capture the advantages of the light pen without its disadvantages, the graphics tablet was devised. A plastic board, about 40–50 cm square has two sets of wires embedded in it, one set parallel to each of two adjacent sides of the square. An associated 'pen' or stylus has a spring loaded switch instead of a ball point. When the stylus is pressed down at any point on the tablet, the two nearby perpendicular wires are affected, and the co-ordinates of that point sent to the computer. Such a device is called a digitizer, as it can 'convert' a curve into a sequence of pairs of numbers in digital form. An existing picture can be input to the computer by laying the paper on the tablet, and tracing the stylus over the lines of the picture. Such a facility has obvious uses in geography and the study of maps, and in biology and the study of cells. It is quite easy to extend the handler to calculate the area enclosed by a curve traced out by the stylus. This could be applied to land areas, leaf areas, etc.

A digitizer used in conjunction with a screen is called a graphics tablet. The screen represents the tablet, in the sense that moving the stylus across the tablet as if drawing a line causes a corresponding line to appear on the screen. Tablet (handlers) provide a range of facilities, including dotted, dashed or continuous lines; a selection of colours for filling in drawn outlines; and basic shapes (such as circles and squares) that can be located at will.

14.5.6   Touch-sensitive screen

A different way of dealing with the clumsiness of using a light-pen on a screen is to use a touch-sensitive screen. The original design had infra red lights shining across the screen from two adjacent sides, with corresponding light detectors on the other two sides. If the screen is touched — with a finger or pencil or whatever — two of the light beams are obstructed, and this enables the position of the finger to be determined. Another commercially available system uses acoustic surface waves on a transparent surface as the generated signals that are modified by a finger presence. Other systems have electrically conductive material on the surface of the touch-sensitive area. The finger on the surface changes the electrical characteristics of the conductive material (cf. Section 7.3).

A recent development is a transparent panel which embodies the touch-sensitivity, and which can be mounted in front of a screen. This is cheaper than a touch-sensitive VDU. The transparent panel need not be mounted in front of a VDU screen, of course. Another possible use is as a simple replacement for push-buttons, mounted on a fixed surface with appropriate symbols below it to indicate where to touch.

A touch pad is also touch-sensitive, but not transparent. This lies on the desk, and bears a similar relation to the screen as does the graphics tablet. Touch pads are usually cheaper and less accurate than touch screens or panels. The major disadvantage of both the touch panel and touch pad is low resolution: obviously the finger is too thick to select accurately between symbols packed so closely as to use all 30 rows and 80 columns of a screen. Typical resolution or

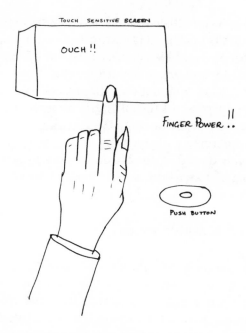

accuracy is the ability to distinguish squares of between 1 and 2 cm across. *The Koala Pad* (American, not Australian, despite the name!) is available for Apple and Commodore computers.

The major advantage of the touch panel is that pointing is natural. Furthermore, for rapid response, it is quicker and easier to touch the screen you are reading, than to have to look down to the keyboard and hunt for the right key. In a sense, it reduces the skill needed to operate a computer. One could envisage, for example, its use with non-readers: pictorial information on the screen can be combined with small pictures (icons) to be touched by the user in

response. (In fact, non-readers quickly learn to make limited use of a keyboard, simply recognizing the marks on the keys as pictures, while ignorant of their significance as letters.) A more likely use in this vein is to refer to things with unfamiliar names. A natural application would be in a tutorial on the structure of a machine: a picture of the machine is displayed, the user touches a part of the picture and the computer displays the name of that part. Yet another useful context would be a factory, where people have gloved hands, too clumsy for keys; or where the dirt in the air may get between and under keys and affect their reliable operation.

14.5.7   Function keys and concept key boards

Some computer keyboards offer programmable keys. This means that pressing the key causes the computer to start carrying out a predetermined program. If this program draws a shape on the screen, then pressing the button will cause that shape to appear on the screen. This system has limited flexibility, but is very useful with young children for precisely this reason.

A similar result is achieved by laying on a touch pad a sheet of paper with only three or four large squares labelled. Pressing anywhere in a large square activates one of the underlying smaller squares of the pad. If the handler is programmed to have the same effect whichever of these small squares is pressed, one has produced a simplified pad with only a small number of functions, each controlled by touching part of a large area of the pad. This device is marketed under the name *Concept Keyboard*. Another recent commercial implementation is *Keyport 717*, a membrane keyboard with up to 717 different 'keys', available for the Apple and Commodore computers, which has a Logo overlay to permit many commands to be issued with a single keypress.

14.5.8   Advantages of computer graphics

All the devices considered in this section have been designed for input. They offer a great variety of ways of using a computer, and considerably extend its utility. A trend is much easier to see on a graph than from lists of figures; a complicated blueprint might be easily accommodated on the screen, but take pages and pages to describe verbally; and so on. Another application is in 'incremental drawing'. Often one wishes, not a final picture right at the start, but a picture to which additions are gradually made. This can be messy on a blackboard; overhead projector overlays can be intricate; re-drawing the picture every time is time-consuming and may be confusing. The computer graphics screen is an ideal instrument for this. It also facilitates a heuristic (trial and error) approach to problem solving. It is easy to add or remove lines and shapes, to rotate or translate them, to magnify or diminish them. This can be used to encourage exploration, the development of new ideas, and the identification of good problem-solving strategies.

Graphics facilities will be enhanced by the use of the videodisc. The 'video' in this name refers not to these discs being a graphical medium (like a VDU), but to the means of writing to them and reading from them. Data are encoded into binary form, and a laser is used to burn the consequent binary patterns into the surface of the disc. The resulting pattern of holes can then be read by means of a laser. This system can store a great deal of data, with highly reliable recovery characteristics. The large storage capacity allows the digitizing and storage of a very large amount of graphical (or acoustic) data.

14.5.9   Use of graphical input devices

Most of the devices described have an accompanying printed circuit board or card which plugs into the computer and handles the basic communication between the device and the computer. The device handler (i.e. the program that interprets the signals from the device) may be costed separately. This is because there are many handlers for each device (or, equivalently, many programs which use that device as an input mechanism). 'Handler' is a technical term; the commercial term is more likely to be 'Graphics Processing System' or 'Special Effects' to name two products at random. Conversely, similar effects may often be achieved by the use of different input devices (although not necessarily so conveniently), so, for example, the Graphics Processing System comes in three versions, for use with a graphics tablet, light pen, or paddles or joystick. Alternatively, the more advanced user may write his or her own handler to obtain the precise effects desired.

The thoughtful teacher who bears in mind these devices and their capabilities will subsequently recognize, during the course of lesson planning, ways in which they can be used. This, of course, is the right approach to any teaching aid, namely to be aware of it all the time, but to employ it only when appropriate. The problem in the case of these aids, however, is that your school may not have one. When the school's (first) computer is bought, it usually represents a significant financial outlay, and consideration should be given to buying a variety of software and peripherals at the start. Otherwise an unpleasant shock can be experienced when one decides to purchase a peripheral or handler. It is better to refer to the initial discussions on the purpose(s) the computer is to serve, and use these as the basis for the purchase of both the basic system and its extra hardware and software. A careful selection might result in the purchase of a computer system with 64k bytes of memory and a joystick, and 10 programs that run in that memory space and require either the joystick or the keyboard. Incautious selection may hit upon 10 programs whose catalogue descriptions look good, only to find that two need joysticks, three need paddles, one involves a graphics tablet, and so on. The school's stock of computer-based teaching material (both hardware and software) must be built up over time as finances permit.

14.6   GRAPHICS OUTPUT DEVICES

14.6.1   Turtle (cf. Section 2.5 and Chapter 5)

The turtle is a small wheeled vehicle which, under computer control can move forward and back, turn left and right, hoot, switch on its lights, and can move with its pen up or down. If the turtle is placed on a sheet of paper on the floor, and the pen is down, then it draws on the paper, leaving a record of its travels. Users can control the turtle to make various shapes. This gives a good insight into problem-solving, with immediate and graphical feed back on the success or otherwise of the turtle's perambulation. The turtle is often associated with a terminal screen which displays a symbolic representation of the turtle, and lines to show where it has travelled.

14.6.2   Sprites (cf. Section 5.3.2)

The screen turtle concept has been extended by the invention of the sprite. This is an invisible screen 'creature' that can be instructed, by commands typed at the keyboard, to 'carry' objects of different shapes, sizes and colours, and to move in different directions at different speeds. Since there are usually 32 sprites, some very impressive screen effects are possible. Also using Logo, it is possible to re-draw alphabetic, numeric and other characters, obtaining again the equivalent of a typist changing golf ball or daisy wheel.

14.6.3   Plotter

Like the turtle, this works by moving a pen over a sheet of paper. In this case, however, the pen movement is restricted to straight lines in two perpendicular directions. The pen can be moved across or along the paper, and, by combining these movements, can also draw curves. Some plotters have pens of different colours, selectable by instruction from the computer. Some of the most advanced (and expensive) plotters have small jets of coloured paint instead of pens.

The use of a plotter enables the computer to produce pictures directly. For example, analysis of data might produce a set of pairs of values to be plotted on a graph. With a plotter, the computer can produce the graph directly. Other, far more complicated pictures, would be useless in numeric form, and it is only the invention of the plotter that has enabled the computer to be used for such purposes. Satellite photographs of the earth, for example, are coded numerically to represent the lights and darks and colours, and these numbers are broadcast back to earth, where a computer interprets the numbers and plots the corresponding picture.

Plotters are often used in conjunction with a VDU to output a picture which the user has created on the screen, using one of the devices described above.

14.6.4   Printer

Some printers have whole print characters (like a typewriter). Some, however, have a matrix of wires, each of which can print a dot on the paper. These are called dot-matrix printers. The wires are controlled (by hardware or software) so as to strike the paper in the appropriate combination to produce letters, numbers etc. However, one can write a program to re-interpret the screen memory map, so that a dot on the screen becomes a dot printed on the paper. This allows us to produce pictures that are crude (because lines are not continuous but are composed of dots) but which are faithful reflections of the pictures on the screen.

14.6.5   Robots

There are already some interesting robotic devices available, principally robot arms, that can be programmed to do various tasks (Fig. 14.4). The turtle could also be seen as a simple robot. Simple as they are compared to a real arm or turtle, such artefacts provide a good focus for the study of movement, appreciation of spatial relationships, programming to simulate intelligence, and so on. The robot of fiction is self-mobile, with its own on-board computer and the capacities for sight, hearing and speech. Such a machine is still a decade away, so there is plenty of time to consider whether such machines will have any specific role to play in education.

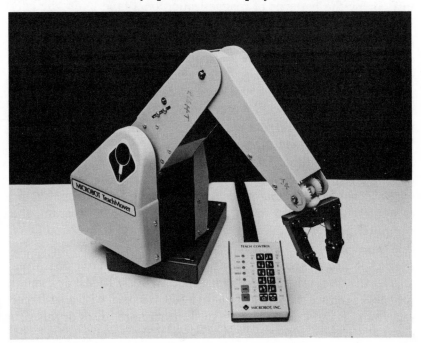

Fig. 14.4

14.7   SOUND INPUT AND OUTPUT

While a lot of communication between people occurs through the media of writing and drawing, reading and looking at pictures, the most common vehicle is sound: talking and listening. Some progress has been made in enabling computers to accommodate humans in this respect. Automatic sound production is easier than sound recognition, and its implementation is further advanced.

14.7.1   Voice output

There are two principal approaches to automatic voice output. One is to record words spoken by a person and produce these as required. The other is to construct appropriate sounds as required. The latter takes a lot of computer time, and is difficult to do naturally, while the former takes a large amount of storage and is thus likely to be slow.

Voice recording

The concept of recording sounds on records or tapes, is a familiar one. The desired sounds are represented by the shape of a groove in a disc, or by the patterns of magnetization on a tape. Now digitally recorded discs are becoming more common. In these, the characteristics of the sound (frequency, pitch, tone, inflexion, etc.) are sampled instantaneously and coded numerically, the numbers converted to binary form, and the corresponding sequences of binary signals encoded on the disc. This system can be used to record speech and store it in the disc store of a computer. However, for accurate reproduction of natural sounding speech, the sampling instants must be very frequent, say 4000 times per second, storing 15 bits of information each time. This means that a 10 megabyte (MB) disc can only hold 20 min of speech. A 500 MB disc could be needed to store a wide vocabulary. Then, when a word is to be spoken by the computer, a command to do this must appear in a program, the computer must work out where the binary sound representation of that word is stored, fetch it from disc, and send it to the audio speaker. Since an arbitrary sentence is likely to require words from all over the disc, this can take a long time. While a 10 MB disc could probably produce them fast enough, a 500 MB disc, with a far larger repertoire, is unlikely to be able to. Furthermore, discs of this size are not currently within the price range of the average school.

Speech synthesis

Again, the concept of electronic sound synthesis is now common in the musical sphere, and can be applied in this context, also. When the letter 'T' occurs in an English word, a human speaker will produce a particular sound, and this sound can be built up electronically by quite a small piece of circuitry (a 'speech chip').

Typically, such a speech chip can accept the specification of a phoneme [such as 'T', or 'A' (as in 'hat'), or 'ZH' (as the 's' in 'measure')] and produce the corresponding sound. This is clearly economical of space, compared to voice recording. Just as hundreds of thousands of (written) English words can be constructed from only 26 letters, so very many (spoken) words can be constructed from only about 60 phonemes. The other necessary component of a speech output device is a text-to-speech chip, which accepts a word, letter by letter, and produces the correct sequence of phonemes. This is quite difficult, because of the vagaries of language pronunciation. However, devices currently available contain 400–500 language rules, and produce an acceptable spelling of a large number of words. Such devices often add the facility for the user to provide a list of 40 or 50 words and their phoneme equivalents. These would presumably be the proper names or technical terms commonly used in the application the particular user has in mind.

Some such devices are quite sophisticated, in automatically varying pitch towards the ends of sentences, questions, clauses, etc. However, all suffer from the problem of not varying adjacent phonemes as the human speaker does. This results in the voice being rather unnatural. Current prices are of the order of $100–200.

Music

Many computers will produce a note whose frequency and length can be specified. By including in a program a sequence of pairs of numbers specifying frequency and duration, a tune can be produced of the level of complexity of a one-finger effort on a piano. This is very naive, but can add interest to the use of the computer.

CAN'T YOU PLAY ANY OTHER TUNE ON THAT COMPUTER?

14.7.2   The use of voice output

Voice output is essential for some applications: there is no point in displaying a word when the exercise is for the student to spell it! Again, in language learning, spoken output is an essential component. It can also make a positive contribution if there are occasions when the user could be looking elsewhere, and his or her attention must be attracted. Production of warning messages of error conditions arising in a piece of machinery is an example.

In other situations, the medium is not essential, but can increase interest through adding diversity. This becomes evident on watching the reaction of the beginner to the naive, barely recognizable, 'one-finger' tunes referred to above (although more sophisticated output is necessary to maintain extended interest). Variety of output is also more natural: human communication uses a variety of media, rather than a bare essential minimum.

14.7.3   Voice input

This is a far more difficult task, computationally, than voice output. Everyone who can speak a foreign language more competently than they can understand it will have an inkling of why this is so. The person or computer receives a continuously varying signal, represented by changes in air pressure, and this has to pass through a lot of translation stages to extract the meaning. In doing so, the human (and hence a speech-perception system) must use knowledge of "the characteristics of speech sounds (acoustic-phonetics), variability in pronunciation (phonology), the stress and intonation patterns of speech (prosodics), the sound patterns of words (lexicon), the grammatical structure of language (syntax), the meaning of words and sentences (semantics), and the context of conversation (pragmatics)" (Arden 1980).

Natural language processing is very difficult, because of the context dependence of so much that is said, because of idioms, and because of the range of words that can be used. Even word recognition is difficult, because people run words together, leave gaps within words, omit sounds, and add extra sounds. They also speak with different accents, speak with different timbre (e.g. typical male/female difference), speak differently in different emotional circumstances, and speak differently with a cold!

Some speech recognition systems have been developed. However, all are either experimental systems, using large quantities of computer power; or they are commercially available systems of restricted scope. An instance of the latter is the type of system that can be 'taught to understand'. The user types a word on the computer keyboard and says it (into a microphone). The computer stores the word and a representation of the sound pattern. When the user says a word, later, the machine compares the sound pattern with the stored ones, selects the one it most resembles, and displays the associated word. This sort of system has been used for parcel sorting in a post office, for example: at the beginning of the shift, the sorter 'teaches the computer to understand' the destination labels on the sorting receptacles. At the other end of the scale, one of the aims of the Japanese Fifth Generation Project (Section 2.7) is to build a machine which can understand continuous human speech with a vocabulary of 50 000 words and 95% accuracy from a few hundred speakers. It should also run a voice-activated typewriter, and conduct a dialogue with users in Japanese or English (McCorduck 1983).

Chapter Fifteen

Preparing for the computer

Politics is perhaps the only profession for which no preparation is thought necessary R.L. Stevenson (1850–1894)

15.1 THE PRINCIPAL

In a roughly chronological development, Chapter 14 discussed the selection of a computer system, and Chapter 16 will deal with its management after installation. In this chapter we cover the period between: the money-raising to purchase the system and the preparation needed before it arrives.

The role of the school principal or head in the introduction and use of computers is vital. One of the principal's major tasks is to provide leadership, and any teacher initiating major developments of which the principal does not approve may be seen as undermining this leadership. Thus, if the principal is opposed or indifferent, enthusiastic teachers will have little incentive to investigate this new area. Since any significant change to curricula or methods involves extra work, such change rarely occurs in the absence of one or two people firmly dedicated to the idea. It is not suggested that the principal need necessarily be one of these people. Indeed, it may be better otherwise, as s/he will have to handle staff who are quite antagonistic to the proposed changes, and this may be easier from a middle ground than from the other end of the spectrum. However, the principal must accept the increasing importance of information and information technology in society and the school, and investigate the possible implications for both curriculum and methods. In so doing s/he will properly take advice from both radicals and conservatives on the issue, and take account of the commitments and fears of both groups. S/he is then well-placed to make decisions in the best interests of students, and provide the necessary leadership (if not necessarily the expertise) to integrate the new developments in information into the school's activities.

Just as the principal need not be the computer evangelist, nor is it expected that all staff will become computer fanatics. However, all staff should be aware of the school's computing programme, and sufficiently involved in it to make rational and well-informed decisions about its implications for their teaching. It is the principal's job to encourage this, and in Section 15.3 we consider the question of professional development. The principal should be involved in the important matter of system selection (Section 14.1), and should maintain communication with parents and the community about the school's computing program.

15.2   FINANCE

When a system has been tentatively chosen, the purchase price must be found. In Section 14.1 we suggested seeking quotations from vendors before obtaining funds. Since the obtaining of funds may be a lengthy business, it may be better to get an approximate figure (from some other owner of a similar system) and raise most of this sum before contacting vendors. Possible sources of funds are

1   the school administration budget;
2   the school budget in a particular academic department;
3   the school council;
4   the parents' association;
5   the Department of Education or other education authority;
6   special government grants;
7   tertiary institutions;
8   community groups, including commercial bodies and charitable foundations;
9   a computer vendor or dealer;
10   any combination of the above.

We have postulated an enthusiastic teacher and a sympathetic principal. The latter (together with the bursar) can make the decision on source 1. If the enthusiastic teacher can inspire the other teachers in his or her department, they can (with the principal's approval) make the decision on source 2. This may need liaison between several departments to supply adequate funds jointly. In fact, the cost of a computer system is usually sufficiently high compared with recurrent funds that a separate capital allocation must be made. To this end, a submission must be prepared, addressed to one or more of the above groups.

When preparing a submission to a prospective donor, ensure that the donation requested is reasonable, the educational benefits expected are consistent with the donor's aims or philosophy, any benefits for the donor are spelled out, and the language used is intelligible. Before making a formal submission, informal contact should be established with some person or persons from the target group. This may be done by the principal or the enthusiastic teacher, as appropriate. (Which is more appropriate will depend partly on the level at which contact is to be made, and partly on individual local knowledge.) Such contact can establish what type and level of support may be expected, the best way of phrasing a request, the person to whom it should be addressed, and any other helpful actions (such as conducting tours of the school, making a presentation on computers in schools, arranging a visit to an existing computer installation in another school, and so on).

15.2.1   Donation

The school council or parents' association, special government funding bodies and charitable foundations may be expected to provide money, a computer company would supply equipment, and a tertiary institution might provide services, such as the use of the institution's computers. Other commercial firms might provide money or goods in kind. The Department of Education may provide funds, possibly only to equal amounts raised locally, or may supply goods at a discount.

15.2.2   Educational benefits

These were spelled out in the original systems selection committee (Section 14.1.1), but should be reinterpreted as appropriate. A special grant body will need to be assured that the benefits are relevant to its particular objectives, such as providing facilities for migrants, the unemployed, gifted children, partially sighted, physically handicapped, etc. The Department of Education will expect the aims to be consistent with its stated policies. The school council and parents' association will need to be convinced of the benefits to their children, and that these benefits are relevant to the children's future employment or further study. A computer company will not need to be convinced of a computer's benefits!

15.2.3   Benefits to the donor

A donor may wish to see some tangible return from the donation. A commercial company may wish to be assured that the students will be better trained for their work force; or to have the school computer room named after them. A tertiary institution may wish to be able to use the school as a test site for educational material or methods. A computer firm may wish to be free to show prospective purchasers around. At the very least, donors expect a report back, and may feel sufficient proprietary interest to expect to be able to inspect the site at will. Those providing special grants will need to be assured that the stated aims have been achieved, as will the school-based groups (although perhaps in more general terms).

15.2.4   Language

Education, like all specialist disciplines, has its own jargon. People from education departments and tertiary institutions are educational professionals, so the technical jargon is appropriate. It is probably also acceptable for special grant bodies, who may be expected to seek professional referees; this may be true of charitable foundations, too, but the initial contacts should check this. Other submissions should be couched in less technical language: after all, who but a professional would guess that 'entering behaviour' does not refer to the way the mob of children pour in through the school doors in the morning? In Australia, the Commonwealth Schools Commission (1983) has suggested a format for the presentation of submissions, in terms of User Requirements and Technical Requirements.

Our consideration of benefits to the donor indicates that a certain indebtedness is established. Other problems can arise if the donor insists on certain conditions being met or particular systems used. Gifts of three different, unsuitable microcomputers can cause more trouble than they are worth.

Before leaving the topic of finance, realize that the initial purchase of the computer system is only the start of the computer spending, not the end of it. Allow, per annum, 30% of the initial hardware cost, as follows:

1 10% for maintenance; this may be a contract, part share in the employment of a technician, or a fund for use when faults arise;
2 10% for new software and consumables; new software includes compilers (Chapter 12) and peripheral handlers (Chapter 14); consumables includes paper, ribbons and floppy discs;
3 10% 'sink fund', allowing for total replacement of equipment, notionally in 10 years time, but this depends on the balance between general inflation and decreasing hardware costs.

15.3   PLANNING FOR IMPLEMENTATION

As with the selection process, the size and composition of the planning organization and the scope of its activities depends on the scale of the innovation. It may comprise a single teacher, or could be a small committee including at least a teacher, a parent and the principal. The principal need not take a large active part in this process, but his or her support must be made evident.

The planning relates to physical and human factors — where shall we put it and what shall we do with it? Of course, the two questions are related, and the latter should be answered first — again stressing the primacy of educational questions. Unfortunately, the former is often anwered first by default, a small system being located in the room of the keenest teacher, or a hastily emptied store room being provided for a larger system. We shall take up this question of location in the next chapter (Section 16.2), in the context of the management of the computer facility.

The question of what to do with the computer depends on the staff, as they must decide. It can be disastrous to insist that certain equipment or approaches be used. In fact, teachers, school administrators and parents should be involved throughout the process of introducing computers to the school. We can identify approximately three stages of this involvement, which we could call initiation, orientation and development. This is not a neat division, as each shades into the next, and at any given moment different staff will be at different stages.

COMPUTER INITIATION

15.3.1   Initiation

Initiation was described in Section 14.1 and occurs when computer use is first considered. Staff are introduced to computers and their potential uses in schools, perhaps through a seminar given by a staff member or an invited speaker. This should include some actual computer use ('hands on') by the teachers. Introductory talks could also be given to parent groups at this time.

Following this introduction, pertinent literature should be gathered and distributed to all staff (by the computer committee), and computer users and computer vendors should be invited to the school to demonstrate their systems and how to use them. By the end of this stage, all staff should be thinking about the possibility of computer use.

15.3.2   Orientation

Orientation takes place when the process of selection and funding is sufficiently advanced that the advent of a computer seems assured. The first priority is to allay the fears of those teachers who are worried about the computer. These fears take various forms:

1 Redundancy: "the computer will take over my job".
2 Inadequacy: "I do not know anything about computers".
3 Insecurity: "the children probably know a lot more than I do".
4 Indignation: "there is nothing wrong with my teaching methods".

At this point it is necessary to get hold of a computer for an extended period. Even if it is the planned computer itself, however, it should not be thrown into service immediately. A much gentler introduction is to set up the computer in the staff room, permanently turned on. The following is one teacher's experience (Hughes 1984).

> "The computer was stationed permanently in the staff room for almost one whole term but this alone was not enough to induce some staff members to do a little key pressing. I set about amassing as much software as possible from varied sources hoping that I would find programs that would appeal and that teachers would think might be of value to students in their class. We had what I considered to be a teaching aid with a great deal of value for the needs of the individual child but unless this could be appreciated by the classroom teacher the purchase of a computer was to no avail. Allowing school children to play Space Invaders on Friday afternoon and then telling the boss that the computer awareness lessons are going well with plenty of 'hands on experience' is a frightful waste!
>
> The program that really broke the ice and encouraged the staff to use the computer estimated the desired weight for any individual, and recommended calorie intake per day and dieting where necessary (cf. chapter 1). As you can well imagine every member of staff allowed their

curiosity to overcome their fear of the keyboard. I was asked several times by different people whether or not the computer actually stored the information or even whether it passed it on to other computers! After all, the program required the exact age and weight of the individual and this knowledge in the staff room compares roughly to the knowledge of nuclear weapons in the world sphere!

Another popular program was 'Apple presents Apple', which gives a very basic introduction to the computer and its use. I encouraged most members of staff to work through this program and once enough people had used it the other more cautious members began to feel that they too must do their bit, or that they were obliged to have a turn.

Even among friends some people felt that they would make fools of themselves or that they would erase the program. Constant reassurance helped to remove these doubts, as also did the ability to take the computer home and experiment alone: this has probably led directly to the high level of usage in the school that we now have. From the outset all members of staff were encouraged to borrow the computer on week nights, weekends and during holidays. To assist in this, I would transport the computer and set it up, if asked to do so. For most staff members, however, just the reassurance that they would not damage the machine and could not erase the programs (without trying deliberately) was enough.

As well as being on call if my advice was required I also produced in the early stages a small book that documented all the programs we had and the instructions for running them. The book was always sent home with the computer as were games. The children of staff members in many cases had contact with computers and could be relied upon to teach their parents something and the games served as a nice incentive."

Although this teacher's experience was very positive, others have had less success with a similar approach.

Other useful packages at this stage are word processors, good simulations (in a variety of subject areas), and Logo. The school council and parents' committee can be kept in the picture quite easily at this stage by being given a similar opportunity to use the computer at a meeting.

Staff development is an extensive and continuous activity, which begins when the computer arrives (or a bit before), and may continue indefinitely. In existing subjects, refresher courses are required from time to time. They are even more necessary in a new and rapidly changing discipline. The next section is devoted to this topic.

15.4   PROFESSIONAL DEVELOPMENT

15.4.1   The aims

The Commonwealth Schools Commission (1983) has suggested competencies required by various teachers in the computer field.

Computer science/computer studies

1 All the competencies listed for Computer Literacy teachers (below).
2 Working knowledge of relevant curriculum guidelines for computer studies, and computer science courses.
3 Teaching skills appropriate for these courses.
4 Familiarity with and competence in using equipment and programming languages suitable for schools.
5 Knowledge of available printed, audiovisual and other teaching resources for such curricula, and of sources of information for keeping this knowledge up to date.
6 Understanding of current trends in information processing, and awareness of developments in both hardware and software.
7 Competence to organize and run a school computer club.
8 Ability to provide advice of a technical nature to other school computer users.
   This would require at least two years of undergraduate computer science study (or equivalent), and a teacher training course including Methods and Practice of Teaching Computer Studies (or equivalent).

Computer literacy

1 Working knowledge of computer awareness/literacy course guidelines.
2 Classroom management skills relating to the control, use of, and equitable access to equipment, and its integration into lessons.
3 Competence in using hardware and software in both demonstration and small group modes.
4 Skills appropriate for teaching social issues arising from use of information technology; these include discussion, social analysis,

use of audio visual and other resources for this purpose, setting and marking of essay work, etc.

5 Confidence with equipment, enough to run and assess package software, to handle simple faults (with power cords, drives, printer connections, etc.), and care of equipment.

6 Knowledge of printed and other resources for teaching computer literacy courses, and of sources for keeping this knowledge up to date.

7 Knowledge of suitable software to support the aims of the courses, and of sources of new software.

8 Skills in selection of suitable software for these courses.

9 Ability to identify and use general sources of current information about computing as it relates to computer awareness courses.

10 Ability to discuss social issues that relate to use of information technology generally, and to educational uses in particular.

11 Enough computer programming skill to be able to teach programming at the level indicated by computer literacy course guidelines.

12 Understanding of and ability to implement good programming practices.

13 Working knowledge of the use of the computer as an information handling tool.

It is envisaged that a minimum of 60 hours coursework would be required.

Other subject teachers

1 Awareness of the potential of computing in the teaching of the subject; familiarity with and understanding of the extent and nature of computer use in the subject area outside schools.

2 Minimum knowledge (similar to that suggested for computer literacy teachers) of equipment operation, maintenance and care.

3 Working knowledge of available software, sources of software, and sources of information to keep this knowledge up to date.

4 Software selection skills.

5 Classroom organization skills; integration of equipment use into lessons; use of demonstration and small group techniques.

6 Awareness of changes in curriculum and shifts in emphases due to new technologies.

7 Ability to discuss the social impacts of information technology as they relate to the subject area.

Primary teachers

1 Understanding of how computing can affect both the process and content of primary education.
2 Basic knowledge of computer hardware: capabilities, limitations; confidence in setting up and using a microcomputer system.
3 Working knowledge of a computer programming language suitable for use with primary school children, and ability to use it to enhance children's learning (to solve problems, learn mathematics, explore language, etc.).
4 Working knowledge of available software suitable for use with primary children, including information handling and word processing packages, and ability to use these to enhance learning.
5 Skills in software selection.
6 Classroom organization skills which enable the integration of computing into classroom practice.
7 Appreciation of wider social and educational implications of use of information technology.

Such lists seem daunting. However, experience shows that it is better to proceed slowly while these competencies are built up, than to rush into computer use insufficiently prepared. It is the task of the school's computer committee to effect, oversee and co-ordinate this expansion of the school's horizons.

15.4.2   The resources

These horizons are being extended by the introduction of new knowledge and expertise, and so outside assistance is required. The following contacts should now be established (even if there are teachers in the school with a high level of competence in computing). Some of these contacts will already have been established, during the initiation and orientation phases.

Education authority

The computer studies consultant of the local education authority, department, or district (or the consultant charged with responsibility for computing). This person (or team) has professional development as a specific responsibility, and so should be the primary contact. S/he may be able to conduct staff seminars, assist in administrative planning, participate in parents' association activities, assist in planning and executing lessons in a team teaching context, suggest curricula and methods, provide further reference and teaching materials, effect introductions to other teachers with relevant experience and expertise, and suggest further contacts in the following categories.

Computer society

A national computer society (such as the Australian Computer Society or the British Computer Society), or its local branch. This may have a subgroup with a special interest in education (such as the American Special Interest Group on Computer Uses in Education).

Teacher associations

The computing teachers association (such as the state or national Computer Education Group or Computer Studies Teachers Association; or the International Council for Computers in Education); also other subject associations may have someone interested in computer use in that subject.

Tertiary institutions

In the local universities and colleges, both the computer science department and the computer studies method staff of the education faculty.

Users' groups

The users' group for the particular computer to be purchased.

Other schools

An excellent source of informed comment is another school that has been through the same process. Beware of the tendency to euphoria, or to gloss over mistakes that were made. (Remember the farmer who asked his neighbour: "What did you give your horse last year when he had colic?" "Bran and molasses". So the farmer gave his horse bran and molasses, and it died. He accosted his neighbour: "I gave my horse bran and molasses, and he died". "So did mine".)

Media

The press, radio and television frequently carry tutorial material. You should at least monitor their proposed programmes, but might also suggest possible future topics.

15.4.3   The means

Courses for new teachers should include material such as that covered in this book, and in more specialized computer science texts. For existing teachers, the Commonwealth Schools Commission (1983) suggests the use of:

1 Conferences.
2 Broadcast courses.
3 Audiovisual tutorials.
4 Courses.
5 School networks.
6 Consultants.
8 Action research.

The school computer committee should use the contacts established (as suggested above) to mediate these to their school staff. The committee's involvement will range from simply obtaining a resource (such as a video tape or notice of a conference) to taking full responsibility for organizing an in-school course.

Conferences are organized by computer societies or teacher associations. They form an excellent forum to share experiences and glean new ideas.

Broadcast, radio or television, courses require a fairly large organization (such as The Open University). They are sometimes presented as an ancillary activity by a tertiary institution or educational radio station.

Audiovisual courses are increasingly available from commercial suppliers, but check the quality carefully before buying or hiring: many are superficial, others are thinly veiled sales pitches, and others take little advantage of the medium. Consider making videotapes of your own courses for on-going training.

Courses come in various shapes and sizes: short (say up to a week) or long (say up to three weeks); in-school or regional (for a group of schools); organized by the school computer committee or regionally (by a consultant or computer centre or tertiary institution). Suggested topics for short courses are:

1   Introduction to the use of microcomputers.
2   Computer use in the classroom.
3   Comparison of computer systems.
4   Computer networks.
5   Software selection.
6   Computer use in subject X.
7   Programming in language Y.
8   Comparison of programming languages.
9   Computer application in a specific industry or business.
10   Careers with computers.

while long courses might address

1   Computer literacy.
2   Concepts of programming and problem-solving.
3   Educational software design.
4   Managing a computer facility.

Staff for these courses may come from the education department (this would be an expected task for a team of consultants), a tertiary institution, computer manufacturers or suppliers, other schools, or the parent body. The committee should approach prospective staff, and design the courses jointly with them. When appropriate, ensure that teachers actually use computers during the course, and that eventually they get a feel for at least one and preferably several computer languages, and for computer use in both a science and a non-science area. Whoever gives these courses should, if possible, be available to answer subsequent questions.

'School network' refers to an informal association designed to share knowledge and expertise. It provides a possible source of staff for courses (see above), sharing of software, loan of equipment in emergency, etc.

Remember that although professional development begins with the advent of the computer, it continues indefinitely. Throughout this professional development, emphasize the probable need for the teachers to seek help, and an attitude of mutual assistance and mutual learning.

15.4.4   Evaluation: action research or action/reflection

It is very important for teachers to experiment, to try new methods and approaches, to learn about the new medium and their handling of it. However, we do not yet have our accustomed level of self-assurance, and so regular evaluation and re-adjustment is essential. Unfortunately, much reported evaluation is no more rigorous than 'the children enjoyed it'. The problem is that the computer does not necessarily replace other methods of teaching, but adds to the total learning experience. As MEP (1982) points out:

"There are four main areas in which we might expect the use of micros to have some effect on children's learning (in some way or other):
1   Social behaviour
2   Learning style
3   Thinking skills
4   Computer literacy.

Social behaviour

Does the computer in your classroom tend to lead to competitiveness or co-operativeness? Are communication skills encouraged or inhibited? Does the use of the micro lead to any sense of depersonalization?

Learning style

Do some children prefer not to use the micro? Does its use seem to lead to independence or passivity? Does the micro continue to motivate children after the novelty has worn off? Are skills learnt through computer use transferable to other situations? Does the use of the micro encourage or discourage group activities? Is it used as a routine learning tool or only as an occasional change of medium? Does computer use lead to a greater or lesser sense of control over learning?

Thinking skills

Does computer use result in more logical thinking? Is creativity inhibited? What effect does the computer have on problem-solving skills? Is it being used to develop the skill of hypothesizing?

Computer literacy

Does the use of the micro result in more realistic attitudes to the limitations of computers? Does it lead to an improvement in information skills? Do the children seem to be becoming aware of appropriate uses? Have their screen-reading and keyboard skills improved? Have they all learnt how to set up and operate the equipment? Do pupils resent using prepackaged learning programs? Have they begun to write programs of their own?

We need to begin to discern some answers to some of these questions, before we shall be really comfortable with computers in the classroom.

Chapter Sixteen

**Managing the
computer system**

*Human beings of today are attacked by so-called manager diseases, high blood pressure,
renal atrophy, gastric ulcers, and torturing neuroses* K. Lorenz (b. 1903)

16.1   THE COMPUTER MANAGER

16.1.1   The hardware

When a computer is installed, it is essential that someone have
ultimate responsibility for it. Since we have emphasized the
involvement of all staff in computer use, this may come as a surprise.
However, if the computer is to be kept permanently or usually in one
special room, that room needs supervision, just as a library needs a
librarian. If the computer is principally peripatetic, it needs someone
to check it over regularly, just as the audiovisual equipment needs a
technician. Like the librarian and the AV technician, this 'computer
manager' may have other duties as well. One of the teaching,
technical or administrative staff (as appropriate) may be given the
responsibility for the computer system as one part of their function in
the school.

Whoever does the job, the manager must know how to operate
the computer, replace ribbons and paper in printers, reset terminals,
check for correct connections, copy discs, and run the most common
programs. S/he should gradually develop sufficient expertise to
diagnose hardware problems, carry out elementary repairs, and
recognize when expert repair is required. This may be done under a
maintenance contract with the supplier. The contract is the
manager's responsibility: s/he may be able to negotiate a more
favourable arrangement by combining equipment onto one contract,
liaising with other schools, etc. Alternatively, special arrangements
may be available through the education authority. The equipment
should also be insured — again, a task for the manager. The manager
also provides for the booking of the computer by staff members for
specific times, co-ordinates the computer's use, and should (initially)
be available to demonstrate the operation of the equipment. Both the

manager and the individual staff members should realize that any specific item of equipment will be out of action from time to time, and must be prepared to handle this situation (just as, when outdoor activities are planned, an emergency alternative is also arranged to cater for wet weather).

We shall use the term 'computer manager', although 'computing resource person' would be a more descriptive title.

16.1.2   The software

The computer manager's role in respect of software is similar to the librarian's in respect of books, and all the following may occur.

1 A staff member hears of a particular program, and asks the manager to arrange to buy it.
2 A staff member seeks the manager's assessment of a particular program.
3 A staff member seeks suggestions for software for a particular purpose.
4 The manager obtains software and informs relevant staff members of its acquisition.

In general, the manager keeps aware of available software, through computer magazines, publishers' catalogues, dealers' catalogues, education department circulars, and discussion with other teachers. S/he maintains a continuous software testing programme, assessing software for purchase. Teachers should gradually be involved in this, so they learn to carry out the software selection process (Section 14.2) themselves. If necessary, the manager should arrange for the maintenance of copies of critical programs in some other location, outside the school.

16.1.3   Staff assistance and development

In Section 15.4, we considered professional development in detail, and pointed out that it is a continuing process. Once a computer manager has been appointed, s/he assumes responsibility for this programme, developing and maintaining an in-school in-service programme which will involve all teachers in the school. The aim is to develop an environment in which all teachers and students feel confident to participate in computing activities, without fear of ridicule or of damaging the computer. Clearly it would be best if the manager were identified in advance, and took a leading part in the planning group (Section 15.3): s/he could be the convenor. The manager would then be well-placed to continue liaison with the support groups and people suggested in Section 15.4.2.

This would assist the gathering of information about computing activities which are relevant to the school. This information would form a basis on which to respond to educational computing questions from teachers, students and parents. The manager should contact software suppliers and solicit regular 'blurbs' of new software, and demonstration visits (such as are carried out by booksellers). Regular bulletins should be circulated, advising teachers of available programs (with abstracts) and courses (with topics); advising parents of school computing activities; and advising students of arrangements for extra-curricular computer use.

16.1.4   The time

It should already be clear that the task of computer manager or resource person is very time-consuming, and the person should be given ample time allowance for the task. Unfortunately, it is not long since the computer enthusiast was looked at askance by the principal, and allowed to pursue his or her new ideas only on sufferance and as an overload. The remains of this attitude may be seen in the miserly amount of time allowed to the computer resource person. A lot of time is required because:

1 the subject is new, so the computer manager must have time for his or her own professional re-training;

2 the subject is changing rapidly, so s/he must have time to keep abreast of the latest products, methods and curricula; and

3 the newness and fluidity mean that the staff will need a lot of hand-holding at first;

4 the manager is combining the roles of teacher, consultant, technician and librarian, all in this new area.

The obvious approach is to (try to) identify a precise time requirement for the above. However, the school will obtain much better results if a (trustworthy) manager is given ample time, within which s/he can try out courseware and other programs, explore new ideas, and adapt these for the particular school. In order to extend the manager's time, some schools 'accredit' interested and competent students to act as computer room housekeepers, consultants (even to staff), software maintenance (i.e. modification) programmers, or software developers. This is excellent for both students and staff.

16.1.5   The person

There is no hard and fast rule about whom to choose for this task — the main requirement is interest in and enthusiasm (but not fanaticism) for the use of computers in schools. The manager should have teaching qualifications, and preferably teaching experience in a range of subject areas. The librarian or audiovisual technician is often chosen for the task because of the similarity of the teaching support role.

16.2   THE COMPUTER ROOM

16.2.1   Where is (are) the computer(s) to live?

The major alternatives are for it to be completely mobile, and move from classroom to classroom like a slide projector; or for it to be permanently set up in some convenient central location. The decision should depend not on convenience, but on the educational objectives spelled out right at the beginning of the system selection process (Section 14.1). A single machine bought for various CAL uses should clearly be mobile. Conversely, a class set bought for word processing should be permanently in a room convenient to the business studies or secretarial studies department. A network or multi-user system is also normally fixed in location, usually with all the computers or terminals in one room. However, they can be connected from different rooms to a central machine. One hopes that, in the very near future, schools will have sufficient equipment to permit more flexible arrangements. [Coburn *et al* (1982) suggest some possibilities.] In schools with a significant commitment to audio-visual support, there is both a central facility, with one or more classrooms, and some mobile equipment. This should be our target for school computer use, also.

The computer room should not be a room that was never used because it is distant or otherwise undesirable. It should be central, and could be in or close to the library and/or audiovisual centre, to encourage and facilitate co-ordinated use of the various educational resources in lesson planning.

16.2.2   Facilities

Establishment of a computer room requires thought, expenditure (over and above the cost of the computer system itself) and preparation.

Security

The room will contain much valuable equipment, and so should be secure and lockable, with barred windows, and a silent, monitored alarm system. Access from corridors should be restricted to reduce through traffic (both for security and decorum).

Power

Plenty of power points should be available, preferably with separate outlets for processors and peripherals, and circuit breakers rather than fuses. If the electricity supply is unreliable, a voltage regulator should be installed to protect equipment from voltage fluctuations. The lighting, both natural and artificial, should be adequate, casting an even light on the terminal screens, with no reflections or glare.

Equipment

Chairs and tables of appropriate heights; white boards, as chalk dust is anathema to disc drives and keyboards; anti-static carpets, to avoid the build-up of static electricity that can destroy recorded data; an assortment of connectors, cables, plugs, tools, etc. Trolleys for moving computers around the school should have lips to prevent equipment sliding off, and be so designed that the equipment need not be removed from the trolley in the class room, but simply plugged in. The room should contain a water and fire resistant data safe.

Reference material

Software (on discs or tapes), software catalogue, supplementary operating instructions for hardware and software, operating check lists, documentation, manuals, books, magazines, posters: indeed, anything that may assist staff and students in their use of the computer. Even if the computer(s) is (are) largely mobile, a computer centre is required as a repository for such items.

16.3   CLASSROOM ORGANIZATION

Organization of the classroom for computer use must take account of the number of computers and their duration of availability. There may be:
1   one computer for the whole class,
2   one computer per small group (of four students), or
3   one computer per student (or pair of students),
and the computer(s) may be
a   available (to any particular class) only at set times during the week, or
b   available the whole time (i.e. part of that class's own equipment).
This gives six possible situations.

(1,a) Only one computer, only intermittently available

We can identify four major types of use, namely: (i) electronic blackboard, (ii) focus for class discussions, (iii) individual occasional use, and (iv) part of a project circuit.

1   Use the computer for demonstrations, for example to plot a graph, draw a map or animate a figure. This requires a large screen or screens connected to the computer so the whole class can see the results. The problem of visibility means that pictorial work is more successful than numerical or literal.
2   Many activities lend themselves to whole class discussions. Simulation of an industrial development involves questions of economics, employment, environment, etc. Different class members can be asked to put the various cases, and provisional decisions are made which the teacher inputs to the computer. The results are apparent to the whole class (again via a large screen) and the discussion continues. A similar approach can be adopted to the building up of a data base. Children having collected specimens (of

various leaves, etc.) or references (to models of cars, etc.), the class discusses how to categorize the data, and the teacher inputs the results of the decisions. Even a more individual activity like Logo programming can be handled in this way, with individuals or small groups writing short programs, and then some being input to the computer, by the teacher, for general inspection and discussion.

3   Use the computer as an auxiliary tool, as described in section 4.7, for example. Usage is not confined to numerical applications: historical and other studies can also make use of the computer in this way. A large screen is not needed.

4   One mode of lesson organization which is independent of the computer is to have several groups working on different tasks simultaneously, and for the groups to rotate around the tasks. The availability of a computer means that it can be the focus of one of the tasks. This, of course, may involve planning a lot of lessons very early, as seven or eight may be in action simultaneously, right from the start.

The occasional use of a single computer is likely to involve moving the computer and setting it up in the classroom. Remember to allow plenty of time for this, and to check all the programs you intend to use. General student use will have to be confined to extra-curricular times (lunch time etc.).

(2,a) Occasional group use of computers

1   Many simulation programs are best used in small groups, as is described in Section 6.2.

2   Work involving data base creation and reference can be carried out (Section 4.5.1).

3   Group project work requiring occasional use of the computer is also relevant. This includes group programming projects, and the use of a word processor to produce a group magazine or newsletter.

4   'Competitive' games can be played within the group.

(3,a) Occasional use of a class set of computers

This level of availability permits most of the work described in this book. The whole class may work on the same thing, such as creative writing through word processing or learning to program. Alternatively, different children can be doing different things. For example, some could be doing small group work, while some individuals are doing some appropriate revision or remedial CAI work.

Use under either (2,a) or (3,a) normally occurs when there is a set of computers in a special purpose computer room. The teacher should realize that the children will not therefore have ready access to the resources in their own classroom while they are using the computer. This contrasts with (1,a), and with the following arrangements.

(1,b) Permanent class use of a single computer

When the class has its own computer, the comments made under (1,a) are also applicable. However, it is also easier to make spontaneous use of the machine, since it is in the class's own room, and permanently set up. It is useful to treat the computer as a learning centre, and have a roster indicating who is using the centre to do what and when.

The most common type of program you will be able to find is the sort designed to provide drill and practice to one or two students working on their own with the computer. This creates problems if you have more than two students in your class! Obviously not all children need practice with, for example, multiplication tables. On the other hand, if only one person ever gets to use the computer, because s/he is the only one who needs practice with tables, and a tables program is the only one you have, then there is going to be some friction in the classroom when suddenly everyone wants to do tables. If some people are going to be assigned to the computer for some drill and practice on such useful programs as you have available, then this needs to be known by all.

If you want the computer at certain defined times to help out with certain planned class lessons, then write this on the roster also. If one group is to use the computer on Wednesday to play a simulation game, then make this known too. If there are any spaces left between assigned computer sessions, then provide an additional blank list on which children can write their own names for 15 minutes of free time at the computer, provided they have completed all their assigned work, and nothing else is happening.

Include a timetable or roster for lunchtime use: computer games are useful for lunchtime especially on wet days. Indeed if we are trying to teach Year 12 computer science or Year 11 typing or word processing on one Apple, it must be accessible for most lunchtimes, as well as all class periods. Provide some unflustered access to the computer for the small group who will become competent programmers given time and encouragement. Allow them at least one, preferably two, full lunch times per week, and lock the games in your drawer!

(2,b) Permanent group use of computers

When a class has permanent use of quite a number of computers then again [as in situation (3,a)] the scope is very wide: certainly all the applications we have described, except those requiring special purpose equipment, are possible with this amount of computer power available. The teacher should plan for some 'hands-on' and some 'hands-off' activities, so that no group's computer is wanted by everyone at once, and so that no-one spends all their time in using a computer.

(3,b) Permanent availability of one computer per person

This is unnecessary. Firstly, there is not enough software being developed to support day by day, week by week computer use by individuals. Secondly, it would destroy the variety of educational approach that we have canvassed as a major benefit of computer use in schools. And thirdly, children (especially primary school children) have plenty of other things to do, like talking, painting, writing, playing, singing, visiting and moving, which should take up more class time than that spent tapping on a computer keyboard.

The computer offers a means to extend teaching possibilities, not replace them. Therefore, successful school use of a computer (or computers) means getting the computer to teachers when they need it, for use at a time when they can justify it, in a lesson where without it they would not be able to achieve the same objectives.

16.4   COMPUTERS: PROMISE AND CHALLENGE IN EDUCATION

The reader who has stayed with us this far will probably agree that computers hold great promise for education. As we have indicated, their effects (both those already felt and those still to be achieved) extend right across the curriculum. Not all these effects have been or promise to be beneficial, of course. However we hope that all teachers can now see potential benefits from the use of computers in their own particular discipline; and that they will take up the challenge to incorporate the computer into their educational decision-making, and be prepared to use it when appropriate. The reader should now be able to decide when computer use is appropriate, and should have some idea of how to make use of it.

The computer will change not only our educational methods, but also our objectives, and hence the curriculum. Not only are new topics (computer studies, etc.) being introduced, but also all other subjects will have to be re-thought as computer use in the 'real world' discipline impinges on its treatment in school. A further challenge is therefore to take a positive role in re-structuring the curriculum. A discussion of curriculum changes deserves a book to itself, though it would be a difficult book to write while the whole area is in such a state of flux.

Appendix   **Resources**

Knowledge is of two kinds. We know a subject ourselves, or we know where we can find information upon it   S. Johnson (1709–1784)

Teaching requires constant renewal, whether we are incorporating new ideas into the existing tapestry or seeking new ways of expressing the existing ideas. We supply some of this renewal ourselves, but also broaden our horizons by making use of the initiatives of others. This is why resource people and organizations are so vital in education. They become even more necessary in a new area, in which the teachers' basic knowledge may be incomplete; and yet more necessary in a rapidly changing area in which yesterday's knowledge is today's ignorance. Computing is such a volatile topic, that relevant information appears in all forms, from learned journals to the daily press, from reports of government committees to publishers' blurbs. The teacher can best handle this by first acquiring sufficient knowledge of the context (from sources such as this book), and then browsing regularly. The school's computer manager should browse most widely, then direct information to other staff as appropriate. This will economize on staff time. Some sources for material of various types are listed below (see also Section 15.4.2)

Education departments and related bodies

Consultants

Most regional, state and national education authorities maintain curriculum groups, research groups and resource centres, and employ subject consultants. Such consultants provide an excellent first point of contact, and can not only provide current information about curricula, courses and resources, but also act as an inter-school information exchange. The appropriate contact address can be found in the local telephone directory.

Computer centres

In Australia, each state has an educational computer centre. This is an extension of the consultancy service, and usually includes software development, review and distribution functions.

Examining boards

Some school assessment boards are distinct from the education department itself. For example, the Victorian Institute of Secondary Education has the task of drawing up curricula for secondary schools, and arranging for the assessment of students who have followed these curricula. Subjects have various titles, including Computer Science, Computer Studies, Computer Awareness, Data Processing, and a range of titles of the form 'X (Computer Option)', where X is Mathematics, Business Studies, and so on. Such syllabi provide a good basis for school-centred curriculum development. In the United Kingdom, there is a large number of such examining bodies.

Special projects

In some places, special project groups have been established. Examples are

1   Microcomputers in Education Project, UK.
2   Computers in the Curriculum Project, Chelsea College, University of London, UK.
3   The ITMA Collaboration (Investigations on Teaching with Microcomputers as an Aid), Shell Centre for Mathematical Education, University of Nottingham, UK, which produces a five volume primary school kit.
   Teachers should contact one that is relevant to their geographical area, and ascertain its objectives and the support it can offer.

Computer societies

1   Australian Computer Society. This has branches in each state, and most have some activities related to computer use in education. The national body (Box 4944, Sydney) also has an education group,

and sponsored the establishment of a national teachers' group in computing (see below).

2 British Computer Society. The headquarters are in London, but it has many local branches, and close links with the Computer Education Group (see below).

3 Association for Computing Machinery (ACM). 11, West 42nd Street, New York, 10036, USA. This association has at least two relevant Special Interest Groups, namely on Computer Science Education (SIGCSE) and on Computer Uses in Education (SIGCUE).

Teacher associations

1 The Australian national group is the National Committee for Computing in Education (NCCE). This may be contacted through the appropriate State Computer Education Group or Computer Studies Teachers' Association.

2 Each of the Australian states has its own association for computing teachers, as follows.

CSTA, O'Connell Education Centre, Stuart St., Griffith, ACT.

CEGNSW, Box 148, Broadway, NSW.

CSTA, Casuarina High School, Darwin, NT.

CEGQ, Box 1669, Brisbane, Qld.

CSTA, Angle Park Computing Centre, Trafford St., Angle Park, SA.

CSTA, Elizabeth Computer Centre, 256, Elizabeth St., Hobart, Tas.

CEGV, Box 88, Balaclava, Vic.

ECA (Educational Computing Assoc.), 12, Lilac Place, Dianella, WA.

3 Computer Education Group, North Staffordshire Polytechnic Computer Centre, Blackheath Lane, Stafford, ST18 0AD, UK.

4 International Council for Computers in Education, Department of Computer and Information Science, University of Oregon, Eugene, Oregon, 97403, USA.

Computer users' groups

These are groups of users of a particular type of computer (for example, a BBC Users' Group), in which the aim is to share experiences, problem solutions and software. The name of a contact person can usually be obtained from the appropriate local computer supplier.

Software suppliers

These fall into different categories, and include both commercial and non-commercial organizations. Education department centres (see below), research and development groups (see below), development and distribution organizations, commercial software writers and distributors, commercial hardware manufacturers and distributors, educational product suppliers (extending their range) and publishers (diversifying their product).

Distribution organizations

1   Conduit, PO Box 388, Iowa City, Iowa, 52244, USA. A software review and distribution centre, mainly for tertiary or upper secondary levels, mainly for mathematics and science. Newsletter is called *Pipeline*.
2   Minnesota Educational Computer Consortium (MECC), 2520, Broadway Drive, St. Paul, Minnesota, 55113, USA. A good source of material for the Apple II.

Software specialists

1   Prologic, 663, Victoria Street, Abbotsford, Victoria. Developing a range of educational courseware, working closely with Longmans and the Victorian Education Department
2   Edsoft, 3a, The Avenue, Blackburn, Victoria. BBC and other software.
3   Seasen Software, 2, Cameron Close, Corio, Victoria. System and other software for Apple and other computers.

Hardware distributors

1   Astro Educational Services, 1, Ruby Street, Burwood East, Victoria. Apple computers

2   Barson Computers, 335, Johnston Street, Abbotsford, Victoria. BBC Acorn computers.

Educational resource suppliers

1   Science Education Resources, Box 130, Blackburn, Victoria.

Information on software sources in the UK is contained in W. Tagg and R. Templeton (1983) 'Computer Software: Supplying It and Finding It', Library and Information, Research Reports, No. 10, British Library. For a USA-oriented list see '19 to Learn By', *Psychology Today* **18**, 9, September 1984.

Publishers

1   Jacaranda Wiley, Box 859, Milton, Queensland. Software is available to support some of Wiley's texts.
2   Pitman Publishing, 158, Bouverie Street, Carlton, Victoria. Pitman supply Chelsea (see above), MECC (see above), and Control Data (Plato) material.
3   Edward Arnold, Heinemann, Macmillan, McGraw-Hill and Nelson are at various stages of establishing and expanding their roles as software suppliers.

Journals

Most of the bodies already mentioned publish journals. We mention particularly *The Computing Teacher* and *Computer Education*. Other publications are as follows.
1   *Computers and Education*, Pergamon Press, Fairview Park, Elmsford, New York, 10523, USA.
2   *Journal of Computer Assisted Learning*, Blackwell Scientific Publications, Box 88, Oxford, UK.
3   *Association for Educational Data Systems Journal*, *1201, Sixteenth Street, NW, Washington, DC 20036, USA.*
4   *Educational Computing*, Oakfield House, Perrymount Road, Haywards Heath, Sussex, PH16 3DH, UK.
5   *Electronic Learning* and *Classroom Computing* Scholastic Inc.,

(Ashton Scholastic in Australia & New Zealand) Box 2001, Englewood Cliffs, New Jersey 07632, USA

6 *Journal of Computer Based Instruction*, Assoc. for Development of CBI Systems, Computer Centre, Western Washington University, USA.

7 *Creative Computing*, PO Box 789-M, Morristown, New Jersey, 07960, USA. Includes educational issues and games listings.

8 *Nibble Magazine*, 10, Lewis Street, Lincoln, Mass. 01773 USA. Contains program listings, mainly Apple oriented.

9 *Softalk for IBM Personal Computer*, Softalk Publishing Co., North Hollywood, California, USA. Similar to *Nibble Magazine*, but with IBM PC program listings.

10 *Byte*, 70, Main Street, Peterborough, New Hampshire, 03458, USA. Not specifically aimed at educational applications, but the articles and advertisements are interesting. An excellent popular magazine for keeping up to date about microcomputing.

11 *Compute! Magazine* (The Journal for Progressive Computing), Compute Publications Inc, PO Box 914, Farmingdale, NY 11737. Home, educational and recreational computing.

12 The local computer press (such as *Computer World*, *Computer Weekly*, *Datamation*).

13 The general national and local press.

Data bases

1 Dialog Information Services Inc., 3460, Hillview Avenue, Palo Alto, California 94304, USA.

2 ERIC Educational Resources Centre, National Institute of Education, Washington, DC 20208, USA.

3 The Source, Reader's Digest, Educational Division, Pleasantville, New York, 10570, USA or 1616, Anderson Road, McLean, Virginia, 22102, USA.

Resource centres

1 Computers in Education as a Resource (CEDAR), Exhibition Road, London, SW7 2BX, UK.

2 MUSE, Ilmington School, Ilmington Road, Wesley Castle, Birmingham, UK.

3 Council for Educational Technology, 3, Devonshire Street, London, W1 2BA, UK.
4 MCS Microcomputer Systems, Sydney, New South Wales. Principally BBC-oriented.

Software

Throughout this book, various CAL programs have been mentioned for various reasons, and they are gathered here for convenience of reference. This list is not comprehensive, and should not be seen as a balanced list for the purpose of setting up a school courseware library.

Bolt, Beranek & Newman (1983) *Quill: Microcomputer-Based Writing Activities*. D.C. Heath.
Chandler D. & Forecast C. (1982) *Factfile*. Cambridge Microsoftware.
Computer Solutions (1981) *Zardax*.
Dresden Associates (1982) *School Microware*. Dresden Associates.
Edens R. *et al* (1982) *Haber*. Edward Arnold.
Eisenstadt M. *et al* (1982) *Micros in Schools: an Awareness Pack for Teachers*. Open University Press.
Gare R. (1983) *Gold Dust Island*. Jacaranda Wiley.
Gare R. *et al* (1983–4) *Scavenger Hunt, Sheep Dog Trials, Cunning Running, Quick Cartage Company*. Jacaranda Wiley.
Geeves P. *et al* (1984) *Birds of Antarctica*. Elizabeth Computer Centre.
ITMA Collaboration (1983) *Micros in the Primary Classroom, Module 3 — Managing the Micro*. Longman (Contains the *Eureka* program.)
Killbery I. *et al* (1983) *Sailing Ships Game*. Longmans.
Kinnear J. (1982) *Catlab*. Conduit.
Kinnear J. (1982) *Birdbreed*. Science Education Resources.
Masterton R.D. *et al* (1982) *Mass Spectrometer*. Longmans.
Mulvey R. & Forecast C. (1983) *Diet*. Cambridge Microsoftware.
Nie N. *et al* (1975) *SPSS: Statistical Package for the Social Sciences*. McGraw-Hill.
Phipps B. & Simpkin G. (1983) *Gas Behaviour*. Stawell Technical School, Victoria.
Rablah P. *et al* (1983) *Acoustics*. Longman.
Smith F. *et al* (1984) *Bank Street Writer*. Broderbund Software.
Software Arts Inc. (1980) *Visicalc*. Personal Software Inc.
Tagg W. *et al* (1983) *Quest*. AUCBE, Hertfordshire.
Watkins C. & Tee D. (1982) *Litter*. MEP.
Wills S. *et al* (1982) *The First Fleet*. Elizabeth Computer Centre.

BIBLIOGRAPHY

Some books are to be tasted, others to be swallowed, and some few to be chewed and digested   F. Bacon (1561–1626)

Abelson H. (1982) *Logo for the Apple II*. Byte/McGraw-Hill.
Abelson H. (1984) Interview reported in *COM-3*, **10**, November, pp. 4–6
Abelson H. & DiSessa A. (1980) *Turtle Geometry*. MIT Press.
Adams T., Adams P. & McDougall A. (1984) *Learning Logo on the TRS-80 Color Computer*. Prentice-Hall.
Ahl D.H. (ed.) (1979) *Computers in Mathematics: A Source Book of Ideas*. Creative Computing Press.
Ahmed K. *et al* (1980) *Software for Educational Computing*. MTP Press.
Akins L. & Oski M. (1982) Year 11 computer studies: course guidelines. Diploma Thesis, Melbourne State College.
Allan B. (1984) *Introducing Logo*. Granada.
Allen J., Davis R. & Johnson J. (1984) *Thinking about TLC Logo*. Holt, Rinehart & Winston.
Allitt C. (1983) Developing a hardware policy. *COM-3*, **34**, August, 10–14.
Alvey Committee Report (1982) *A Programme for Advanced Information Technology*. Department of Industry, HMSO.
Anastasio E.J. & Morgan J.S. (1972) *Factors inhibiting the use of computers in instruction*. Interuniversity Communications Council Inc., Washington
Anderson J. (1984) Computing in schools: An Australian perspective. Australian Education Review No. 21, ACER.
Arden B.W. (ed.) (1980) *What Can Be Automated?* MIT Press.
Atherton R. (1981) Requirements for a general purpose high-level programming language for schools. *Computer Education* June, 14–16.
Bamberger J. (1982) Logo Music. *Byte*, **7**, 8.
Barr A. & Feigenbaum E.A. (eds) (1982) *The Handbook of Artificial Intelligence*, Vol. 2. W. Kaufmann.
Bearden D., Martin K. & Muller J. (1983) *The Turtle's Sourcebook*. Reston.
Beech G. (1978) *Computer Assisted Learning in Science Education*. Pergamon Press.
Billings K. & Gass S. (1981) Adding a micro to your school picture. *Electronic Learning* **1**, 35–40.
Billstein R. *et al* (1984) *A Problem Solving Approach to Mathematics for Elementary School Teachers* (2nd edn). Benjamin/Cummings.
Bishop P. (1982) *Further Computer Programming in Basic*. Nelson.
Bitter G. & Watson N. (1983) *Apple Logo Primer*. Reston.
Bolt, Beranek & Newman (1983) *Quill: Microcomputer-Based Writing Activities*. D.C. Heath.
Borgerson M.J. (1981) *A BASIC Programmer's Guide to Pascal*. Wiley.
Bork A. (1981) *Learning with Computers*. Digital Press.

Boyle D.G. (1969) *A Students' Guide to Piaget*. Pergamon Press.

Brodie L. (1981) *Starting Forth*. Prentice Hall.

Burnett J.D. (1982) *Logo: An Introduction*. Creative Computing Press.

Burton J. *et al* (1983) *Computers in Teaching Mathematics*. Addison-Wesley.

Centre for Educational Research and Innovation (1977) *The Use of the Computer in Teaching Secondary School Subjects*. OECD.

Chambers J.A. & Sprecher J.W. (1980) *CAI:* current trends and critical issues. *CACM*, **23**, 232–243.

Chandor A. (1977) *The Penguin Dictionary of Computers* (2nd edn). Penguin.

Clayson J. (1982) Computer games teach problem-solving. *Impact*, **32**, 435–448.

Coburn P. *et al* (1982) *Practical Guide to Computer Education*. Addison-Wesley.

Cohen H.A. (1982) The La Trobe talking communicator for the severely disabled speechless, Proc. Ninth Aust. Comp. Conf., August, pp. 266–275.

Commonwealth Schools Commission (1983). Teaching, learning & computers, Report of the National Advisory Committee on Computers in Schools, Canberra.

Computer Studies Curriculum Committee (1983a) Computer awareness, Curriculum Branch, Education Department of Victoria.

Computer Studies Curriculum Committee (1983b) Leaving technical computer studies. Curriculum Branch, Education Department of Victoria.

Computer Studies Curriculum Committee (1983c) Leaving technical computer studies — business studies elective. Curriculum Branch, Education Department of Victoria.

Conlan J. & Inman D. (1984) *Sprites, a Turtle, and TI Logo*. Reston.

Cumming G. (1984) The computer and learning to read: towards a discipline of education, *in* A.D. Salvas (ed.) *Computing and Education — 1984 and Beyond, Proc. 6th Ann. Conf. pp. 103–112. Comp. Educ. Gp of Vic.*

DEC(1977) *DECAL Instructor's Guide*. Digital Equipment Corporation.

Deken J. (1983) *Computer Images: State of the Art*. Thames & Hudson.

Dennen D. & Finch C. (1985) *Computers and School Administration*. Addison-Wesley.

Dick W. & Carey L. (1978) *The Systematic Design of Instruction*. Foresman, Glenview, Illinois.

Dijkstra E.W. (1976) *A Discipline of Programming*. Prentice-Hall.

DiSessa A. (1982) A principled design for an integrated computational environment. Tech. Memo. 223, Laboratory for Computer Science, MIT.

DiSessa A. & White B. (1982) Learning physics from a dynaturtle. *Byte*, **7**, 8.

Doerr C. (1979) *Microcomputers and the 3R's*. Hayden.

Dresden Associates (1982) *School Microware*. Dresden Associates.

Dromey R.G. (1982) *How to Solve it by Computer*. Prentice Hall.

Eisenstadt M. *et al* (1982) *Micros in Schools: An Awareness Pack for Teachers*. Open University Press.

Ennals R. (1983) *Beginning Micro-Prolog'*. Ellis Horwood.

Evans C. (1979) *The Mighty Micro*. Gollancz.

Feldman P.R. (1983) What's the big deal about computers?. *The Secondary Administrator* 1–3, June & September.

Flesch R.F. (1948) A new readability yardstick. *J.App.Psych.* **32**, 221–233.

Foulis M.B. (1982) Guidelines for the evaluation of micro-based CAL applications. *in* R. Lewis & E.D.Tagg (eds) *Involving Micros in Education*. North Holland, pp. 53–61.

Frye C.H. (1981) *Planit Reference Handbook*. Frye Software.

Gare R. (1982a) Educational software development: a guide to the design and development of computer-based learning materials. Curriculum Branch, Department of Education, Queensland.

Gare R. (1982b) A guide to the evaluation of computer based learning materials. Curriculum Branch, Department of Education, Queensland.

Gare R. (1982c) Computerising classrooms without computers . *Classroom*, 2, (3), 14-17.

Gare R. & Gredden G. (1982) Computers in the classroom: reflections and projections. *Classroom*, 2,(5), 25-27.

Garson J.W. (1979) The case against multiple choice. *The Computing Teacher*, December.

Goldenberg E.P. (1979) *Special Technology for Special Children*. University Park Press.

Griffiths M. & Tagg E.D. (eds) (1985) *The Role of Programming in Teaching Informatics*. Proc. IFIP TC3 Working Conference on Teaching Programming. North Holland.

Hade D.D. (1982) Literacy in an information society. *Ed. Tech*. August, 7-12.

Hall D. (1980) Logo, mathematics and problem solving, Working Paper 73, Dept of Artificial Intelligence, University of Edinburgh.

Harper D.O. & Stewart J. (1983) *Run, Computer Education*. Brookes/Cole.

Harvey B. (1982) Why Logo? *Byte* 7, 8.

Hayes B. (1983) Computer recreations. *Scientific American* **249**,24-30.

Henderson-Lancett L. (1984) Year 6 learn to write using the word processor, in A.D. Salvas (ed.) *Computing and Education — 1984 and Beyond, Proc. 6th Ann. Conf*. 126-19. Comp. Educ. Gp of Vic.

Hill B. (1977) *The Schools*. Penguin.

Hofmeister A. & Maggs A. (1984) *Microcomputer Applications in Education and Training*. Holt, Rinehart & Winston.

Howe J.A.M. (1980) Teaching mathematics through programming. Research Paper 129, Dept of Artificial Intelligence, University of Edinburgh.

Howe J.A.M. & du Boulay B. (1979) Microprocessor assisted learning: turning the clock back? *PLET* 16, 240-246.

Howe J.A.M. & O'Shea T. (1978) Learning mathematics through Logo. *ACM SIGCUE Bulletin*, **12**, 1.

Howe J.A.M., O'Shea T. & Plane F. (1980) Teaching mathematics through logo programming: an evaluation study. *in* Lewis R. & Tagg E.D. (eds) *Computer Assisted Learning*. North Holland.

Howe J.A.M. & Ross P.M. (1981) *Microcomputers in Secondary Education: Issues and Techniques*. Kogan Page.

Howe J.A.M., Ross P., Johnston K., Plane F. & Inglis R. (1981) Teaching mathematics through programming in the classroom. Research Paper 157, Dept of Artificial Intelligence, University of Edinburgh.

Hudgins B.B. (1966) *Problem Solving in the Classroom*. Macmillan.

Hughes J. (ed.) (1984) *Computers and Education: Dreams and Reality. Proc. Aust. Comp. Educ. Conf.Comp. Educ. Gp of New South Wales.*

Hughes O. (1984) Personal communication.

Huizinga J. (1955) *Homo Ludens: A Study of the Play-Element in Culture.* Beacon Press.

Illich I.D. (1971) *De-Schooling Society.* Calder & Boyars.

Johnston V.R. (1984) Timetabling and computers. Technical Report No.7, Department of Computer Science, La Trobe University.

Jones B.O. (1982) *Sleepers, Wake!* Oxford University Press.

Kelly A.V. (ed.) (1984) *Microcomputers and the Curriculum.* Harper & Row.

Kelman P. *et al* (1983) *Computers in Teaching Mathematics.* Addison-Wesley.

Kemmis S., Atkin R. & Wright E. (1977) How do students learn? Working Papers on CAL, Occasional Paper No. 5, Centre for Applied Research in Education, University of East Anglia, UK.

Kleiman G., Humphrey M. & Lindsay P. (1981) Microcomputers and hyperactive children. *Creative Computing*, March.

Knuth D.E. (1969) *The Art of Computer Programming. Vol. 2: Seminumerical Algorithms.* Addison-Wesley.

Kolstad R. & Lidtke D. (1981) Gifted and Talented. *ACM SIGCSE/SIGCUE*, January.

Kurtz T.E. (1978) Basic. in R.L. Wexelblat (ed.) *History of Programming Languages. ACM SIGPLAN Notices*, 13, 101–18, August.

Lally M. & Macleod I. (1982) Development of skills through computers: achieving an effective, enjoyable learning environment. *Impact of Science on Society* 32, 449-460.

Lamb D. (1983) *Help! It's a Computer.* Yarra Valley Anglican School, Entry in La Trobe University Computer Fayre.

Lawler R. (1980a) One child's learning: introducing writing with a computer. *ACM SIGCUE Bulletin*, June.

Lawler R. (1980b) Extending a powerful idea. Logo Memo 58, Artificial Intelligence Laboratory, M.I.T.

Lawler R. (1982) Designing computer-based microworlds. *Byte*, 7, 8.

Lawless S. (1982) Basic skills for 1982: word literacy, numeracy and Computer Literacy. *JFHE*, 6, 36-39.

Lewis R. & Tagg E.D. (eds) (1980) *CAL: Scope, Progress and Limits. Proc. IFIP TC3 Conference on CAL.* North Holland.

Lewis R. & Tagg E.D. (eds) (1981) *Computers in Education. IFIP 3rd World Conf. on Computer Education*, North Holland.

Lewis R. & Tagg E.D. (eds) (1982) *Involving Micros in Education.* North Holland.

Lewis R. & Want D. (eds) (1981) CAL materials: design, guidelines and standards. Computers in the Curriculum, Project Paper 20.

Lewis W.E. (1980) *Problem Solving Principles for Ada Programs: Applied Logic, Psychology and Grit.* Hayden.

Luehrmann A. (1980) Computer literacy: a national crisis and a solution for it. *Byte*, 5 (7), 98–102.

McCorduck P. (1983) Introduction to the fifth generation. CACM, 26, 629-630.

McDougall A. (1980) Computers and post-primary education in Victoria: a study of needs. Department of Education, Victoria.

McDougall A. (1981) Problems in the preparation of computer studies teachers. *in* R. Lewis & E.D. Tagg (eds) *Computers in Education*. North Holland, pp. 693-6.

McDougall A. & Adams T. (1984) Teaching a computer to write poetry, *in* Salvas A.D. (ed.) *Computing and Education — 1984 and Beyond*. Proc. 6th Ann. Conf., 130–136, Comp. Educ. Gp of Vic.

McDougall A., Adams T. & Adams P. (1982) *Learning Logo on the Apple II*. Prentice-Hall.

McDougall A., Adams T. & Adams P. (1984) *Learning Logo on the Commodore 64*. Pitman.

McDougall A., Adams T. & Adams P. (1985) *Learning Logo on the BBC Micro*. Prentice-Hall.

McKenzie J. (1978) *Interactive Computer Graphics in Science Teaching*. Halstead Press.

Malone T.W. (1981) What makes computer games fun? *Byte* **6**, December, pp. 258–277.

Microelectronics Education Programme (MEP) (1982) *Micro Primer*. Tecmedia.

Microsift (1982) *Evaluator's Guide for Microcomputer-Based Instructional Packages*. International Council for Computers in Education.

Minnesota Educational Computing Consortium (1983) *Apple Logo in The Classroom*. MECC.

Mitchell L. (1984), quoted in the *Victorian Bulletin, Aust. Comp. Soc.*, March.

Moore O.K. (1966) Autotelic-responsive environments and exceptional children, *in* O.J. Hervey (ed.) *Experience, Structure and Adaptability*, pp. 169–77 Springer.

Moursund D.(1981) *Introduction to Computers in Education for Elementary & Middle School Teachers*. International Council for Computers in Education.

Mowshowitz A. (1977) *Inside Information: Computers in Fiction*. Addison-Wesley.

Murphy R.T. & Appel L.R. (1977) *Evaluation of the Plato IV Computer-Based Education System in the Community College*, Ed. Testing Service, Princeton, N.J.

Nevile L. (1984) Turtle Talk. *COM-3*, **10**, 2.

Nevile L. & Dowling C. (1983) *Let's Talk Turtle*. Prentice-Hall.

Nicholls A. & Nicholls S.H. (1972) *Developing a Curriculum: A Practical Guide*. Allen & Unwin.

Ninedek A. (1984) *Word Processing in Primary Schools*, *in* A.D. Salvas (ed.) *Computing and Education — 1984 and Beyond*, Proc. 6th Ann. Conf. Comp. Educ. Gp of Vic.

Oldknow A. & Smith D. (1984) *Learning Mathematics with Micros*. Ellis Horwood.

O'Neil H.F. (1981) *Computer Based Instruction: A State of the Art Assessment*. Academic Press.

O'Shea T. & Self J. (1983) *Learning and Teaching with Computers*. Prentice-Hall.

Overall T., Lola P., Murphy K., Dafoe M., Housey J., & Leventhal S. (1981) Learning with Logo at the Lamplighter School. *Microcomputing*, Sept.

Oxford (1984), *Oxford Dictionary of Computers*. Oxford University Press.

Papert S. (1972) Teaching children to be mathematicians versus teaching about mathematics. *Int. J. Math. Educ. Sci. Technol.*, **3**, 1972, reprinted in Taylor R.P. (ed.) *The Computer in the School: Tutor, Tool, Tutee*. Teachers College Press, New York, 1980, pp. 177–196.

Papert S. (1976) An evaluative study of modern technology in education. Logo Memo. 26, Artificial Intelligence Laboratory, MIT.

Papert S. (1977) Assessment and documentation of a children's computer laboratory. Logo Memo 48, Artificial Intelligence Laboratory, MIT.

Papert S., Abelson H., Bamberger J., DiSessa A., Weir S., Watt D., Hein G. & Dunning S. (1978) Interim report of the Logo project in the Brookline public schools. Logo Memo 49, Artificial Intelligence Laboratory, MIT.

Papert S. (1980) *Mindstorms*. Harvester.

Parker D.B. (1976) *Crime by Computer*. Charles Scribner.

Peterson J.L. (1980) Computer programs for detecting & correcting spelling errors. *CACM*, **3**, 676–687.

Piaget J. (1951) *Play, Dreams and Imitation in Childhood*. Norton.

Piaget J. (1972) *The Science of Education and the Psychology of the Child*. Viking.

Pollard J. (1983) Direct Helper. Dataflow Computer Services, Burwood, New South Wales.

Pratt D. (1980) *Curriculum Design & Development*. Harcourt Brace Jovanovich.

Preece J. & Squires D. (1984) Selecting CAL Packages. *Comp. Educ.* February, pp. 20–21.

Reinecke I. (1982) *Micro Invaders*. Penguin.

Richards T.J. (1983) Teaching a fully-computerized course. *The Record*, La Trobe University.

Ross P. (1983) *Logo Programming*. Addison-Wesley.

Rowbottom M.E. *et al* (1983). The schools information retrieval (SIR) project. British Library, Library and Information Research Report 15.

Rushby N.J. (1979) *Introduction to Educational Computing*. Croom Helm.

Rushby N.J. (1981) *Selected Readings in Computer Based Learning*. Kogan Page.

Rushby N.J. (ed.) (1983) *State of the Art Report on Computer Based Learning*. Pergamon Infotech.

Salvas A.D. (ed.) (1983) *Could You Use a Computer? Proc. Aust. Comp. Educ. Conf.* Comp. Educ. Gp of Vic.

Salvas A.D. (ed.) (1984) *Computing and Education — 1984 and Beyond. Proc. Sixth Annual Conf.* Comp. Educ. Gp of Vic.

Samways B. & Byrne-Jones T. (1985) *A First Computer Dictionary*. Macmillan.

Scottish Computer Project. *Yours Obediently* series. Chambers.

Scottish Microelectronics Development Programme (SMDP) Program Documentation: Interim Standards. SMDP, 74 Victoria Crescent Road, Glasgow.

Seidel, R.J. & Rubin M.L. (eds) (1977) *Computers and Communications: Implications for Education*. Academic Press.

Sharp P. (1984) The aesthetics of Logo and instruction in the arts: lesson plans and procedures, paper presented at the LOGO84 Conf., MIT.

Sharples M. (1980) *A Computer Written Language Lab*. Research Paper 134, Dept. of Artificial Intelligence, University of Edinburgh.

Sharples M. (1981) A computer-based teaching scheme for creative writing, *in*

Lewis R. & Tagg E.D. (eds) *Computers in Education*. North Holland.

Shaw K.A. (1982) Computer-based learning: the creation of software through in-service training. *Proc. 9th Aust. Comp. Conf. Schools' Symposium*, Hobart, Tasmania, September.

Shaw L.G. (1982) *Why Touch Sensing?* Datamation.

Sherwood B.A. (1977) *The TUTOR Language*. Control Data Corporation.

Short J. *et al* (1982) The application of microcomputers to English essay writing: a comparison of two authoring systems, *in* R. Lewis & E.D. Tagg (eds) *Involving Micros in Education*, pp. 53–61, North Holland.

Skinner B.F. (1968) *The Technology of Teaching*. Appleton-Century-Crofts.

Skinner B.F. (1971) *Beyond Freedom and Dignity*. A.A. Knopf.

Smith S. & Sherwood B. (1976) Educational uses of the PLATO computer system. *Science*, **192**, April.

Squires D., McDougall A., Adams T. & Adams P. (in press) *Learning Logo on the RML 480Z*. Prentice-Hall.

Steely D. (1980) Instructional design and CAI. *The Computing Teacher*, September.

Stonier T. (1982) The emerging information society, *Proc. Ninth Aust. Comp. Conf.*, August, 25–34.

Sugarman R. (1978) A second chance for CAI. *ICEE Spectrum*, August, pp. 29–37.

Sullivan P. (1984) Using the power of the computer in language teaching, *in* A.D. Salvas (ed.) *Proc. 6th Ann. Conf., Comp. Educ. Gp of Vic.*, pp. 139–142.

Suppes P. (1981) *University Level Computer Assisted Instruction at Stanford: 1968–1980*. IMSSS, Stanford University.

Sussex R. *et al* (1982) *Mentor: a Computer-Based Teaching System*. University of Melbourne.

Tagg E.D. (ed.) (1980) *Microcomputers in Secondary Education*. Proc. IFIP TC3 Conference 1980. North Holland.

Tatnall A.D. (1982) *Pilot Interactive Computer Language*. Seasen Software.

Taylor R.P. (ed.) (1980) *The Computer in the School: Tutor, Tool, Tutee*. Teachers' College Press, 1234, Amsterdam Ave, New York 10027.

Thornburg D.D. (1982) *Picture This!* Addison-Wesley.

Thornburg D.D. (1982) *Picture This, Too!* Addison-Wesley.

Thornburg D.D. (1983) *Discovering Apple Logo*. Addison-Wesley.

Vanderheiden G. (1982) Computers can play a dual role for disabled individuals. *Byte*, **7**, pp. 136–62.

Wang A.C. (1981) *Index to Computer Based Learning*. Instructional Media Laboratory, University of Wisconsin-Milwaukee.

Want D.L. (1982) Keyword driven interaction in computer assisted learning, *in* R. Lewis & E.D. Tagg (eds) *Involving Micros in Education*, pp. 125–132. North Holland.

Watson D. (1982) Some implications of micros on curriculum development, *in* R. Lewis & E.D. Tagg (eds) *Involving Micros in Education*, pp. 197–206, North Holland.

Watt D. (1979a) Final report of the Brookline Logo project, Part III: profiles of individual students' work. Logo Memo 54, Artificial Intelligence Laboratory, MIT.

Watt D. (1979b) A comparison of the problem solving styles of two students learning Logo, a computer language for children. *Creative Computing*, **5**, 12.

Watt D.H. (1980) Computer Literacy: what should schools be doing about it?. *Classroom Computer News*, **1**, pp. 26–27.
Watt D. (1983) *Learning with Logo*. McGraw Hill.
Webster T. & Champion R. (1984) *Microcomputer Software Buyer's Guide*. Computer Reference Guide, 284 Victoria Avenue, Chatswood, New South Wales.
Weizenbaum J. (1966) ELIZA — A computer program for the study of natural language communication between man and machine. *CACM*, **9**, 36–44, January.
Wills S. (1980) Computer education in Tasmanian schools. *The Australian Computer Bulletin*, August.
Wilkinson A.C. (ed.) (1983) *Classroom Computers and Cognitive Science*. Academic Press.
Withers S. (1983) Home computer overview. *Australian Personal Computer*, **4**, 69f, October.
Wheeler J.H. (ed.) (1973) *Beyond the Punitive Society*. W. H. Freeman.
Williams J.G., Thorkildsen R. & Crossman E. (1982) Application of computers to the needs of handicapped persons, *in* Harper D.O. & Stewart J. *RUN: Computer Education*. Brooks/Cole.
Woodhouse D. (1981) A short Pascal course for high schools. *COM-3*, No. 24, May, pp. 5–18.
Woodhouse D. (1982) Mathematics for computer science, *in* J. Dowsey (ed.) *Working With Mathematics*. Proc. Math. Assoc. of Vic. Conf., pp. 280–290.
Woodhouse D. (1983) Introductory courses in computing. Aims and languages. *Computers & Education*, **7**, 79–89.
Woodhouse D., Johnstone G. & McDougall A. (1984) *Computer Science*. (2nd edn.) Jacaranda Wiley.
Woodhouse D. (1984) Planning for the day after tomorrow. *Aust. Foundation for Computer Literacy*, Vol. 1.
Yazdani M. (1984) *New Horizons in Educational Computing*. Ellis Horwood.

INDEX